Good Housekeeping

Doing up the Christmas parcels. Brother will receive a necktie of flamboyant hue from Santa Claus . .

AMERICAN
FAMILY
CHRISTMAS

Good Housekeeping

AMERICAN

FAMILY
CHRISTMAS

An Allen D. Bragdon Book

Hearst Books, New York

Photography, Illustration, and Design Credits

Cover (design) Herbert Bleiweiss, (photo, front) Keith Scott Morton, (illus, back) Jessie Wilcox Smith; pages 9, 154, 156, 157 (photo) Jerry Abramowitz; pages 10-37, 39, 41-43, 45, 47, 61, 64, 66, 69, 86-87, 97, 115, 118-126, 133, 136-137, 140-141, 144, 146, 164-165 (photo) Victor Scocozza; pages 1, 6, 131 (illus) Maud Tousey; pages 2, 3, 24 (illus) Jessie Wilcox Smith; page 5 (illus) James Preston; page 38 (photo) Paul Dome; page 46 (photo) Manuel Denner; pages 48-49 (photo) George Cochran; pages 52-53 (photo) John Paul Endress; pages 56-57, 62-63, 162 (illus) Robert Penny; pages 74, 82 (upper right), 84, 85 (lower left), 90, 95, 99, 106-107, 153 (upper left), 155 (lower right), 158, 160, 161 (upper left), 163 (photo) Charles Gold; page 81 (photo) Barbara Bersell; pages 82 (upper left), 83, 85 (upper right, photo) Andr'e Gillardin; pages 94, 100-1, 102, 155 (upper left), 161 (right) (photo) Myron Miller; page 97 (design) Ollie Alpert; page 98, 149, 152, 159 (photo) Richard Jeffery; page 104 (photo) Barbara and Justin Kerr; page 153 (lower right, photo) Neil Portnoy; pages 128-129 (photo) Karen Leeds; pages 134-135 (photo) Ray Coggen; page 145 (photo) Gus Francisco; page 150 (photo) Susan Wood. Back-issue pages photographed by Allen Clifford Bragdon.

Publisher's Acknowledgements

The text and photographs for this book were selected by the editors of Allen D. Bragdon Publishers Inc., from issues of Good Housekeeping magazine and Good Housekeeping Needlework & Crafts magazine published in the 100-years from 1885 to 1985. We acknowledge with respect the consistently high level of editorial judgement required to shape and maintain the appeal of a magazine successfully for that long. Specifically we appreciate the skills of the magazine's current editorial staff and the staff of the Good Housekeeping Institute whose work is reflected in this book: John Mack Carter, Editor-in-Chief; Mary Fiore, Managing Editor; Mina Mulvey, Executive Editor; Herbert Bleiweiss, Art Director; A. Elizabeth Sloan, Director, the Institute; Mildred Ying, Food Editor; Cecelia Toth, Needlework & Crafts Editor; Donna Liotto, Director Appliances and Microwave Cookery; Amy Barr, Director Nutrition, Diet & Fitness Center; James M. Lopez, Director Editorial Production. They and their associates listed below went to considerable effort to make available to us the best work that they and their predecessors produced. Our thanks for your searches and researches: Valentina A. Snell, Susan Deborah Goldsmith, Julia Gant, Janet Hoffman Akhtarshenas, Arthur Adams, Lori Stollerman, Lyn McFarland

Staff for this book:

Editor in Chief—Allen D. Bragdon
Senior Editor—Sidney Burstein
Art Director—Stephanie Schaffer
Text Production—Hans Schmitt
Proofreader—Evelyn Wheeler

Distributed to the book trade by
Hearst Books
A division of William Morrow Co. Inc.
New York

Designed, Produced, and Published by
Allen D. Bragdon Publishers, Inc.
153 West 82nd Street
New York, NY 10024

Library of Congress Cataloging in Publication Data
Main entry under title:

Good housekeeping American family Christmas.
  Includes index.
    1. Christmas cookery. 2. Christmas decorations. 3. Handicraft. 4. Gifts.
5. Christmas—United States.
I. Good housekeeping (New York, N.Y.)
TX739.G63 1985   641.5'68   85-80221
ISBN 0-916410-29-3

Printed in the U.S.A.
10 9 8 7 6 5 4 3 2 1

Good Housekeeping   December 1904

TABLE OF CONTENTS

INTRODUCTION   7

I.   SIT-DOWN MENUS
      FOR CHRISTMAS DAY   8

      Great Beginnings   12
      Enticing Entrees   17
      Glorious Go-Alongs   25
      Super Salads   27
      From the Bakery   29
      Perfect Endings   31
      Party Punches   39

II.   BUFFETS FOR FRIENDS
      AND NEIGHBORS   40

      Simple Starters   42
      Party Time   47
      Christmas Cheer   52

III.   TRADITIONAL FAVORITES
      MADE EASY AND LIGHT   60

      Old Favorites Made New   62
      Old Favorites Made Light   72
      Old Favorites Made in the   75
        Microwave

IV.   GIFTS FROM HAND,
      HEART AND HEARTH   80

      From the Hearth   82
      From the Hand and Heart   92
      The Big Chirstmas Wrap-Up   106

V.   BOUNTIFUL BATCHES   114

      Cascades of Cookie Recipes   116
      Gingerbread Christmas   126

VI.   SWEET TOUCHES, NIBBLES,
      BREADS AND PASTRIES   132

VII.   TREES, TREATS
      AND TRIMMINGS   148

      Top the Table   151
      Deck the Wall   155
      Trim the Tree   161
      Garlands Good Enough to Eat   164

INDEX   166

GOOD HOUSEKEEPING

CHRISTMAS IS COMING!

The children's pleasure must be planned for. There is nothing like a rag doll for making a child happy. The finest wax or china baby Paris ever produced will not be treasured like a clumsy, roly-poly doll that can be thrown around and abused and loved all day long, and will only cease to smile when her face is so dirty that the smile is blotted out. COOK'S FLAKED RICE CO. has thousands of these dolls all ready to make Xmas happy for thousands of little people. They are the size of a small child (25 inches high), are printed in natural colors on strong muslin, and only need to be sewed up and stuffed with a few cents' worth of cotton to be perfect. One will be mailed to any address on receipt of the coupon contained in every package of COOK'S FLAKED RICE and 10 cts. to cover expenses of mailing, etc. Address COOK'S FLAKED RICE CO., 1 Union Square, New York City. The Rice is never sent by mail.

COOK'S FLAKED RICE is a perfect food for every member of the family. Delicious and tempting, it may be prepared on the table in less than a minute. ABSOLUTELY NO COOKING. Can be served in countless different ways for Breakfast, Luncheon and Dinner. It is equally satisfactory as Breakfast cereal, entree and dessert. It is not a new food, simply the very best Rice, sterilized and steam cooked. Book of tested receipts in every package. You must buy a package of COOK'S FLAKED RICE of your Grocer, and get the coupon. We will not supply the rice to consumers.

25 INCHES HIGH

COOK'S FLAKED RICE CO.,
1 UNION SQUARE,   .·.   NEW YORK CITY

When you write advertisers please mention Good Housekeeping.

Good Housekeeping   December 1900

INTRODUCTION

American Family Christmas, these three simple words describe our book and the story it tells. On the front cover the double doors, wreathed in pine, invite you in to our Christmas celebration. It is a time to bake things and make things that will adorn our homes and bring smiles to the lips of those we invite to share with us. Come in, have a cup of Christmas cheer and we'll entertain you with the recipes that best represent American cooking—from Maine to Florida and from Washington State to Southern California—as well as recipes that were molded and adapted by people who came here from other lands.

Enter and join our family because that, too, is Christmas—a celebration and expression of love for all who are dear to us, for all who gather for the holiday festivities. For some, it is the only time during the year when long lost relatives suddenly reappear. For others, it's a congregation of familiar and cherished faces. A time when all—friends and neighbors of every faith—are invited in for a slice of fruitcake and a cup of mulled cider.

So let's get started. Pull down the sewing basket, the paint set and the scissors. Let's bring the Christmas atmosphere indoors (as well as out!) and begin cutting, sewing and painting the toys, dolls, crafts, and decorations—symbols of the holiday season.

We hope, like the little boy on our back cover, to bring the love and light of Christmas into your home this, and every, year.

John Mack Carter
Editor-in-Chief,
Good Housekeeping Magazine

I. SIT-DOWN MENUS FOR CHRISTMAS DAY

Christmas dinner and the family is about to assemble—kids from college, visiting grandparents, a great aunt or uncle. It is a time of celebration and of course feasting where the table is set for four or twenty-four. Soon the first course will be served. But what will it be? Traditional, or an old favorite with a new twist? How about a soup this year? And the main course? A Christmas Goose or a Country Pot Roast with Winter Vegetables? Choose a very personal Christmas Menu from the following pages that will appeal to all (but remember, you can't please everyone!). We have a favorite six-course Good Housekeeping Christmas Dinner and we've marked each recipe.

This unusually elaborate setting includes fine china, crystal, silk flowers and candlelight. What's missing are the sumptuous courses you will choose from our CHRISTMAS A LA CARTE menu on the following pages.

Christmas à la Carte

Here's everything you need—from great beginnings to perfect endings—for your own idea of a fabulous Christmas feast. Just choose the dishes you prefer from the dozens listed on our menu

Great Beginnings

Crab Strudel
Pâté in Aspic
Chilled Lemony Mushrooms
Avocado and Shrimp in Butter Sauce
Tomato Boats
Sour Cream and Cabbage Pie
Velvety Pumpkin Bisque
Salmon-Sole Mousse

Enticing Entrées

Christmas Goose with Glazed Oranges
Chicken Legs with Rice-Sausage Stuffing
Seafood Newburg
Holiday Rock Cornish Hens
Roast Pork with Parsley Crumb Crust
Beef and Oyster Pie
Beef Bourguignon with Chestnuts
Tenderloin en Croûte
Breast of Duckling with Green Peppercorns
Pork Loin Chops with Prune Stuffing
Country Pot Roast with Winter Vegetables

Glorious Go-Alongs

Sautéed Red Cabbage
Party Potato Casserole
Jasmine Rice
Roasted Potato Fans
Broccoli Puffs
Gingery Apple Rings

Super Salads

Julienne of Vegetables Rémoulade
Cold Vegetable Salad with Zucchini Dressing
Artichoke and Mushroom Salad
Orange and Avocado Salad

From the Bakery

Colonial Oatmeal Bread
Greek Christmas Bread
Old-Fashioned Dinner Rolls
Crunchy Onion Twists
Cranberry-Almond Muffins

Perfect Endings

Christmas Wreath Cheesecake
Mixed-Nut Fruitcake
Raspberry-Strawberry Cream Ca
Holiday Pear-Peach Pie
Almond Cream Pie
Spicy Crumb Cake
Cheese-Filled Crepes with Chocola
Espresso Nut Mousse
Creamy Cheese Triangles
Marzipan Apples
Frozen Almond Bonbons
Maple Crunch Squares

Party Punches

Orange Cream Punch
Espresso Eggnog

CRAB STRUDEL

	butter or margarine
1	tablespoon minced green onion
3	tablespoons all-purpose flour
1/4	teaspoon salt
1/8	teaspoon coarsely ground black pepper
1 1/3	cups milk
2	6-ounce packages frozen Alaska King or Snow crabmeat, thawed and drained
3	tablespoons dry sherry
	about 1/3 pound phyllo (strudel leaves)
1/4	cup dried bread crumbs
	radish roses for garnish
	parsley sprigs for garnish

About 1½ hours before serving:

1. In 2-quart saucepan over medium heat, in 4 tablespoons hot butter or margarine, cook minced green onion until tender, stirring occasionally. Stir in flour, salt, and pepper until blended; cook 1 minute. Gradually stir milk into flour mixture; cook, stirring constantly, until mixture is thickened and smooth. Stir in crabmeat and sherry; remove saucepan from heat.

2. In small saucepan over low heat, melt 4 tablespoons butter or margarine.

3. On waxed paper, overlap a few sheets of phyllo to make a 16″ by 12″ rectangle, brushing each sheet of phyllo with some melted butter or margarine. Sprinkle with 1 tablespoon bread crumbs. Continue layering, brushing each sheet of phyllo with some butter or margarine and sprinkling every other layer with 1 tablespoon bread crumbs.

4. Preheat oven to 375°F. Starting along a short side of phyllo, evenly spoon crabmeat mixture to cover about half of rectangle. From crabmeat-mixture side, roll phyllo, jelly-roll fashion.

5. Place roll, seam-side down, on cookie sheet; brush with remaining butter or margarine. Bake 40 minutes or until golden. For easier slicing, cool strudel about 15 minutes on cookie sheet on wire rack.

6. To serve, cut strudel into 1-inch-thick slices. Arrange a slice of strudel on a small plate; garnish with a radish rose and some parsley sprigs. Makes 12 first-course servings.

PATE IN ASPIC

	butter or margarine
1/2	pound chicken livers
1/4	pound mushrooms, thinly sliced
2	tablespoons minced green onions
1/8	teaspoon dill weed
	salt
1/8	teaspoon hot pepper sauce
	dry sherry
3	cups water
3	chicken-flavor bouillon cubes or envelopes
1/8	teaspoon pepper
2	envelopes unflavored gelatin
2	small cucumbers
1	small carrot
1	lemon

Early in day or day ahead:

1. In 10-inch skillet over medium-high heat, in 2 tablespoons hot butter or margarine, cook chicken livers, sliced mushrooms, minced green onions, dill weed, and 1/4 teaspoon salt until chicken livers are lightly browned but still pink inside, about 5 minutes, stirring mixture frequently. Stir in hot pepper sauce and 1/4 cup sherry; cover and simmer 5 minutes to blend flavors.

2. In food processor with knife blade attached or in blender at medium speed, blend chicken-liver mixture and 4 tablespoons butter or margarine until smooth, stopping blender occasionally and scraping sides with rubber spatula. (Mixture will be thin.) Pour mixture into small bowl; cover and refrigerate 2½ hours or until firm.

3. Prepare aspic: In 2-quart saucepan, mix water, chicken-flavor bouillon, pepper, 1/3 cup sherry, and 1/4 teaspoon salt; sprinkle gelatin evenly over chicken-broth mixture. Over medium heat, heat mixture stirring constantly, until gelatin is completely dissolved.

4. For ease in handling, arrange eight 6-ounce custard cups in 15½" by 10½" jelly-roll pan. Pour about 1 teaspoonful gelatin mixture into each cup; refrigerate until gelatin is set, about 10 minutes.

5. Thinly slice 1 cucumber and carrot. With vegetable peeler, shave some peel from lemon; cut peel into eight 2" by ⅛" strips. In bottom of each custard cup on aspic, arrange a few cucumber slices, a carrot slice, and a strip of lemon peel to make a pretty design; cover with ⅛-inch-thick layer of gelatin mixture; refrigerate until gelatin is set, about 10 minutes.

6. With two spoons, shape chicken-liver mixture into 8 balls, using about 1 rounded tablespoonful mixture for each ball. Place a chicken-liver ball on aspic in center of each custard cup. Pour remaining gelatin mixture over pâté to cover completely. Refrigerate until gelatin is set, about 2 hours.

7. To serve, unmold each onto a small plate. Thinly slice remaining cucumber. Garnish aspic with cucumber slices. Makes 8 first-course servings.

CHILLED LEMONY MUSHROOMS

1	*pound medium mushrooms*
1	*medium lemon*
¼	*cup salad oil*
2	*tablespoons water*
1½	*teaspoons soy sauce*
¼	*teaspoon salt*
¼	*teaspoon sugar*
¼	*teaspoon rubbed sage*
2	*small heads Bibb lettuce*

About 2 hours before serving or early in day:

1. Rinse mushrooms under running cold water; trim tough stem ends and slice mushrooms. Cut 6 very thin slices and squeeze 2 teaspoons juice from lemon; set aside.

2. In 3-quart saucepan over medium-high heat, in hot salad oil, cook mushrooms, stirring frequently, until mushrooms are coated with oil. Stir in water, soy sauce, salt, sugar, rubbed sage, lemon slices, and lemon juice; heat mixture to boiling. Reduce heat to medium; continue cooking 3 minutes longer or until mushrooms are tender, stirring mixture often. Spoon mushroom mixture into bowl; cover and refrigerate until well chilled.

3. To serve, cut each head of Bibb lettuce into 4 wedges. Arrange lettuce wedges and mushrooms on 8 small plates. Makes 8 first-course servings.

AVOCADO AND SHRIMP IN BUTTER SAUCE

¾	*pound large shrimp*
2	*cups water*
½	*cup dry white wine*
2	*teaspoons white wine vinegar*
1	*medium green onion, cut into 1-inch pieces*
1	*small garlic clove, cut in half*
½	*cup butter*
1	*ripe avocado, at room temperature sliced green onion for garnish*

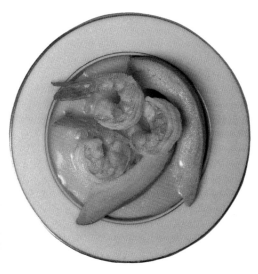

About 30 minutes before serving:

1. Shell and devein shrimp, but leave tail part of shell on. In 2-quart saucepan over high heat, heat water to boiling. Add shrimp; heat to boiling. Reduce heat to medium; cook shrimp 2 to 3 minutes until shrimp are tender and pink; drain; keep warm.

2. In same saucepan, combine white wine, wine vinegar, green onion, and garlic. Over high heat, heat mixture to boiling. Boil about 5 minutes or until liquid is reduced to about 2 tablespoons. Discard green onion and garlic. Reduce heat to medium; add butter, 2 tablespoons at a time, beating constantly with wire whisk until butter is melted and mixture is thickened. Keep butter sauce warm. (Do not use margarine; sauce will not be thick.)

3. To serve, peel and remove seed from avocado; cut avocado into 12 wedges. On each of 6 warm small plates, spoon some butter sauce; arrange 2 avocado wedges and a few shrimp. Garnish with sliced green onion. Serve immediately. Makes 6 first-course servings.

TOMATO BOATS

2 large tomatoes
1 small eggplant (½ pound)
1 small onion
1 small green pepper
1 small zucchini
¼ cup salad oil
1½ teaspoons salt
1 teaspoon oregano leaves
¾ teaspoon sugar
   Crusty Bread Flowers
   spinach leaves for garnish

About 2 hours before serving or early in day:

1. Cut each tomato into 4 wedges. With spoon, scoop out pulp from tomato wedges, leaving a ¼-inch-thick shell; cover and refrigerate tomato shells. Chop tomato pulp.

2. Cut eggplant into ½-inch cubes. Dice onion and green pepper. Cut zucchini crosswise into ¼-inch-thick slices; cut slices into thin strips.

3. In 4-quart saucepan over medium heat, in hot salad oil, cook eggplant, onion, and chopped tomato pulp until vegetables are tender, about 20 minutes, stirring occasionally. Stir in green pepper, zucchini, salt, oregano, and sugar; cook 5 minutes

or until green pepper and zucchini are tender-crisp, stirring occasionally. Spoon mixture into medium bowl; cover and refrigerate until mixture is chilled.

4. Meanwhile, prepare Crusty Bread Flowers.

5. To serve, fill each tomato shell with some eggplant mixture. Garnish each serving with spinach leaves and Crusty Bread Flowers. Makes 8 first-course servings.

Crusty Bread Flowers

In small bowl, stir *4 teaspoons butter* or margarine, softened, *1 teaspoon sesame seeds,* and *¼ teaspoon garlic powder* until well mixed. With 1½-inch flower-shaped cookie or canapé cutter, cut *4 thin slices white bread* into 16 flowers. (Reserve bread trimmings for bread crumbs another day.) Spread one side of bread flowers with butter mixture; arrange bread flowers, butter-side up, on cookie sheet. Broil about 3 minutes to toast bread. Remove cookie sheet from oven; set aside.

SOUR CREAM AND CABBAGE PIE

¼ cup salad oil
6 cups finely shredded cabbage (about 1 pound)
¼ pound medium mushrooms, sliced
1 medium onion, diced
1 teaspoon salt
1 teaspoon sugar
⅛ teaspoon pepper
   piecrust mix for two 9-inch piecrusts
½ cup sour cream
1 pint cherry tomatoes
   small lettuce leaves

About 1 hour before serving:

1. In 5-quart Dutch oven over medium heat, in hot salad oil, cook cabbage, mushrooms, onion, salt, sugar, and pepper until vegetables are tender, about 20 minutes, stirring occasionally. Keep warm.

2. Preheat oven to 425°F. Prepare piecrust mix as label directs. Roll half of pastry into circle to line 12-inch pizza pan. Cut remaining pastry into four equal portions. With hands, roll each into an 18-inch-long strand; gently twist each 2 strands together to make a rope. Moisten edge of pastry in pizza pan with water; top with pastry rope, pressing gently in place. Bake piecrust 10 minutes or until lightly browned.

3. Stir sour cream into cabbage mixture; spoon mixture into piecrust. Bake 10 minutes longer or until crust is golden brown and pie is hot.

4. Meanwhile, cut each cherry tomato into 5 wedges but not all the way through; gently spread wedges apart to resemble a flower.

5. To serve, cut pie into 12 wedges. Garnish each serving with a lettuce leaf and one or two tomato flowers. Makes 12 first-course servings.

Here's a quick, glorious holiday appetizer, dessert too: Prick a half wheel or any size wedge of **Brie** with a fork; sprinkle with *brandy* and *confectioners' sugar;* then broil until top is golden and sugar is caramelized—just a minute or two. Serve immediately—with *crackers* as an appetizer; with *fresh fruit,* like orange sections or wedges of apple or pear, for dessert.

VELVETY PUMPKIN BISQUE

2 tablespoons butter or margarine
1 tablespoon minced green onion
1 16-ounce can pumpkin
1 cup water
2 teaspoons brown sugar
½ teaspoon salt
⅛ teaspoon white pepper
⅛ teaspoon ground cinnamon
2 chicken-flavor bouillon cubes or
     envelopes
2 cups half-and-half
1 lemon, thinly sliced for garnish
     minced parsley for garnish

About 30 minutes before serving:

1. In 2-quart saucepan over medium heat, in hot butter or margarine, cook green onion until tender, stirring occasionally. Stir in pumpkin, water, brown sugar, salt, pepper, cinnamon, and bouillon until blended and mixture begins to boil; cook 5 minutes to blend flavors. Stir in half-and-half; heat through.

2. To serve, ladle soup into soup bowls; garnish each serving with a lemon slice and some minced parsley. Makes about 5 cups or 10 first-course servings.

There's no better way to chase winter's chill away than with a bowl of **hot soup.** To make sure the soup stays hot, prewarm the soup bowls, mugs, or cups by filling them with boiling water and letting them stand a minute to heat. Then drain them and ladle in the piping-hot soup.

SALMON-SOLE MOUSSE

¼ cup dry sherry
   water
1 pound fresh or frozen sole fillets
1 envelope unflavored gelatin
½ teaspoon salt
1 7¾-ounce can salmon, drained
½ bunch watercress
1 cup heavy or whipping cream
   Caper Mayonnaise

Early in day or day ahead:

1. In 10-inch skillet over medium heat, heat sherry and about ½ inch water to boiling. Add sole fillets; cover and cook 15 minutes or until fish flakes easily when tested with a fork. With pancake turner, remove sole to plate; set aside. Reserve ½ cup poaching liquid; discard remaining liquid.

2. In small saucepan, evenly sprinkle gelatin over ¼ cup cold water; let stand 1 minute to soften; stir in reserved poaching liquid. Over medium heat, cook mixture, stirring constantly, until gelatin is completely dissolved.

3. In blender at medium speed or in food processor with knife blade attached, blend sole with any liquid in plate, gelatin mixture, and salt until sole is very smooth. Pour mixture into large bowl; cover and refrigerate until well chilled and almost set, about 45 minutes.

4. Meanwhile, in medium bowl, finely flake drained salmon. Mince enough watercress to make ⅓ cup; place in small bowl. Reserve remaining watercress for garnish.

5. In small bowl with mixer at medium speed, beat heavy or whipping cream until stiff peaks form. Fold whipped cream into sole mixture until blended. Fold ½ cup sole mixture into flaked salmon. Fold another ½ cup sole mixture into minced watercress. Evenly spoon half of remaining sole mixture into 9" by 5" loaf pan; top with salmon mixture, then watercress mixture. Spoon remaining sole mixture on top. Cover and refrigerate until mousse is set, at least 3 hours.

6. Prepare Caper Mayonnaise; cover and refrigerate.

7. To serve, unmold mousse onto cutting board; cut into 10 slices. For each serving, spoon some Caper Mayonnaise onto a small plate; place a slice of mousse on top. Garnish with watercress leaves. Makes 10 first-course servings.

Caper Mayonnaise
In small bowl with wire whisk or fork, mix well *1 cup mayonnaise, ⅓ cup milk, 3 tablespoons catchup,* and *1 tablespoon capers, minced.*

ENTICING ENTREES

CHRISTMAS GOOSE WITH GLAZED ORANGES

Rye-Bread Stuffing
1 10- to 12-pound goose
1 teaspoon salt
¼ teaspoon pepper
8 small oranges
   water
⅓ cup light corn syrup
2 tablespoons sugar
   Mushroom Sauce
   parsley sprigs for garnish

About 4½ hours before serving:

1. Prepare Rye-Bread Stuffing.

2. Remove giblets and neck from goose. Refrigerate giblets and neck to use in soup another day. Discard fat from body cavity; rinse goose with running cold water and drain well. Spoon some stuffing into neck cavity. (Do not pack stuffing; it expands during cooking.) Fold neck skin over stuffing; fasten neck skin to the back with 1 or 2 skewers. With goose breast-side up, lift wings up toward neck, then fold under back of goose.

3. Spoon stuffing lightly into body cavity. (Bake any leftover stuffing in covered greased small casserole during last 40 minutes of roasting time.) Fold skin over opening; skewer closed if necessary. With string, tie legs and tail together. With fork, prick skin of goose in several places.

4. Place goose, breast-side up, on rack in open roasting pan. Rub goose with salt and pepper. Insert meat thermometer into thickest part of meat between breast and thigh, being careful that pointed end of thermometer does not touch bone. Roast goose in 350°F. oven about 3 hours. Start checking doneness during last 30 minutes.

5. About 1 hour before goose is done, prepare glazed oranges: With knife, carefully remove peel and white membrane from oranges; set aside. Trim off white membrane from few pieces of peel; then cut peel into long, thin strips to make about ½ cup, firmly packed. In 10-inch skillet over high heat, heat orange peels and 3 cups water to boiling; cook 15 minutes. Drain; rinse. With 3 cups more water, cook peels 15 minutes again; drain.

6. In same skillet over high heat, heat corn syrup and sugar until boiling and sugar is dissolved. Add oranges and peels to coat well with corn-syrup mixture. Reduce heat to medium-low and cook until oranges are heated through, about 10 minutes; keep warm.

7. Prepare Mushroom Sauce; keep warm.

8. Goose is done when thermometer reaches 190°F. and thickest part of leg feels soft when pinched with fingers protected by paper towels.

9. To serve, remove skewers and strings; place goose on warm large platter; garnish with parsley sprigs and glazed oranges. Brush goose with corn-syrup mixture remaining in skillet. Serve goose with sauce. Makes 8 to 10 servings.

Rye-Bread Stuffing

In 5-quart Dutch oven or saucepot over medium heat, melt ½ cup butter or margarine. Add 2 celery stalks, diced and 1 medium onion, diced; cook until vegetables are tender, stirring frequently. Remove Dutch oven from heat; stir in 10 cups rye-bread cubes, 1¼ cups milk, 2 tablespoons minced parsley, ½ teaspoon thyme leaves, ¼ teaspoon rubbed sage, and ¼ teaspoon pepper.

Mushroom Sauce

In 3-quart saucepan over medium heat, melt 3 tablespoons butter or margarine. Add ½ pound mushrooms, thinly sliced, and 1 green onion, sliced, and cook until vegetables are tender, stirring occasionally. Stir in 2 tablespoons all-purpose flour, ¼ teaspoon salt, and ⅛ teaspoon pepper. Gradually stir in 2 cups milk and 1 chicken-flavor bouillon cube; cook, stirring frequently, until mixture thickens.

CHICKEN LEGS WITH RICE-SAUSAGE STUFFING

1 cup regular long-grain rice
1 16-ounce package pork-sausage meat
1 large celery stalk, diced
1 small onion, minced
¾ cup milk
¼ teaspoon salt
8 large chicken legs (about 4 pounds)
2 tablespoons soy sauce
   honey
   watercress sprigs for garnish

About 2 hours before serving:

1. Prepare stuffing: Prepare rice as label directs. Meanwhile, in 5-quart Dutch oven or saucepot over medium heat, cook pork-sausage meat until browned, stirring to break up sausage. With slotted spoon, remove sausage to medium bowl. To drippings in Dutch oven, add celery and onion and cook until tender, stirring occasionally. Remove Dutch oven from heat; stir in cooked rice, cooked sausage, milk, and salt.

2. Preheat oven to 400°F. Carefully loosen skin on each chicken leg by pushing fingers between skin and meat to form a pocket; spoon some stuffing into each pocket. Place chicken in large, open roasting pan; brush with soy sauce. Bake 50 minutes or until chicken is fork-tender.

3. To serve, remove chicken to warm platter; brush lightly with honey. Garnish with watercress. Makes 8 servings.

SEAFOOD NEWBURG

Rich Biscuits
1 pound fresh or frozen cod, flounder, or
    haddock fillets
1 *pound medium shrimp or 1 12-ounce*
    package frozen shelled and
    deveined shrimp, thawed and
    drained
    butter or margarine
1 *pound mushrooms, sliced*
1/3 *cup all-purpose flour*
1 *teaspoon salt*
1/8 *teaspoon pepper*
4 *cups half-and-half*
1 *cup milk*
1 *10-ounce package frozen peas*
1 *6-ounce package frozen Alaska King*
    or Snow crabmeat, thawed
1/4 *cup dry sherry*
3/4 *cup shredded Swiss cheese*
2 *4-ounce jars pimento, drained and*
    cut into thin strips
    paprika

About 1¼ hours before serving:

1. Prepare Rich Biscuits; keep warm.

2. If using frozen, let fish stand at room temperature 15 minutes to thaw slightly, then cut into bite-size chunks. Meanwhile, if using fresh shrimp, shell and devein shrimp; set aside.

3. In 4-quart saucepan over medium-high heat, in 3 tablespoons hot butter or margarine, cook mushrooms until tender, stirring occasionally. With slotted spoon, remove mushrooms to bowl.

4. In same saucepan over medium heat, melt 4 more tablespoons butter or margarine. Stir in flour, salt, and pepper until blended; cook 1 minute. Gradually stir in half-and-half and milk until mixture is

Delicate mix of fish, shrimp, crabmeat, mushrooms, green peas, and pimento in a smooth cheese-flavored sauce, served over feathery-light biscuits.

smooth. Add fish chunks, shrimp, frozen peas, crabmeat with its liquid, sherry, and mushrooms; cook, stirring frequently, until fish flakes easily when tested with a fork and shrimp are tender and mixture is slightly thickened. Stir in cheese and pimento; cook until cheese is melted. Sprinkle lightly with paprika. Serve with biscuits. Makes 10 servings.

Rich Biscuits
Preheat oven to 450°F. In medium bowl with fork, mix *2 cups all-purpose flour, 1 tablespoon baking powder,* and *1 teaspoon salt.* With pastry blender or two knives used scissor-fashion, cut in *⅓ cup shortening* until mixture resembles coarse crumbs. With fork, stir in *⅔ cup milk* just until mixture forms soft dough and leaves side of bowl.

On lightly foured surface with lightly floured hands, knead dough 10 times. Pat dough into ½-inch-thick circle. With floured 3-inch flower-shaped cookie cutter (or, use 3-inch round cookie cutter), cut out as many biscuits as possible. Place biscuits, about ½ inch apart, on large cookie sheet. Press dough trimmings together; pat and cut as above until all dough is used. In cup with fork, beat *1 egg.* Brush biscuits with beaten egg. Bake 10 to 12 minutes until golden.

HOLIDAY ROCK CORNISH HENS

6 *1-pound fresh or frozen (thawed)*
    Rock Cornish hens
6 *tablespoons butter or margarine*
1/2 *pound mushrooms, sliced*
2 *celery stalks, diced*
1 *small onion, diced*
1/2 *pound chicken livers, cut into 1-inch*
    pieces
3 *cups white-bread cubes (6 slices)*
2 *tablespoons dry sherry*
    salt
    pepper
    salad oil
    paprika
    Gingered Peaches
    watercress sprigs for garnish

About 2 hours before serving:

1. Remove livers from Rock Cornish hens; set aside; refrigerate gizzards, hearts, and necks to use in soup another day. Rinse hens with running cold water; pat dry with paper towels; refrigerate.

2. Prepare stuffing: In 12-inch skillet over medium heat, in hot butter or margarine, cook mushrooms, celery, and onion until vegetables are tender, stirring occasionally. Push vegetables to one side of pan; add chicken livers and Rock Cornish hen livers; cook just until livers lose their pink color. Remove skillet from heat. Stir in bread cubes, sherry, ¼ teaspoon salt, and ⅛ teaspoon pepper.

3. Lightly spoon some stuffing into body cavity of each hen. Fold neck skin to back; lift wings up toward neck, then fold under back. With string, tie legs and tail of each hen together. Place hens, breast-side up, on rack in open roasting pan.

4. Brush hens with salad oil; lightly sprinkle with salt, pepper, and paprika. Roast hens in 350°F oven about 1¼ hours, brushing occasionally with drippings in pan. Hens are done when legs can be moved up and down easily, or when fork is inserted between leg and body cavity and juices that escape are not pink.

5. When hens are done, discard strings. Place hens on warm large platter; keep warm. Prepare Gingered Peaches.

6. To serve, arrange peaches on platter with hens. Garnish with watercress. Makes 6 servings.

Gingered Peaches
In 2-quart saucepan over medium heat, stir *one 29- to 30-ounce can sliced cling peaches* with their liquid and *1 tablespoon slivered preserved ginger.* Cook until peaches are heated through, stirring occasionally.

ROAST PORK WITH PARSLEY CRUMB CRUST

1   14-pound pork leg (fresh ham), whole
¼   teaspoon pepper
     salt
¼   cup prepared mustard
1   teaspoon Worcestershire
¼   teaspoon ground ginger
4   tablespoons butter or margarine
3   slices white bread
¼   cup chopped parsley
     water
3   tablespoons all-purpose flour
1   cup milk

About 6½ hours before serving:

1. With knife, remove skin and excess fat from pork leg, leaving only a thin fat covering. Place pork leg, fat-side up, on rack in open roasting pan. Rub pork with pepper and 1 teaspoon salt. Insert meat thermometer into center of thickest part of pork, being careful that pointed end of thermometer does not touch fat or bone. Roast in 325°F. oven about 5½ hours or until thermometer reaches 170°F. Remove pork leg from oven.

2. In small bowl, mix mustard, Worcestershire, and ginger. In 1-quart saucepan over medium heat, melt butter or margarine; remove saucepan from heat. Into saucepan, tear bread into small pieces. Add chopped parsley; mix well.

3. Skim off 1 tablespoon fat from drippings in roasting pan; add to mustard mixture. With pastry brush, brush mustard mixture onto pork leg. With hands, carefully pat bread-crumb mixture onto pork. Return pork to oven; bake 15 minutes longer or until bread is lightly browned. Place pork on warm large platter or cutting board. Let stand 15 minutes for easier carving.

4. Meanwhile, prepare gravy: Remove rack from roasting pan; pour drippings into 4-cup measure or medium bowl (set pan aside); let stand a few seconds until fat separates from meat juices. Skim 3 tablespoons fat from drippings into 2-quart saucepan; skim off and discard any remaining fat. Add ¼ cup water to roasting pan; stir until brown bits are loosened; add to meat juice in cup with additional water to make 2 cups.

5. Into fat in saucepan over medium heat, stir flour and ¼ teaspoon salt until blended; gradually stir in meat-juice mixture and milk; cook, stirring, until gravy is thickened. Pour gravy into gravy boat.

6. To serve, if you like, wrap small end of pork leg with a clean napkin to conceal shank bone. Serve gravy with pork. Makes 28 servings.

BEEF AND OYSTER PIE

1   beef kidney (about 1 pound)
1/4   cup all-purpose flour
2   pounds beef for stew, cut into 1-inch chunks
    salad oil
1   garlic clove, cut in half
4   medium carrots, cut into 1-inch chunks
1   large onion, chopped
1   12-ounce can or bottle beer
2   tablespoons steak sauce
1/2   teaspoon salt
1/4   teaspoon pepper
    water
1   8-ounce container shucked oysters
    piecrust mix for one 9-inch piecrust
1   egg yolk

About 2 hours before serving:

1. Rinse kidney. With knife, remove membranes and hard white parts from kidney; cut kidney into 1-inch chunks. On waxed paper, coat kidney chunks with 1 tablespoon flour; place in small bowl. Coat beef for stew with remaining flour; place on plate.

2. In 5-quart Dutch oven over medium-high heat, in 1/4 cup hot salad oil, cook garlic until golden; discard garlic. In same Dutch oven, cook kidney until well browned. With slotted spoon, remove kidney to bowl; set aside.

3. In oil remaining in Dutch oven, cook beef for stew until well browned. With slotted spoon, remove beef for stew to plate. In drippings remaining in Dutch oven (add 2 tablespoons salad oil if necessary) over medium heat, cook carrots and onion until lightly browned, stirring frequently. Return beef for stew to Dutch oven; stir in beer, steak sauce, salt, pepper, and 1/2 cup water; over high heat, heat to boiling. Reduce heat to low; cover and simmer 1 1/2 hours or until beef is fork-tender.

4. When beef is tender, stir kidney and oysters with their liquid into beef mixture; spoon into 2 1/2-quart round casserole.

5. Prepare piecrust mix as label directs. Preheat oven to 400°F. On lightly floured surface with lightly floured rolling pin, roll dough into a circle about 1 1/2 inches larger all around than top of casserole. Place pastry loosely over meat mixture. With kitchen shears, trim pastry edge, leaving 1-inch overhang. Fold overhang under and press gently all around casserole rim to make a high stand-up edge. With tip of knife, cut several slits in pastry top. In cup with fork, mix egg yolk with 1 teaspoon water. Brush crust with egg-yolk mixture. If you like, reroll scraps and use a cookie cutter to cut out shapes to decorate top of pie; brush cut-outs with yolk mixture. Bake pie 20 minutes or until crust is golden and mixture is heated through. Makes 10 servings.

BEEF BOURGUIGNON WITH CHESTNUTS

    salad oil
2 1/2   pounds beef for stew, cut into 1 1/2-inch chunks
1 1/2   pounds mushrooms, each cut in half or in quarters
6   slices bacon, diced
1   pound small white onions
2   medium carrots, diced
1   medium celery stalk, diced
1   cup dry red wine
2   teaspoons sugar
1   teaspoon salt
1/4   teaspoon pepper
1   beef-flavor bouillon cube or envelope
    water
1   pound chestnuts
2   tablespoons all-purpose flour
1   tablespoon minced parsley for garnish

About 3 hours before serving:

1. In 5-quart Dutch oven over medium-high heat, in 2 tablespoons hot salad oil, cook beef for stew, half at a time, until well browned on all sides. With slotted spoon, remove meat to plate; set aside. In drippings remaining in Dutch oven (add salad oil if necessary) over medium heat, cook mushrooms 5 minutes; with slotted spoon, remove mushrooms to medium bowl.

2. In same Dutch oven over medium heat, cook bacon, onions, carrots, and celery until bacon and vegetables are browned, stirring frequently. Stir in wine, sugar, salt, pepper, bouillon, and 1 1/4 cups water. Return meat to Dutch oven; over high heat, heat to boiling. Reduce heat to low; cover and simmer 1 1/2 hours or until meat is almost tender, stirring occasionally.

3. Meanwhile, in 2-quart saucepan over high heat, heat chestnuts and enough water to cover to boiling. Reduce heat to medium; cover and cook 15 minutes. Remove saucepan from heat. Immediately, with slotted spoon, remove 4 chestnuts from water. With kitchen shears, carefully cut each chestnut on flat side through shell. With fingers, peel off shell and skin, keeping chestnuts whole if possible. Repeat with remaining chestnuts. (Chestnuts will be difficult to peel when cool.)

4. When meat is ready, stir mushrooms and chestnuts into meat mixture. Continue cooking until meat is fork-tender, about 15 minutes.

5. To serve, skim off fat from liquid in Dutch oven. In cup with fork, stir flour and 1/4 cup water until blended. Gradually stir flour mixture into beef mixture in Dutch oven; cook over medium heat, stirring, until mixture is thickened. Spoon meat mixture into warm bowl; sprinkle with parsley. Makes 10 servings.

TENDERLOIN EN CROUTE WITH CAPER SAUCE

1 medium eggplant (about 1½ pounds)
  salad oil
  salt
2 tablespoons butter or margarine
1 2- to 2½-pound beef loin tenderloin roast, well trimmed and tied with string
1 medium onion, minced
¼ cup dried bread crumbs
  coarsely ground black pepper
  piecrust mix for two 9-inch piecrusts
1 egg, slightly beaten
½ cup water
1 tablespoon capers
½ cup heavy or whipping cream
¼ cup dry vermouth
2 teaspoons all-purpose flour
2 teaspoons prepared mustard
¼ teaspoon sugar
  watercress sprigs for garnish

About 2 hours before serving:

1. Slice eggplant lengthwise into ¼-inch-thick slices. In 12-inch skillet over medium heat, in 3 tablespoons hot salad oil, cook eggplant, a few slices at a time, until tender and browned on both sides, adding more salad oil as needed. With pancake turner, remove eggplant slices as they brown to paper towels to drain. Sprinkle eggplant slices lightly with salt.

2. In same skillet over medium-high heat, in hot butter or margarine, cook beef loin tenderloin roast until well browned on all sides, about 5 minutes. Remove meat to plate; set aside.

3. In drippings in skillet over medium heat, cook onion until tender, stirring occasionally. Remove skillet from heat; stir in bread crumbs, ½ teaspoon salt, and ¼ teaspoon coarsely ground black pepper; set aside.

4. Prepare piecrust mix as label directs. On lightly floured surface with floured rolling pin, roll pastry into a 15″ by 15″ square. With knife, cut 2-inch strip of pastry from one edge; reserve for decorating the crust.

5. Preheat oven to 425°F. With kitchen shears, cut string from roast. Pat onion mixture on top of roast; wrap roast with eggplant slices. Center eggplant-wrapped roast, crumb-side down, lengthwise on pastry. Bring one long side of pastry up over roast; brush with some beaten egg. Bring other long side up, overlapping edges, pressing edges lightly to seal. Fold up both ends; brush with egg to seal. Place pastry-wrapped roast, seamside down, in 15½″ by 10½″ jellyroll pan. Brush pastry crust with egg.

6. With canapé cutter or knife, cut reserved pastry to make pretty design; arrange on top of pastry crust; brush with egg. Bake pastry-wrapped roast 30 to 35 minutes until meat thermometer reaches 140°F. With two pancake turners, carefully transfer roast to warm platter. Let stand 10 minutes for easier slicing.

7. Meanwhile, prepare Caper Sauce: In blender at medium speed or in food processor with knife blade attached, blend water and capers until capers are pureed. In same skillet mix caper mixture, heavy or whipping cream, vermouth, flour, mustard, sugar, and ¼ teaspoon coarsely ground black pepper until smooth; over medium heat, heat until sauce is slightly thickened, stirring mixture frequently.

8. To serve, garnish platter with watercress. Cut roast into 1-inch-thick slices. Pass caper sauce to serve with roast. Makes 6 servings.

It's always best to wait a bit before **carving** a roast. The temperature inside the meat will continue to rise even after the roast has been removed from the oven. Letting it stand 15 to 20 minutes will allow the meat to stabilize, making carving easier and preventing juices from running out, so meat stays juicy and tender.

Beef Bourguignon with Chestnuts, classic French stew of tender beef, onions, and mushrooms in a dark, rich wine sauce with a delicious extra for Christmas. Recipe on page 21.

BREAST OF DUCKLING WITH GREEN PEPPERCORNS

1 4½- to 5-pound fresh or frozen (thawed) duckling
  butter or margarine
1 small green onion, minced
2 tablespoons dry white wine
2 tablespoons water
1 teaspoon green peppercorns
  watercress for garnish
½ 14-ounce jar spiced apples

About 40 minutes before serving:

1. Remove breasts from duckling: Remove giblets and neck from duckling; set aside. Rinse duckling with running cold water; pat dry with paper towels. Place duckling, breast-side up, on work surface. With sharp knife, working with one side of duckling at a time, insert tip of knife between meat and breast-bone and cut and scrape meat away from bone and rib cage, gently pulling meat back in one piece as you cut. Repeat with other side. Remove and discard skin and any fat on breasts. Reserve remaining duckling, giblets, and neck for use in soup or salad another day.

2. In 7- to 8-inch skillet over medium-high heat, in 2 tablespoons hot butter or margarine, cook duckling breasts until underside is browned, about 4 minutes; turn breasts and cook about 3 minutes longer for medium-rare or until of desired doneness. Remove breasts to warm platter; slice into thin slices; keep warm.

3. Reduce heat to medium-low. In drippings in skillet and 1 more tablespoon hot butter or margarine, cook green onion until tender. Add wine, water, and green peppercorns, stirring to loosen brown bits on bottom of skillet. Drain any juice from duckling in platter into sauce in skillet. Remove skillet from heat; stir in 1 tablespoon butter or margarine until melted. Pour sauce over duckling breasts. Garnish platter with watercress and spiced apples. Makes 2 servings.

PORK LOIN CHOPS WITH PRUNE STUFFING

2 tablespoons butter or margarine
1 small onion, diced
1½ cups whole-wheat bread cubes (about 3 slices)
1½ cups pitted prunes, coarsely chopped
¼ teaspoon sage leaves
water
salt
pepper
6 pork loin rib chops, each cut about 1 inch thick
2 chicken-flavor bouillon cubes or envelopes
¼ cup milk
1 tablespoon all-purpose flour

About 2 hours before serving:

1. In 12-inch skillet over medium heat, in hot butter or margarine, cook onion until tender, stirring occasionally. Remove skillet from heat. Add whole-wheat bread cubes, prunes, sage, ⅓ cup water, 1 teaspoon salt, and ¼ teaspoon pepper; mix well.

2. With sharp knife, trim several pieces of fat from edge of pork loin rib chops; reserve fat. Cut each pork chop, from fat side, horizontally almost to the bone to form pocket. Spoon some prune mixture firmly into each pocket; close pockets with toothpicks. Lightly sprinkle pork chops on both sides with salt and pepper.

3. In same skillet over medium-high heat, heat reserved fat until lightly browned; using spoon, press and rub fat over bottom of skillet to grease it well; discard fat. Add 3 chops to skillet; over high heat, cook until well browned on both sides, removing chops from skillet as they brown. Repeat with remaining chops.

4. Return chops to skillet; add bouillon and 1 cup water; over high heat, heat to boiling. Reduce heat to low; cover and simmer 1½ hours or until pork chops are fork-tender, turning chops once. Remove pork chops to large platter; discard toothpicks. Keep pork chops warm.

5. Skim off fat from liquid in skillet. In cup, mix milk and flour until blended. Gradually stir flour mixture into liquid in skillet. Cook over medium heat, stirring constantly, until gravy is slightly thickened. Pour gravy over chops. Makes 6 servings.

COUNTRY POT ROAST WITH WINTER VEGETABLES

2 tablespoons salad oil
1 4- to 4½-pound beef chuck cross rib pot roast, boneless
1 medium onion, diced
1 small garlic clove, minced
1 10¾-ounce can condensed cream of mushroom soup
1 cup dry red wine
½ cup water
1 teaspoon salt
½ teaspoon pepper
½ teaspoon sugar
6 medium potatoes (about 2 pounds)
2 large acorn squash (about 1 pound each)
2 10-ounce packages frozen Brussels sprouts

About 3½ hours before serving:

1. In 8-quart Dutch oven over medium-high heat, in hot salad oil, cook beef chuck cross rib pot roast until well browned on all sides; remove meat to plate; set aside.

2. In same Dutch oven in drippings over medium heat, cook onion and garlic until tender, stirring occasionally. Stir in undiluted cream of mushroom soup, wine, water, salt, pepper, and sugar. Return meat to Dutch oven; over high heat, heat to boiling. Reduce heat to low; cover and simmer about 2½ hours, stirring occasionally.

3. About 1 hour before meat is done, peel potatoes; cut into bite-size chunks. Cut each acorn squash in half; remove seeds; cut into bite-size chunks. Add potatoes and squash to meat mixture; over high heat, heat to boiling. Reduce heat to low; cover and simmer 30 minutes. Add Brussels sprouts; cook 15 minutes longer or until meat and vegetables are fork-tender.

4. To serve, arrange meat and vegetables on warm deep platter. Skim off fat from liquid in Dutch oven. Serve liquid with meat and vegetables. Makes 12 to 14 servings.

Good Housekeeping   December 1912

GLORIOUS GO-ALONGS

🏷 SAUTEED RED CABBAGE

1	*large head red cabbage (about 3 pounds)*
¼	*cup salad oil*
1	*medium onion, diced*
1	*teaspoon salt*
¼	*teaspoon pepper*
2	*tablespoons white wine vinegar*
1½	*teaspoons brown sugar*

About 45 minutes before serving:

1. Discard any tough outer leaves from cabbage. Reserve 6 large leaves from cabbage; set aside. Finely shred enough cabbage to make ¼ cup; set aside. Coarsely shred remaining cabbage.

2. In 5-quart saucepot or Dutch oven over high heat, in hot salad oil, cook coarsely shredded cabbage, onion, salt, and pepper until vegetables are tender-crisp, about 10 minutes, stirring frequently. Remove saucepot from heat; add vinegar and brown sugar; toss to mix well.

3. To serve, line platter with reserved cabbage leaves. Spoon cabbage mixture on leaves; garnish with finely shredded cabbage. Makes 8 accompaniment servings.

PARTY POTATO CASSEROLE

8	*medium potatoes (2½ pounds)*
	water
1	*8-ounce container sour cream*
2	*tablespoons milk*
	butter or margarine, softened
	salt
	pepper
1	*12-ounce package frozen cooked squash, thawed*
1	*egg*
1	*10-ounce package frozen chopped spinach, thawed and drained*
2	*teaspoons grated onion*
¼	*cup shredded Cheddar cheese*

About 2 hours before serving:

1. In 5-quart saucepot over high heat, heat potatoes and enough water to cover to boiling. Reduce heat to medium-low; cover and cook potatoes 30 minutes or until fork-tender; drain. Cool potatoes slightly; peel potatoes.

2. In large bowl with mixer at low speed, beat potatoes, sour cream, milk, 2 tablespoons butter or margarine, ½ teaspoon salt, and ⅛ teaspoon pepper until smooth and fluffy. Set aside.

3. Preheat oven to 350°F. In small bowl, mix well thawed frozen squash with 1 tablespoon butter or margarine and ⅛ teaspoon salt; set aside.

4. In second small bowl, beat egg slightly; add thawed frozen spinach, grated onion, 1 tablespoon butter or margarine, and ⅛ teaspoon salt; mix well; set aside.

5. In 2-quart deep glass casserole or glass soufflé dish, evenly spread one-third of mashed potatoes; top with squash mixture in an even layer, then with another one-third of potatoes, then with spinach mixture, then with remaining potatoes.

6. Bake casserole 40 minutes or until heated through. Remove from oven; sprinkle Cheddar cheese over top of potatoes and let stand few minutes until cheese melts. Makes 10 accompaniment servings.

GINGERY APPLE RINGS

- 1   *large lemon*
- 6   *tablespoons butter or margarine*
- ¼   *cup packed brown sugar*
- 2   *tabelspoons water*
- 2   *teaspoons minced, peeled ginger root or ½ teaspoon ground ginger*
- ⅛   *teaspoon salt*
- 4   *medium Golden Delicious apples, cored and cut into ½-inch rings*

About 30 minutes before serving:

1. Grate 1 tablespoon peel and squeeze 2 tablespoons juice from lemon.

2. In 12-inch skillet over medium heat, heat lemon peel, lemon juice, butter or margarine, brown sugar, water, ginger, and salt until butter is melted and sugar is dissolved. Add apples; cook about 10 minutes or until apples are tender, gently turning apple rings occasionally with pancake turner. Makes 6 accompaniment servings.

ROASTED POTATO FANS

- 6   *medium potatoes (2 pounds)*
- 6   *tablespoons butter or margarine*
- ½   *teaspoon salt*
- ¼   *teaspoon basil*
- ¼   *teaspoon marjoram leaves*
- ⅛   *teaspoon pepper*

About 1¼ hours before serving:

1. Peel potatoes. Cut each potato crosswise into ¼-inch-thick slices, being careful to cut each slice only ¾ of the way through potato.

2. In 13″ by 9″ baking pan in 400°F. oven, melt butter or margarine. Arrange potatoes, cut-side up, in pan; brush with melted butter; sprinkle with salt, basil, marjoram, and pepper.

3. Bake 1 hour or until potatoes are golden and slices are fanned out, occcasionally brushing potatoes with butter in pan. Makes 6 accompaniment servings.

✍ BROCCOLI PUFFS

- 4   *slices bacon*
- 4   *eggs*
- 2   *cups milk*
- 1¾   *cups all-purpose flour*
- ¾   *teaspoon salt*
- 1   *10-ounce package frozen chopped broccoli, thawed and patted dry*

About 1½ hours before serving:

1. In 10-inch skillet over medium-low heat, cook bacon until browned; remove to paper towels to drain. Crumble bacon. Reserve 2 tablespoons bacon drippings.

2. Preheat oven to 375°F. Grease ten 6-ounce custard cups; set in jelly-roll pan for easier handling. In large bowl with wire whisk or fork, beat eggs until foamy. Beat in milk, flour, salt, bacon; and reserved drippings until smooth. Stir in chopped broccoli.

3. Fill each custard cup three-quarters full with egg mixture. Bake 45 minutes or until golden and toothpick inserted in center comes out clean. Serve Broccoli Puffs immediately. (Puffs will fall upon standing.) Makes 10 accompaniment servings.

JASMINE RICE

- 3   *cups water*
- 3   *jasmine or oolong tea bags*
- 1½   *cups regular long-grain rice*
- 4   *tablespoons butter or margarine*
- 1   *teaspoon salt*
    celery leaves for garnish

About 1 hour before serving:

1. In 3-quart saucepan over high heat, heat water to boiling. Remove saucepan from heat; add tea bags; let steep 15 minutes. Discard tea bags.

2. Over high heat, heat tea in saucepan to boiling; add rice, butter or margarine, and salt. Reduce heat to low; cover and simmer 20 minutes or until rice is tender and all liquid is absorbed. Remove saucepan from heat.

3. If you like, divide rice into 8 portions. Pack one portion of rice at a time into 5-ounce timbale mold or a small custard cup; unmold rice onto warm plate. (Or use an ice-cream scoop.) Garnish each with a celery leaf. Makes 8 accompaniment servings.

JULIENNE OF VEGETABLES REMOULADE

🐚 COLD VEGETABLE SALAD WITH ZUCCHINI DRESSING

4	medium potatoes
	water
1	bunch broccoli
4	hard-cooked eggs
1	16-ounce can sliced beets, drained
3/4	cup olive or salad oil
1/3	cup red wine vinegar
2	tablespoons chopped parsley
1	tablespoon prepared mustard
1	teaspoon sugar
1/2	teaspoon salt
1/2	teaspoon coarsely ground black pepper
1	small zucchini, shredded (about 3/4 cup)
1/2	medium green pepper, minced

About 2 hours before serving or early in day:

1. Cook potatoes: In 3-quart saucepan over high heat, heat unpeeled potatoes and enough water to cover to boiling. Reduce heat to medium-low; cover and cook 25 to 30 minutes until potatoes are fork-tender; drain. Cool potatoes slightly until easy to handle. Peel and cut potatoes into 1/4-inch-thick slices.

2. Cut broccoli into 2" by 1" pieces. In 12-inch skillet over high heat, in 1 inch boiling water, heat broccoli to boiling. Reduce heat to low; cover and simmer about 5 minutes or until broccoli is tender-crisp; drain.

3. Slice each hard-cooked egg in half. Arrange eggs, potatoes, broccoli, and beets in separate piles on large chilled platter. Cover and refrigerate at least 1 hour.

4. Meanwhile, in small bowl with fork, mix olive oil, vinegar, parsley, mustard, sugar, salt, and pepper until blended. Stir in zucchini and green pepper; cover; refrigerate.

5. To serve, stir zucchini dressing to mix. Pour dressing over vegetables and eggs. Makes 8 accompaniment servings.

ORANGE AND AVOCADO SALAD

1/4	cup orange juice
3	tablespoons lemon juice
3	tablespoons olive or salad oil
2	teaspoons sugar
1	teaspoon salt
4	large oranges, peeled and cut into sections
2	medium avocados, sliced
1	medium head romaine lettuce
1	large head Boston lettuce

About 30 minutes before serving:

1. large bowl, mix orange juice, lemon juice, olive oil, sugar, and salt. Stir in oranges and avocados.

2. Into fruit mixture, tear lettuce into bite-size pieces. Gently toss to mix well. Makes 8 accompaniment servings.

ARTICHOKE AND MUSHROOM SALAD

2	9-ounce packages frozen artichoke hearts
1	pound medium mushrooms
2	4-ounce jars pimento, drained
1/2	cup salad oil
3	tablespoons cider vinegar
1	tablespoon lemon juice
1	tablespoon prepared mustard
1/2	teaspoon salt
1/8	teaspoon pepper
	lettuce leaves

About 1 1/2 hours before serving or early in day:

1. Prepare frozen artichoke hearts as labels direct, but prepare both packages together and omit salt; drain. Meanwhile, thinly slice mushrooms; cut pimento into thin strips.

2. In large bowl with fork or wire whisk, mix salad oil, vinegar, lemon juice, mustard, salt, and pepper. Add artichoke hearts, mushrooms, and pimento; toss gently to coat with dressing. Cover and refrigerate at leat 1 hour, stirring occasionally.

3. To serve, line chilled platter with lettuce leaves; spoon vegetables and dressing onto lettuce. Makes 8 accompaniment servings.

JULIENNE OF VEGETABLES REMOULADE

4	large zucchini (about 3 pounds)
4	medium carrots
1	medium green pepper
1/4	medium head red cabbage
	salt
3/4	cup mayonnaise
1	tablespoon minced parsley
1	tablespoon prepared mustard
1	teaspoon capers, minced
1/2	teaspoon tarragon
	lettuce leaves

About 2 1/2 hours before serving or early in day:

1. Cut zucchini, carrots, and green pepper into matchstick-thin strips. Finely shred cabbage to make about 1 1/2 cups.

2. In large bowl, toss zucchini, carrots, green pepper, and 3/4 teaspoon salt until well mixed. In small bowl, toss red cabbage and 1/4 teaspoon salt until well mixed. Cover bowls and let stand 1 hour.

3. Drain vegetables: Tip bowls one at a time, over sink, pressing vegetables with hand to drain as much liquid as possible.

4. Add red cabbage, mayonnaise, parsley, mustard, capers, and tarragon to vegetables in large bowl; toss gently to coat with dressing. Cover and refrigerate at least 1 hour.

5. To serve, line platter with lettuce leaves; arrange salad on lettuce. Makes 6 accompaniment servings.

FROM THE BAKERY

COLONIAL OATMEAL BREAD

1½   teaspoons salt
2   packages active dry yeast
4   cups whole-wheat flour
      about 2¾ cups all-purpose flour
2¼   cups water
½   cup honey
4   tablespoons butter or margarine
1   egg
1   cup quick-cooking oats, uncooked

About 4 hours before serving or day ahead:

1. In large bowl, combine salt, yeast, 2 cups whole-wheat flour, and 1 cup all-purpose flour. In 2-quart saucepan over low heat, heat water, honey, and butter or margarine until very warm (120° to 130°F.). (Butter or margarine does not need to melt completely.) With mixer at low speed, gradually beat liquid into dry ingredients just until blended. Increase speed to medium; beat 2 minutes, occasionally scraping bowl with rubber spatula. Gradually beat in egg and 1 cup whole-wheat flour to make a thick batter; continue beating 2 minutes, scraping bowl often. With wooden spoon, stir in oats, 1 cup whole-wheat flour, and 1 cup all-purpose flour to make a soft dough.

2. Lightly sprinkle work surface with all-purpose flour; turn dough onto surface and knead until smooth and elastic, about 10 minutes, working in more all-purpose flour (about ¾ cup) while kneading. Shape dough into a ball and place in greased large bowl, turning dough over so that top is greased. Cover and let rise in warm place (80° to 85°F.) away from draft, until dou-

bled, about 1 hour. (Dough is doubled when two fingers pressed lightly into dough leave a dent.)

3. Punch down dough. Turn dough onto lightly floured surface; cover with bowl and let dough rest 15 minutes for easier shaping.

4. Grease large cookie sheet. Cut dough in half; shape each half into a 7″ by 4″ oval, tapering ends slightly; place on cookie sheet. Cover with towel and let rise in warm place until doubled, about 1 hour. (Dough is doubled when one finger very lightly pressed against dough leaves a dent.)

5. Preheat oven to 350°F. With knife, cut 3 to 5 crisscross slashes across top of each loaf; lightly dust tops of loaves with some all-purpose flour. Bake 35 to 40 minutes until loaves sound hollow when lightly tapped with fingers. Remove loaves from cookie sheet and cool on wire rack. Makes two 1¾-pound loaves.

GREEK CHRISTMAS BREAD

1   cup sugar
1½   teaspoons anise seeds, crushed
1   teaspoon salt
2   packages active dry yeast
      about 7¾ cups all-purpose flour
2   cups milk
1   cup butter or margarine
3   eggs
16   candied red cherries

About 4 hours before serving or day ahead:

1. In large bowl, combine sugar, anise seeds, salt, yeast, and 2 cups flour. In 1-quart saucepan over low heat, heat milk and butter or margarine until very warm (120° to 130°F.). (Butter or margarine does not need to melt completely.) With mixer at low speed, gradually beat liquid into dry ingredients just until blended. Increase speed to medium; beat 2 minutes, occasionally scraping bowl with rubber spatula.

2. Reserve 1 egg white for brushing top of loaves. To mixture in large bowl, gradually beat in egg yolk, remaining 2 eggs, and 2 cups flour to make a thick batter; continue beating 2 minutes, scraping bowl often. With wooden spoon, stir in 3 cups flour to make a soft dough.

3. Turn dough onto well-floured surface and knead until smooth and elastic, about 10 minutes, working in more flour while kneading (about ¾ cup). Shape dough into a ball and place in greased large bowl, turning dough over so that top is greased. Cover and let rise in warm place (80° to 85°F.), away from draft, until doubled, about 1 hour. (Dough is doubled when two fingers pressed lightly into dough leave a dent.)

4. Punch down dough. Turn dough onto lightly floured surface; cover with bowl and let rest for 15 minutes for easier shaping. Meanwhile, grease two cookie sheets.

5. Prepare loaves: Cut dough in half; cut off and reserve ½ cup dough from each half. Shape each half into a 6-inch-round loaf; place loaves on cookie sheets. Roll 1 piece of reserved dough into two 12-inch-long ropes; cut a 3-inch-long slash into each end of the two ropes. Place ropes on top of loaf to make a cross; do not press down. Curl slashed ends of each rope; place a candied red cherry in each curl. Repeat with remaining reserved dough and second loaf. Cover loaves with towels and let rise in warm place until doubled, about 45 minutes. (Dough is doubled when one finger very lightly pressed against dough leaves a dent.)

6. Preheat oven to 350°F. In cup with fork, beat reserved egg white. With pastry brush, brush loaves with egg white. Place cookie sheets with loaves on 2 oven racks; bake 15 minutes; switch cookie sheets between upper and lower racks so both loaves brown evenly; bake about 15 to 20 minutes longer until loaves sound hollow when lightly tapped with fingers. (If loaves start to brown too quickly, cover loosely with foil.) Remove loaves from cookie sheets and cool on wire racks. Makes two 2-pound loaves.

In the bread basket (left to right) : Crunchy Onion Twists, Greek Christmas Bread, Cranberry-Almond Muffins, Old-Fashioned Dinner Rolls. Also "from the bakery" on our menu, Colonial Oatmeal Bread.

✒ OLD-FASHIONED DINNER ROLLS

½ cup sugar
1 teaspoon salt
2 packages active dry yeast
  about 6 cups all-purpose flour
2 cups water
½ cup butter or margarine
2 eggs
  salad oil

Early in day or up to 3 days ahead:

1. In large bowl, combine sugar, salt, yeast, and 2¼ cups flour. In 1-quart saucepan over low heat, heat water and butter or margarine until very warm (120° to 130°F.). (Butter or margarine does not need to melt completely.) With mixer at low speed, gradually beat liquid into dry ingredients just until blended. Increase speed to medium; beat 2 minutes, occasionally scraping bowl with rubber spatula. Gradually beat in 1 egg and 1¼ cups flour to make a thick batter; continue beating 2 minutes, scraping bowl often with rubber spatula. With wooden spoon, stir in 2 cups flour to make a soft dough.

2. Turn dough onto well-floured surface and knead until smooth and elastic, about 10 minutes, working in more flour while kneading (about ¼ to ½ cup). Shape dough into a ball and place in greased large bowl, turning dough over so that top is greased. Cover and let rise in warm place (80° to 85°F.), away from draft, until doubled, about 1½ hours. (Dough is doubled when two fingers pressed lightly into dough leave a dent.)

3. Punch down dough. Turn dough over; brush lightly with salad oil. Cover bowl tightly with plastic wrap and refrigerate, punching down dough occasionally, until ready to use.

About 2 hours before serving:

4. Remove dough from refrigerator. Grease 2 large cookie sheets. Cut dough into 30 pieces. On lightly floured surface, with lightly floured hands, shape half of dough pieces into ovals; shape remaining dough pieces into balls. Place rolls on cookie sheets. Cover and let rise in warm place until doubled, about 1 hour. (Dough is doubled when one finger very lightly pressed against dough leaves a dent.)

5. Preheat oven to 400°F. With razor, cut lengthwise slash along top of each oval roll; cut a cross on top of each round roll. In cup with fork, beat remaining egg. With pastry brush, brush rolls with egg. Bake rolls 15 minutes or until golden. Remove rolls from cookie sheet; cool on wire racks. Makes 30 rolls.

CRUNCHY ONION TWISTS

1¼ cups all-purpose flour
½ cup yellow cornmeal
½ teaspoon salt
¼ cup shortening
⅓ cup instant minced onions
  cold water

About 45 minutes before serving or day ahead:

1. In medium bowl, mix flour, cornmeal, and salt. With pastry blender or two knives used scissor-fashion, cut in shortening until mixture resembles coarse crumbs. With fork, stir in onions and ⅓ cup water. With hands, shape dough into a ball. (If mixture is too dry, add more water, a teaspoon at a time, until moist enough to hold together.)

2. Preheat oven to 425°F. On lightly floured surface with floured rolling pin, roll half of pastry into 12″ by 10″ rectangle. Cut dough into 5″ by ½″ strips. Remove each strip; holding ends, make twist by turning ends in opposite directions. Arrange twists on cookie sheet; press ends to sheet to prevent uncurling.

3. Bake twists 6 to 8 minutes until golden. Remove twists to wire racks to cool. Repeat with remaining dough. Store in tightly covered container. Serve as breadsticks. Makes 8 dozen.

CRANBERRY-ALMOND MUFFINS

3 cups all-purpose flour
½ cup sugar
2 teaspoons baking powder
1 teaspoon baking soda
¼ teaspoon salt
1 16-ounce container sour cream
⅓ cup milk
¼ cup salad oil
½ teaspoon almond extract
2 eggs
1½ cups fresh or frozen cranberries, coarsely chopped
2 tablespoons sliced blanched almonds

About 45 minutes before serving or early in day:

1. Grease and flour twelve 3-inch muffin-pan cups. (Or, use twenty-four 2½-inch muffin-pan cups; bake 25 minutes. Makes 24 muffins.) Set aside.

2. Preheat oven to 375°F. In large bowl with fork, mix first 5 ingredients. In medium bowl with fork, beat sour cream, milk, salad oil, almond extract, and eggs until blended. Stir sour-cream mixture into flour mixture just until flour is moistened. (Batter will be lumpy.) With rubber spatula, gently fold in cranberries.

3. Spoon batter into muffin-pan cups; sprinkle with sliced almonds. Bake 30 minutes or until toothpick inserted in center of muffin comes out clean. Immediately remove from pans. Serve muffins warm or cool on wire rack to serve later. Makes 12 muffins.

PERFECT ENDINGS

CHRISTMAS WREATH CHEESECAKE

6   tablespoons butter or margarine,
       softened
     all-purpose flour
     sugar
3   8-ounce packages cream cheese,
       softened
3   eggs
¼   cup milk
1   tablespoon grated lemon peel
¼   teaspoon salt
     Chocolate Leaves for garnish
     other garnishes: 1 slice candied
       pineapple, about 6 dried apricot
       halves, 4 candied green cherries,
       and 12 cranberries

Early in day or day ahead:

1. Preheat oven to 400°F. In small bowl with mixer at low speed, beat butter or margarine, ¾ cup flour, and 2 tablespoons sugar until well mixed. Press mixture into bottom of 10″ by 3″ springform pan. Bake 10 minutes or until crust is lightly browned. Cool on wire rack.

2. Turn oven control to 325°F. In large bowl with mixer at low speed, beat cream cheese just until smooth. Add eggs, milk, lemon peel, salt, ¾ cup sugar, and 2 table-spoons flour; beat 3 minutes longer, oc-casionally scraping bowl with rubber spat-ula.

3. Pour cream-cheese mixture into pan. Bake 45 minutes. Cool in pan on wire rack. Cover and refrigerate at least 4 hours or until well chilled.

4. Meanwhile, prepare Chocolate Leaves.

5. To serve, remove cake from pan. With small star-shaped canapé cutter, cut stars from candied pineapple and dried apricot halves; cut each candied green cherry in half. Arrange garnishes on cheesecake to resemble a wreath. Makes 12 servings.

Chocolate Leaves

In double boiler over hot, *not boiling, water* (or in heavy 1-quart saucepan, over low heat), heat *one-half 6-ounce package semi-sweet-chocolate pieces* (½ cup) and *2 teaspoons shortening* until chocolate is melted and smooth, about 5 minutes stirring occa-sionally. With small metal spatula, spread a layer of chocolate mixture on underside of *10 medium lemon leaves*. (If other kinds of leaves are used, make sure that they are also nontoxic.) Place coated leaves, choc-olate-side up, on cookie sheet or plate; re-frigerate at least 20 minutes or until choc-olate is firm. Carefully peel off lemon leaves from chocolate. Refrigerate Chocolate Leaves until ready to use.

RASPBERRY-STRAWBERRY CREAM CAKE

1¾ cups cake flour
¾ cup milk
¾ cup butter or margarine, softened
1 tablespoon baking powder
¾ teaspoon salt
½ teaspoon baking soda
4 eggs
   sugar
   vanilla extract
   Raspberry Custard Filling
   about ¼-pound piece whole citron
      (Whole citron is sold in specialty
      food stores.)
2 pints strawberries
3½ cups heavy or whipping cream

Early in day or day ahead:

1. Preheat oven to 375°F. Grease and flour two 9-inch round cake pans. Into large bowl, measure flour, milk, butter or margarine, baking powder, salt, baking soda, eggs, 1½ cups sugar, and 1 tablespoon vanilla. With mixer at low speed, beat just until mixed, constantly scraping bowl with rubber spatula. Increase speed to high; beat 4 minutes, occasionally scraping bowl.

2. Pour batter into pans. Bake 25 minutes or until toothpick inserted in center of cake comes out clean. Cool cake in pans on wire racks 10 minutes. Remove from pans; cool completely.

3. Meanwhile, prepare Raspberry Custard Filling.

4. Prepare citron leaves for garnish: Cut peel from whole citron; cut peel into 10 small leaves; cover and set aside. Reserve remaining citron to use in fruitcake or sprinkle on ice cream another day.

5. Reserve 6 large whole strawberries to garnish top of cake. Slice each remaining strawberry in half; set aside. With serrated knife, cut each cake horizontally in half to make 2 layers; set aside.

6. In large bowl with mixer at medium speed, beat heavy or whipping cream, 2 teaspoons sugar, and 1 teaspoon vanilla until stiff peaks form. Place 1 cake layer on cake platter; spread with about 1 cup whipped cream; arrange ⅓ halved straw-

berries on top of cream. Top with second cake layer, pressing down gently but firmly. Spread raspberry custard mixture over layer; top with third cake layer. Repeat with whipped cream and halved strawberries. Top with remaining cake layer.

7. Frost top and side of cake with ⅓ of remaining whipped cream. Spoon remaining whipped cream into decorating bag with large star tip; use to decorate top and side of cake. Garnish top of cake with citron leaves and reserved whole strawberries, side of cake with remaining halved strawberries. Refrigerate until serving time. Makes 16 servings.

Raspberry Custard Filling

Drain *one 10-ounce package quick-thaw red raspberries*, reserving ½ cup juice; set aside. In heavy 2-quart saucepan, stir *4 teaspoons sugar, 4 teaspoons all-purpose flour, 1 envelope unflavored gelatin*, and ¼ *teaspoon salt*. In medium bowl with fork, beat *2 egg yolks* with *1 cup milk* and reserved raspberry juice until blended; stir into gelatin mixture. Cook over medium-low heat until gelatin is completely dissolved and mixture thickens and coats a spoon, stirring constantly, about 15 minutes. (Do not boil or custard will curdle.) Remove from heat; stir in raspberries. Refrigerate until mixture mounds slightly when dropped from a spoon, about 30 minutes to 1 hour, stirring occasionally.

In small bowl, with mixer at medium speed, beat ½ *cup heavy or whipping cream* until stiff peaks form. With rubber spatula or wire whisk, fold whipped cream into custard. Cover and refrigerate until filling is firm enough to spread, about 20 minutes.

MIXED-NUT FRUITCAKE

2 6½- to 8-ounce containers candied
      red cherries
1 12-ounce package pitted prunes
1 10-ounce container pitted dates
1 3½- to 4-ounce container candied
      green cherries
½ cup cream sherry
2 12-ounce cans salted mixed nuts
1 6-ounce can pecans
1½ cups all-purpose flour
1 cup sugar
1 teaspoon baking powder
6 eggs, slightly beaten

Day ahead or up to 1 month ahead:

1. In very large bowl or 6-quart saucepot, combine first 5 ingredients; let stand 15 minutes or until almost all liquid is absorbed, stirring occasionally.

2. Meanwhile, line 10-inch tube pan with foil; press out wrinkles as much as possible so cake surface will come out smooth after baking.

3. Stir mixed nuts and pecans into fruit mixture in bowl. Remove 1½ cups fruit mixture; set aside. Stir flour, sugar, and baking powder into fruit mixture in large bowl until well coated. Stir in eggs until well mixed.

4. Spoon batter into prepared pan, packing firmly to eliminate air pockets. Sprinkle reserved fruit mixture on top.

5. Cover pan loosely with foil. Bake in 300°F oven 2 hours. Remove foil and bake ½ hour longer or until knife inserted into center of cake comes out clean and top of cake is lightly browned.

6. Cool cake in pan on wire rack 30 minutes; remove from pan and carefully peel off foil. Cool cake completely on rack. Wrap fruitcake tightly with foil or plastic wrap. Refrigerate. Makes one 4½-pound fruitcake.

Here's a favorite holiday **dessert**—it's elegant yet **easy** to prepare, light enough to serve after a sumptuous feast. Combine cut-up seasonal fruits such as oranges, grapefruit, strawberries, pineapple. Just before serving, arrange fruit in stemmed glasses and pour in chilled, dry champagne.

HOLIDAY PEAR-PEACH PIE

2   29-ounce cans sliced pears
1   29- to 30-ounce can sliced cling
    peaches
2   tablespoons lemon juice
½   teaspoon ground cinnamon
⅛   teaspoon ground cloves
    all-purpose flour
    salt
¾   cup shortening
5   to 6 tablespoons cold water
1   pint vanilla ice cream, slightly
    softened (optional)

About 3½ hours before serving or early in day:

1. Into sieve over large bowl, pour canned fruit to drain well. Pour off all but 2 tablespoons syrup. Into syrup in large bowl, add fruit slices, lemon juice, cinnamon, cloves, 2 tablespoons flour, and ¼ teaspoon salt. With rubber spatula, toss gently to mix.

2. In medium bowl, stir 2 cups flour and 1 teaspoon salt. With pastry blender or two knives used scissor-fashion, cut shortening into flour until mixture resembles coarse crumbs. Add water, a tablespoon at a time, mixing with fork until pastry holds together; shape pastry into 2 balls, one slightly larger.

3. On lightly floured surface with floured rolling pin, roll larger pastry ball into a circle about 2 inches larger than 9-inch pie plate. Line pie plate with pastry; with kitchen shears, trim pastry, leaving 1-inch overhang. Spoon fruit mixture into pie plate.

4. Preheat oven to 425°F. Roll remaining pastry into 12-inch circle; cut into ½-inch-wide strips. Place some strips about 1 inch apart across pie filling; do not seal ends. Fold every other strip back halfway from center. Place center cross-strip on pie and replace folded part of strips. Fold back alternate strips and place second cross-strip in place. Repeat to "weave" lattice. Trim strips; seal ends; make a fluted edge.

5. Bake pie 45 minutes or until fruit is heated through and crust is golden. Cool pie on wire rack. If you like, serve pie with ice cream. Makes 10 servings.

ALMOND CREAM PIE

1   3½-ounce can flaked coconut
½   cup graham-cracker crumbs
3   tablespoons butter or margarine,
    softened
4   eggs, separated
1   cup milk
¾   cup sugar
1   envelope unflavored gelatin
1   teaspoon almond extract
¼   teaspoon salt
1   cup heavy or whipping cream
1   tablespoon thinly sliced cranberries for
    garnish

Early in day or day ahead:

1. Preheat oven to 375°F. Spread coconut evenly in 15½" by 10½" jelly-roll pan. Bake 10 minutes or until lightly browned, stirring occasionally. Reserve ¼ cup toasted coconut for garnish. In 9-inch pie plate with hand, mix graham-cracker crumbs, butter or margarine, and remaining toasted coconut. Press mixture firmly onto bottom and up side of pie plate, making a small rim. Bake 5 minutes or until golden brown. Cool.

2. In heavy 2-quart saucepan with wire whisk, beat egg yolks, milk, and sugar until well mixed. Sprinkle gelatin evenly over egg mixture. Cook over medium-low heat until gelatin is completely dissolved and mixture is thickened and coats a spoon, about 20 minutes (do not boil or mixture will curdle). Stir in almond extract. Refrigerate until chilled but not set, about 45 minutes.

3. In large bowl with mixer at high speed, beat egg whites and salt until stiff peaks form; set aside. In small bowl, using same beaters, with mixer at medium speed, beat heavy cream until stiff peaks form.

4. With wire whisk, gently fold egg-yolk mixture and whipped cream into egg-white mixture. Spoon into piecrust; refrigerate until set, about 3 hours.

5. To serve, garnish top of pie with reserved toasted coconut and sliced cranberries. Makes 10 servings.

SPICY CRUMB CAKE

Crumb Topping
1¾ cups all-purpose flour
1 cup butter or margarine, softened
½ cup sugar
¼ cup milk
2 teaspoons baking powder
3 eggs
1 tablespoon honey
¼ teaspoon ground allspice
¼ teaspoon ground cinnamon

About 2 hours before serving or day ahead:

1. Prepare Crumb Topping; set aside. Grease and flour 9-inch springform pan.

2. Preheat oven to 350°F. In large bowl with mixer at low speed, beat flour and next 5 ingredients until just blended, constantly scraping bowl with rubber spatula. Continue beating 2 minutes, occasionally scraping bowl. Spoon batter into prepared pan.

3. In cup, mix honey, allspice, and cinnamon; drizzle over batter. With fork, swirl honey mixture just on top of batter; sprinkle with Crumb Topping. Bake cake 55 to 60 minutes until toothpick inserted in center of cake comes out clean and Crumb Topping is golden brown. Cool cake in pan on wire racks 10 minutes. Remove cake from pan; serve cake warm. Or cool cake to serve later. Makes 10 servings.

Crumb Topping

In medium bowl with fork, stir ½ cup all-purpose flour, ¼ cup California walnuts, finely chopped, and 2 tablespoons sugar. With pastry blender or two knives used scissor-fashion, cut ¼ cup butter or margarine into flour mixture until mixture resembles coarse crumbs.

CHEESE-FILLED CREPES WITH CHOCOLATE SAUCE

Crepes
1½ cups milk
⅔ cup all-purpose flour
½ teaspoon salt
3 eggs
about 6 tablespoons butter or margarine, melted

Cheese Filling
1 15- to 16-ounce container ricotta cheese
½ cup sour cream
¼ cup confectioners' sugar
2 teaspoons grated orange peel
¾ cup peach preserves

Chocolate Sauce
⅓ cup cocoa
⅓ cup sugar
¼ cup milk
¼ cup light corn syrup
3 tablespoons butter or margarine
1 tablespoon almond-flavor liqueur

About 3½ hours before serving:

1. Prepare Crepe batter: In medium bowl with wire whisk or fork, beat milk, flour, salt, eggs, and 2 tablespoons melted butter or margarine until well blended. Cover and refrigerate at least 2 hours.

2. Meanwhile, prepare Cheese Filling: In blender at medium speed or in food processor with knife blade attached, blend half of ricotta at a time, until very smooth; spoon into medium bowl. Stir in remaining filling ingredients except preserves until blended. Cover and refrigerate until ready to use.

3. Cook Crepes: Brush bottoms of 7-inch crepe pan and 10-inch skillet with some melted butter or margarine. Over medium heat, heat pans. Pour scant ¼ cup crepe batter into hot crepe pan, tipping pan to coat bottom. Cook until top of crepe is set and underside is lightly browned, about 2 minutes. With metal spatula, loosen crepe; invert crepe into hot skillet; cook other side, about 30 seconds. Slip crepe onto waxed paper. Meanwhile, start cooking another crepe. Stack crepes between waxed paper. Repeat making crepes until all batter is used. (You will have 12 crepes.)

4. Prepare Chocolate Sauce: In 1-quart saucepan over medium heat, heat all sauce ingredients except almond-flavor liqueur until mixture is smooth and boils, stirring frequently. Remove saucepan from heat; stir in liqueur; set aside; keep warm.

5. Assemble Crepes: Spread 1 tablespoon peach preserves evenly over a crepe. Top with about 2 tablespoons cheese filling, spreading filling almost but not all the way to edge of crepe. Fold crepe into quarters; arrange on heat-safe platter. Repeat with remaining crepes, preserves, and filling. Cover platter with foil.

6. To serve, preheat oven to 350°F. Bake crepes until just heated through, about 10 minutes. Serve with Chocolate Sauce. Makes 12 servings.

ESPRESSO NUT MOUSSE

1¾	cups California walnuts
3	cups milk
	sugar
	instant espresso-coffee powder
2	envelopes unflavored gelatin
¼	teaspoon salt
4	egg whites, at room temperature
2	cups heavy or whipping cream

About 5 hours before serving or day ahead:

1. Reserve about 1 tablespoon walnuts for garnish. In blender at medium speed or in food processor with knife blade attached, finely grind walnuts, half at a time.

2. In 1-quart saucepan, mix 1½ cups milk, ½ cup sugar, and 3 tablespoons instant espresso-coffee powder; sprinkle gelatin evenly over mixture; over medium-low heat, cook, stirring constantly, until gelatin is completely dissolved. In medium bowl, mix gelatin mixture, walnuts, salt, and remaining 1½ cups milk. Cover and refrigerate until mixture mounds when dropped from a spoon, about 45 minutes.

3. Meanwhile, prepare collar for 1½-quart soufflé dish: Fold a 20-inch strip of waxed paper or foil lengthwise into 20″ by 6″ strip; wrap around outside of dish so collar stands 2 inches above rim. Secure with tape.

4. In small bowl with mixer at high speed, beat egg whites until soft peaks form. Beating at high speed, gradually sprinkle in ¼ cup sugar, beating until sugar is completely dissolved. (Whites should stand in stiff, glossy peaks.)

5. In large bowl with mixer at medium speed, beat 1¾ cups heavy or whipping cream until stiff peaks form (reserve remaining ¼ cup cream for garnish). With rubber spatula or wire whisk, fold walnut mixture and egg whites into whipped cream until blended. Spoon mixture into soufflé dish; cover and refrigerate until set, about 2½ hours.

6. To serve, coarsely chop reserved walnuts. In small bowl with mixer at medium speed, beat reserved ¼ cup heavy cream with ½ teaspoon sugar until soft peaks form. Remove collar from soufflé dish. Garnish top of mousse with whipped cream and walnuts. Makes 12 servings.

CREAMY CHEESE TRIANGLES

½	cup butter or margarine, softened
1½	cups all-purpose flour
½	cup packed brown sugar
¾	cup California walnuts, finely chopped
2	8-ounce packages cream cheese, softened
⅓	cup sugar
2	tablespoons grated orange peel
1	teaspoon orange extract
1	egg

About 3 hours before serving or early in day:

1. Preheat oven to 350°F. Grease 12″ by 8″ baking pan; set aside.

2. In small bowl with mixer at low speed, beat butter or margarine, flour, and brown sugar until well blended, occasionally scraping bowl with rubber spatula. (Mixture will be crumbly.) Stir in walnuts. Reserve 1¼ cups crumb mixture; evenly pat remaining mixture into bottom of baking pan. Bake 20 minutes or until lightly browned.

3. Meanwhile, in large bowl with mixer at medium speed, beat cream cheese, sugar, grated orange peel, orange extract, and egg until well blended, occasionally scraping bowl with rubber spatula. Evenly spread cream-cheese mixture over baked layer in pan. Sprinkle with reserved crumb mix-

ture. Bake 30 minutes longer or until golden. Refrigerate until well chilled, at least 2 hours.

4. To serve, cut dessert into 2″ by 2″ squares; cut squares into triangles. Makes 48.

MARZIPAN APPLES

1½	cups blanched whole almonds
1½	cups confectioners' sugar
1	egg white
1¼	teaspoons almond extract
¼	teaspoon salt
	green food color
	red food color
	water
	about 20 whole cloves

About 1½ hours before serving or up to 1 week ahead:

1. In blender at medium speed or in food processor with knife blade attached, blend almonds, ½ cup at a time, until very finely ground. (If using food processor, add confectioners' sugar, egg white, almond extract, salt, and green food color to ground almonds; blend to make a stiff paste.) In medium bowl with fork, mix ground almonds, confectioners' sugar, egg white, almond extract, salt, and enough green food color to tint a pretty apple-green color. With hands, knead to make a stiff paste.

2. Shape 1 tablespoonful dough into an apple (cover remaining dough with plastic wrap); repeat until all dough is used. Using a small artist's brush, tint apples with red food color diluted with water. Press stems from cloves partway into tops of apples. Let apples dry on wire rack, about 30 minutes. Makes about 20 marzipan apples.

FROZEN ALMOND BONBONS

1	pint vanilla ice cream
1	4½-ounce can whole blanched almonds, finely chopped
1	6-ounce package semisweet-chocolate pieces

3 tablespoons butter or margarine
1 tablespoon light corn syrup
½ teaspoon almond extract
crystallized lilacs or violets for garnish

Early in day or up to 2 weeks ahead:

1. Place ice cream in refrigerator to soften slightly, about 30 minutes. Chill small cookie sheet in freezer. Meanwhile, toast almonds. Remove skillet from heat. Cool; place toasted almonds on waxed paper.

2. Line chilled cookie sheet with waxed paper. Working quickly, with small ice-cream scoop or two spoons, scoop a ball of ice cream; roll in almonds; place on waxed-paper-lined cookie sheet. Repeat with remaining ice cream and almonds to make 12 ice-cream balls. Freeze until firm, about 1½ hours.

3. In double boiler over hot, *not boiling,* water, heat chocolate pieces, butter or margarine, corn syrup, and almond extract until chocolate is melted and mixture is smooth, stirring occasionally. Turn off heat, but leave top of double boiler over hot water in bottom of double boiler to keep the chocolate warm for easier dipping.

4. With two forks, quickly dip each ice-cream ball in chocolate mixture to coat completely; return to same cookie sheet; lightly press a crystallized lilac on top of each for garnish. Return to freezer; freeze until chocolate is firm, about 1 hour.

5. If not serving bonbons on same day, wrap with foil or plastic wrap to use within 2 weeks.

6. To serve, let bonbons stand at room temperature 10 minutes to soften slightly. Makes 12 servings.

MAPLE CRUNCH SQUARES

butter or margarine
¾ cup California walnuts, finely chopped
¾ cup packed light brown sugar
¾ cup vanilla-wafer crumbs
1 cup cake flour
½ cup buttermilk
⅓ cup sugar

¼ cup water
½ teaspoon baking soda
½ teaspoon salt
¼ teaspoon baking powder
2 squares unsweetened chocolate, melted
1 egg
1 cup heavy or whipping cream
1¼ teaspoons maple extract
1 square semisweet chocolate, shaved, for garnish

About 4 hours before serving or early in day:

1. In 13″ by 9″ baking pan in 350°F. oven, melt ½ cup butter or margarine; remove pan from oven. Reserve 1 tablespoon finely chopped walnuts for garnish. Into melted butter in pan, stir brown sugar, vanilla-wafer crumbs, and remaining walnuts until well blended. Pat mixture evenly on bottom of pan; set aside.

2. Into large bowl, measure flour, next 8 ingredients, and ¼ cup softened butter or margarine. With mixer at low speed, beat ingredients until blended, constantly scraping bowl with rubber spatula. Increase speed to high; beat 3 minutes, occasionally scraping bowl.

3. Pour batter over crumb mixture in pan. Bake 20 minutes or until toothpick inserted into center of cake comes out clean. Cool cake in pan on wire rack 10 minutes. With spatula, loosen edge of cake from pan; invert cake onto wire rack to cool completely.

4. Cut cake into about 30 squares. In small bowl with mixer at medium speed, beat heavy or whipping cream with maple extract until stiff peaks form. Spoon whipped cream into decorating bag with large rosette tip. With cake squares crumb-side up, pipe a large rosette of whipped cream onto top of each. Sprinkle half of rosettes with reserved chopped walnuts; half with shaved semisweet chocolate. Makes 30.

Good Housekeeping

INSTITUTE
APPLIANCES and HOME CARE
FOODS and COOKERY

IT ISN'T *Christmas*
WITHOUT *Coffee*

1. Glass top-stove percolator. 2. Aluminum drip pot. 3. Candle-warmer percolator. 4. Automatic percolator. 5. Instant-coffee maker. 6. Electric teakettle (for quick instant coffee). 7 and 8. Top-stove percolators. 9. Big automatic party pot (20 to 50 cups). 10. Automatic percolator with coffee-level indicator. 11. Automatic vacuum pot. 12. Electric coffee mill. 13. Spoutless automatic percolator.

PARTY PUNCHES

ORANGE CREAM PUNCH

3   large oranges
4   eggs separated
¼   cup sugar
¼   cup orange-flavor liqueur
2   cups half-and-half
1   cup heavy or whipping cream
    ground cinnamon for garnish

About 2 hours before serving or early in day:

1. Grate 1 teaspoon peel and sqeeze juice from oranges (about 1 cup). Wrap peel with plastic wrap; reserve for garnish.

2. In large bowl with wire whisk, beat egg yolks and sugar until sugar is dissolved; beat in orange juice, orange-flavor liqueur, half-and-half, and heavy cream until well blended. Cover and refrigerate until well chilled.

About 20 minutes before serving:

3. In small bowl with mixer at high speed, beat egg whites until soft peaks form. With rubber spatula or wire whisk, gently fold egg whites into yolk mixture just until blended. Pour into 2-quart chilled punch bowl. Sprinkle cinnamon and reserved orange peel over punch. Makes 8 cups or sixteen ½-cup servings.

ESPRESSO EGGNOG

¼   cup instant espresso-coffee powder
1   cup boiling water
2   cups iced water
3   eggs, separated
1   cup coffee-flavor liqueur
1   pint coffee ice cream
2   cups half-and-half
    grated chocolate for garnish

About 2 hours before serving or early in day:

1. In medium bowl, stir instant espresso-coffee powder with boiling water until dissolved. Add iced water; refrigerate until well chilled.

2. In small bowl with mixer at high speed, beat egg yolks until thick and lemon-colored, frequently scraping bowl with rubber spatula. Reduce speed to medium; gradually beat in coffee-flavor liqueur (egg yolks may curdle if liqueur is beaten in too quickly). Cover and refrigerate until well chilled.

About 30 minutes before serving:

3. Remove coffee ice cream from freezer; let stand at room temperature to soften slightly.

4. In large bowl with mixer at high speed, beat egg whites until soft peaks form.

5. In chilled 3-quart punch bowl, stir egg-yolk mixture, coffee ice cream, and half-and-half until blended. With rubber spatula or wire whisk, gently fold egg whites into yolk mixture just until blended. Lightly sprinkle grated chocolate over eggnog. Makes 9 cups or eighteen ½-cup servings.

II. BUFFETS FOR FRIENDS AND NEIGHBORS

*W*hen the 'season to be jolly' is upon us, entertaining friends and family is a popular activity. But not all feasts are served with guests seated around the dining room table. Help-yourself buffets can be fun, quick and practical for all involved, whether the event is a morning brunch, an afternoon tea, a Trim-the-Tree Supper, or a Come-for-Dessert celebration. What about an informal evening of simple and elegant hors d'oeuvres with a punch bowl of egg nog or mulled cider? This chapter includes useful information about wine, assorted punch recipes with and without Christmas cheer, and buffet menus that keep you out of the kitchen at party time.

A large platter overflowing with Cream-Cheese Scrambled Eggs, crisp bacon, sliced smoked salmon, mushrooms and avocados; Fruit in Orange Cups and coffee make this a quick, elegant party brunch.

Open-House Hors d'Oeuvres

SAVORY ENDIVE

About 2¼ hours before serving or early in day:

1. Prepare *Lemony Salmon Filling, Creamy Liverwurst Filling,* or *Peppery Avocado Filling.* Cover and refrigerate until filling is firm, at least 1 hour.

2. Meanwhile, separate leaves from *6 medium Belgian endives* (for each filling). You should be able to get 6 pretty leaves from each endive; reserve small leaves and centers for salad another day. Rinse leaves under running cold water; pat dry with paper towels; cover and refrigerate.

About 30 minutes before serving:

3. Spoon filling into decorating bag with large rosette tube. Pipe some filling on wide end of each endive leaf. Garnish filling with *watercress, capers, radish slices,* and/or *pimento strips.* Makes 3 dozen hors d'oeuvres (each filling).

Lemony Salmon Filling

In blender at medium speed or in food processor with knife blade attached, blend *one 7¾-ounce can salmon,* drained, *one 3-ounce package cream cheese,* softened, *1 tablespoon capers,* drained, *1½ teaspoons lemon juice, ¼ teaspoon salt,* and *⅛ teaspoon dill weed* until smooth. Spoon mixture into small bowl. Makes about 1 cup.

Creamy Liverwurst Filling

In blender at medium speed or in food processor with knife blade attached, blend *one 8-ounce package braunschweiger* or liverwurst, *one 3-ounce package cream cheese,* softened, and *1 tablespoon dry sherry* until very smooth. Spoon liverwurst mixture into small bowl. Makes about 1½ cups.

Peppery Avocado Filling

In blender at medium speed or in food processor with knife blade attached, blend *1 ripe medium avocado, 6 tablespoons butter* or margarine, softened, *1 tablespoon lime juice, ¾ teaspoon salt, ⅛ teaspoon onion powder,* and *hot pepper sauce* to taste until smooth. Spoon mixture into small bowl. Makes about 1½ cups.

RUSSIAN PASTRIES

1	*8-ounce package cream cheese, softened*
1½	*cups all-purpose flour*
½	*cup butter or margarine, softened*
2	*eggs*
½	*pound ground beef*
1	*medium onion, diced*
¼	*cup water*
¼	*cup sour cream*
3	*tablespoons sweet pickle relish*
½	*teaspoon salt*
½	*teaspoon dill weed*
⅛	*teaspoon pepper*

About 2 hours before serving or early in day:

1. In medium bowl with hand, knead cream cheese, flour, and butter or margarine until smooth. Shape dough into ball; wrap in plastic wrap or foil; refrigerate until chilled, about 1 hour.

2. Meanwhile, hard-cook 1 egg; chop.

3. In 10-inch skillet over high heat, cook ground beef and onion until meat is browned and all pan juices evaporate. Remove skillet from heat; stir in water, sour cream, pickle relish, salt, dill weed, pepper, and chopped egg; set aside.

4. On floured surface with floured rolling pin, roll half of dough ⅛ inch thick. With floured 2¾-inch round cookie cutter, cut out 20 dough circles. Repeat with remaining dough and trimmings to make about 50 dough circles in all.

5. Onto one half of each dough circle, place a teaspoon of meat mixture. In cup with fork, beat remaining egg; brush edges of dough circle with some egg; fold dough over filling. With fork, firmly press edges together to seal; prick tops; brush with remaining egg. Arrange pastries on ungreased cookie sheet, about 1 inch apart. If not serving right away, cover with foil and refrigerate.

6. To serve, preheat oven to 425°F. Bake pastries 10 minutes or until golden. Makes 50 pastries.

To Freeze And Use Up To 1 Month Later

Place unbaked pastries in freezer container with waxed paper between each layer; seal; label; and freeze. About 25 minutes before serving, preheat oven to 425°F. Arrange frozen pastries on ungreased cookie sheet and bake 15 minutes or until pastries are golden.

Tasty **potato-skin hors d'oeuvres** are simple to make. Here's how: Peel *uncooked potatoes* with knife, cutting off strips about ⅛-inch thick; toss with *melted butter* or margarine, if you like; sprinkle lightly with salt. Bake skin-side up on a cookie sheet in preheated 475°F. oven for 8 to 10 minutes until crisp.

CARAWAY CHEESE CRISPS

1½ cups all-purpose flour
½ cup butter or margarine, softened
½ teaspoon caraway seeds
¼ teaspoon salt
¾ pound Cheddar cheese, shredded
   (about 3 cups)

About 1½ hours before serving or up to 3 days ahead:

1. Preheat oven to 425°F. In large bowl with hand, knead all ingredients until blended.

2. Shape dough into ½-inch balls. On ungreased cookie sheet, place three dough balls in a cluster. With fingers, flatten cluster to ¼ inch thickness. Repeat with remaining balls, placing clusters about 2 inches apart. Bake 10 to 12 minutes until lightly browned. With pancake turner, remove cheese crisps to wire racks; cool. Store cheese crisps in tightly covered container to use up within 3 days. Serve cheese crisps as cocktail snack. Makes about 5 dozen.

CAVIAR AND CHEESE FINGERS

½ cup water
4 tablespoons butter or margarine
⅛ teaspoon salt
½ cup all-purpose flour
2 eggs
1 8-ounce package cream cheese, softened
½ cup sour cream
1½ teaspoons grated onion
¾ teaspoon dill weed
1 2-ounce container red salmon caviar, drained

About 1½ hours before serving or early in day:

1. Grease large cookie sheet. In 2-quart saucepan over medium heat, heat water, butter or margarine, and salt until butter melts and mixture boils. Remove saucepan from heat. Add flour all at once. With wooden spoon, vigorously stir until mixture forms ball and leaves side of pan. Add eggs to flour mixture, one at a time, beating well after each addition until mixture is smooth.

2. Preheat oven to 375°F. Spoon mixture into decorating bag with medium writing tube. Pipe mixture onto cookie sheet into 2½" by ½" strips, about 1 inch apart. Bake 20 minutes or until golden. Cool pastry fingers on wire rack.

3. To serve, in small bowl with mixer at medium speed, beat cream cheese, sour cream, onion, and dill until smooth. With serrated knife, cut each pastry finger horizontally in half. Spoon some cream-cheese mixture into each half; top with some caviar. Makes about 60 hors d'oeuvres.

ZESTY ZUCCHINI ROUNDS

1 10-ounce package extra-sharp Cheddar cheese, shredded (2½ cups)
½ cup beer
¼ cup mayonnaise
1 teaspoon Worcestershire
¼ teaspoon salt
3 medium zucchini (about 1½ pounds)
¼ teaspoon ground red pepper

About 2½ hours before serving or day ahead:

1. In blender at medium speed or in food processor with knife blade attached, blend first 5 ingredients until smooth. Cover and refrigerate at least 2 hours or until firm.

About 15 minutes before serving:

2. Slice zucchini crosswise into ¼-inch-thick slices. Spoon cheese mixture into decorating bag with small rosette tube. Pipe some cheese mixture on each zucchini slice. Lightly sprinkle with ground red pepper. Makes about 4 dozen hors d'oeuvres.

SCALLOP KABOBS

2 tablespoons salad oil
1 pound bay scallops
¼ cup mayonnaise
1 tablespoon milk
1 tablespoon lemon juice
½ teaspoon salt
½ teaspoon hot pepper sauce
1 6-ounce jar pickled cocktail corn, drained
   cocktail picks
   lemon leaves for garnish

About 1½ hours before serving or early in day:

1. In 10-inch skillet over medium-high heat, in hot salad oil, cook scallops until they turn opaque and are just tender when tested with a fork, about 3 minutes, stirring frequently. With slotted spoon, remove scallops to medium bowl; add mayonnaise, milk, lemon juice, salt, and hot pepper sauce. With rubber spatula, stir gently to mix sauce and coat scallops. Cover and refrigerate at least 1 hour to develop flavor, stirring occasionally.

2. To serve, cut each cocktail corn crosswise into bite-sized pieces. On each cocktail pick, arrange 2 scallops and a piece of cocktail corn. Line chilled platter with lemon leaves; arrange kabobs on leaves. Makes about 1½ dozen kabobs.

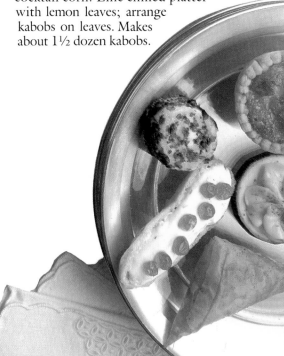

BLUE-CHEESE PINWHEELS

¼ pound blue cheese, at room temperature
½ cup minced parsley
4 tablespoons butter or margarine, softened
6 slices soft white bread

About 1 hour before serving or early in day:

1. In small bowl, mix blue cheese, ¼ cup minced parsley, and 2 tablespoons butter or margarine until well blended.

2. Trim crusts from bread slices; reserve bread trimmings for making crumbs another day. With rolling pin, roll bread slices flat. Evenly spread about 1 rounded tablespoonful cheese mixture on each bread slice; roll up, jelly-roll fashion.

3. On waxed paper, place remaining ¼ cup minced parsley. Spread outside of cheese rolls with remaining butter or margarine; coat lightly with parsley. Wrap rolls tightly in plastic wrap; refrigerate at least 30 minutes for easier slicing.

4. To serve, slice each parsley-coated cheese roll crosswise into six slices. Place slices, cut-side up, on platter. Makes 3 dozen hors d'oeuvres.

BITE-SIZED BACON QUICHES

piecrust mix for two 9-inch piecrusts
1 tablespoon butter or margarine, melted
1 8-ounce package sliced bacon, diced
3 eggs
1 cup half-and-half
¼ teaspoon salt
⅛ teaspoon pepper
¼ pound Swiss cheese, shredded (1 cup)

About 1½ hours before serving or early in day:

1. Grease and flour thirty-six 1¾-inch muffin-pan cups. Prepare piecrust mix as label directs.

2. On lightly floured surface with floured rolling pin, roll dough about ⅛ inch thick. Using 3-inch round fluted cookie cutter, cut dough into 36 circles, rerolling trimmings.

3. Line muffin-pan cups with pastry circles; brush pastry lightly with melted butter or margarine; cover and refrigerate.

4. In 2-quart saucepan over medium heat, cook diced bacon until crisp and browned. With slotted spoon, remove bacon to paper towels to drain; cool. Wrap in plastic wrap; refrigerate until ready to use.

About 35 minutes before serving:

5. Preheat oven to 400°F. In small bowl with wire whisk or fork, beat eggs, half-and-half, salt, and pepper until well blended. Into each pastry cup, sprinkle some cooked, diced bacon and some shredded cheese. Spoon about 1 tablespoon egg mixture into each cup. Bake 20 to 25 minutes until knife inserted in center of a quiche comes out clean. Remove quiches from pan and serve immediately. Makes 3 dozen hors d'oeuvres.

MINIATURE REUBENS

1 8-ounce loaf party rye-bread slices
¼ cup mayonnaise
1 tablespoon chili sauce
½ teaspoon prepared horseradish
½ small green pepper, minced
¼ pound thinly sliced corned beef
1 8-ounce can sauerkraut, drained
1 8-ounce package sliced Swiss cheese

About 35 minutes before serving:

1. Preheat oven to 350°F. Arrange bread slices on large cookie sheet. Bake 5 minutes or until lightly browned on one side. Remove cookie sheet from oven.

2. Meanwhile, in small bowl, stir mayonnaise, chili sauce, horseradish, and green pepper until blended.

3. With knife, spread some mayonnaise mixture on toasted side of each bread slice. Top each slice with some corned beef, sauerkraut, then cheese, cutting corned beef and cheese slices to fit. Bake about 10 minutes or until cheese is melted. Serve immediately. Makes 3 dozen canapés.

SAUSAGE TRIANGLES

½ 16-ounce package pork sausage meat
¼ pound mushrooms, diced
¼ pound Monterey Jack cheese, shredded (1 cup)
about ⅓ pound phyllo (8 strudel leaves)
½ cup butter or margarine, melted

About 1½ hours before serving or early in day:

1. In 10-inch skillet over medium-high heat, cook pork sausage meat and mushrooms until sausage is well browned and mushrooms are tender, stirring occasionally. With slotted spoon, remove sausage mixture to paper towels to drain. In large bowl mix sausage mixture and shredded cheese.

2. With knife, cut phyllo lengthwise into 2-inch-wide strips. Place strips on waxed paper; then cover with slightly damp paper towel to prevent phyllo from drying out.

3. Place 1 strip of phyllo on work surface; brush top lightly with melted butter or margarine. Place about 1 teaspoonful sausage mixture at end of strip. Fold one corner of strip diagonally over filling so that short edge meets the long edge of strip, forming a right angle. Continue folding over at right angles until you reach the end of the strip to form a triangular-shaped package. Place package, seam-side down, in 15½" by 10½" jelly-roll pan; brush with butter or margarine. Repeat with remaining phyllo strips and sausage mixture. If not serving right away, cover with foil and refrigerate.

4. To serve, preheat oven to 425°F. Bake triangles 15 minutes or until golden. Makes about 3½ dozen hors d'oeuvres.

Open-House Hors d'Oeuvres: Caviar and Cheese Fingers, Zesty Zucchini Rounds, Caraway Cheese Crisps, Scallop Kabobs, Blue-Cheese Pinwheels, Russian Pastries, Bite-Sized Bacon Quiches, Savory Endive, Sausage Triangles, Miniature Reubens. Recipes on pages 42-44.

COUNTRY PATE

2 tablespoons salad oil
¼ pound mushrooms, chopped
1 medium onion, minced
1 garlic clove, minced
¼ cup dry sherry
1 teaspoon salt
½ teaspoon pepper
½ teaspoon thyme leaves
⅛ teaspoon nutmeg
½ pound ground pork
½ pound ground chicken (1 whole
    chicken breast)
2 ounces ground pork fat
¼ cup shelled pistachios
1 egg
⅓ cup chopped parsley
1 8-ounce package sliced bacon
    assorted crackers, grapes

Day ahead or up to 1 week ahead:

1. In 10-inch skillet over medium heat, in hot salad oil, cook mushrooms, onion, and garlic until tender. Add sherry, salt, pepper, thyme, and nutmeg; heat to boiling. Reduce heat to low; simmer 5 minutes.

2. In bowl, combine mushroom mixture, pork, chicken, pork fat, pistachios, egg, and 2 tablespoons parsley. Wrap and refrigerate remaining parsley. With wooden spoon, beat until well mixed.

3. Line bottom and sides of 8½" by 4½" loaf pan with bacon, letting bacon slices hang over sides of pan.

4. Spoon mixture into pan, packing to press out air pockets. Fold bacon over mixture. Bake in 350°F oven 1¼ hours. Cover pâté with foil-wrapped cardboard; place cans on top to weigh down pâté. Refrigerate overnight.

5. To serve, remove cans and cardboard. Dip pan in hot water 15 seconds; lift from water and run metal spatula between pâté and sides of pan; invert. Scrape off excess fat. Garnish with reserved parsley. Serve with crackers and grapes. Makes about 2 pounds pâté; 16 first-course servings.

PARTY BRIE

1 17¼-ounce package frozen puff
    pastry
1 egg yolk
1 tablespoon water
1 2¼-pound wheel Brie (8 inches in
    diameter)
    seedless grapes and nuts for garnish

About 3 hours before serving or early in day:

1. Let frozen puff pastry stand at room temperature 20 minutes to thaw slightly.

2. Unfold one sheet of pastry on lightly floured surface. With floured rolling pin, roll pastry to 13" by 10" rectangle. Cut a 13" by 1½" strip and an 8½-inch round from the rectangle. Repeat with remaining sheet of pastry.

3. In cup with fork, beat egg yolk and water. Place one pastry round on ungreased cookie sheet; center Brie on pastry.

Brush side of Brie with some yolk mixture. Wrap the two long pastry strips around side of Brie; press strips firmly to Brie so they stay in place. Brush pastry strips with some yolk mixture.

4. Place second pastry round on top of Brie. Press edges of rounds to pastry strips to seal Brie in pastry.

5. Preheat oven to 425°F. With tip of knife, cut top of pastry into 1½-inch diamonds. Brush top and side of pastry with remaining yolk mixture. Bake 30 to 35 minutes until pastry is golden brown.

6. Refrigerate Brie about 1 hour until Brie is room temperature. (If served hot, cheese will be too soft and runny.) Or, if made early in day, keep Brie refrigerated. About 2 hours before serving, remove Brie from refrigerator and let stand at room temperature to soften to serving consistency.

7. To serve, with pancake turner, transfer Brie to large platter. Garnish with grapes and nuts. Let each person cut chunks of Brie with pastry. Makes 24 appetizer servings.

Party Brunch

Pictured on page 41.

FRESH FRUIT IN ORANGE CUPS

8	large oranges
1	cup sugar
½	cup water
¼	teaspoon salt
4	kiwi fruits
1	pint strawberries
¼	cup brandy
	lemon leaves for garnish

Day ahead:

1. Prepare orange cups: With sharp knife, cut off one-third of each orange from stem end. Then cut thin slice off opposite end of each orange so oranges can stand upright. With spoon, carefully separate fruit from inside walls of top and bottom pieces of oranges; remove fruit in one piece if possible. Place half of fruit in large bowl (reserve other half for fruit salad another day); cover and refrigerate.

2. With kitchen shears, trim rim of each bottom orange shell into sawtooth pattern; cover and refrigerate orange cups.

3. From top orange shells, remove thin slices of peel with vegetable peeler; cut enough peel into 1-inch-long julienne strips to make about 1 tablespoon. In 1-quart saucepan over high heat, heat sugar, water, and salt to boiling. Add strips of peel; reduce heat to low; simmer 5 minutes to blend flavors. Cover and refrigerate syrup until well chilled.

About 1½ hours before serving or early in day:

4. Prepare fruit: Section peeled oranges in bowl. Return sections to bowl. Peel kiwifruits; cut crosswise into slices; cut each slice in half. Add to oranges in bowl. Wash and hull strawberries; cut each strawberry in half or into quarters if they are large. Add to fruit in bowl.

5. Stir brandy into chilled syrup. Pour syrup over fruit in bowl. Cover and refrigerate until well chilled, stirring occasionally.

6. To serve, spoon fruit mixture with some syrup into orange cups. Place each orange cup on a small plate; garnish with lemon leaves. Makes 8 first-course servings.

CREAM-CHEESE SCRAMBLED EGGS

3	8-ounce packages thick-sliced bacon
	Seasoned Avocados
	Sautéed Mushrooms
14	eggs
¼	teaspoon pepper
6	tablespoons butter or margarine
2	3-ounce packages cream cheese, diced
3	3-ounce packages sliced smoked salmon

About 1½ hours before serving:

1. Cook bacon: Preheat broiler if manufacturer directs. Arrange bacon slices, overlapping slightly, on rack in broiling pan. About 5 inches from source of heat, broil bacon at 300°F 10 to 15 minutes or until golden. With tongs or fork, turn bacon, separating slices. Broil about 10 minutes longer or until bacon is browned and crisp. Remove bacon to paper towels to drain; keep warm.

2. Meanwhile, prepare Seasoned Avocados; cover and refrigerate, stirring occasionally. Prepare Sautéed Mushrooms; keep warm.

3. Prepare Cream-Cheese Scrambled Eggs: In large bowl with fork, beat eggs and pepper until just blended. In 12-inch skillet over medium-high heat, melt butter or margarine. Add egg mixture. As egg mixture begins to set, with spatula, stir slightly so uncooked egg flows to bottom. When eggs are partially cooked, add diced cream cheese. Continue cooking until egg mixture is set but still moist. Remove skillet from heat.

4. To serve, spoon egg mixture into warm bowl; place on large platter. Arrange Seasoned Avocados, Sautéed Mushrooms, bacon strips, and smoked salmon around eggs on platter. Makes 8 main-dish servings.

Seasoned Avocados
In medium bowl, mix *1 tablespoon sugar, 3 tablespoons white wine vinegar, 2 tablespoons salad oil, 1 tablespoon chopped parsley,* and *¾ teaspoon salt.* Peel and remove seed from *2 large avocados.* Cut avocados lengthwise in half, then crosswise into ¼-inch-thick slices. Add avocados and *one 2-ounce jar sliced pimentos,* drained, to dressing in bowl; toss to coat well with dressing.

Sautéed Mushrooms
In 5-quart saucepot over medium-high heat, melt *6 tablespoons butter* or margarine. Add *3 green onions,* sliced, *1½ pounds mushrooms,* thickly sliced, *¾ teaspoon lemon-pepper seasoning,* and *¼ teaspoon thyme leaves* and cook until mushrooms are tender and almost all juices are absorbed, stirring frequently.

Grandma's Classic Colonial Feast

CHEDDAR CHEESE SOUP

- 3 medium carrots
- 3 medium celery stalks
  butter or margarine
- 1 large onion
- 1 medium green pepper
- 3 13¾-ounce cans chicken broth
- 1 8-ounce package shredded Cheddar cheese
- 2 cups milk

About 1 hour before serving:

1. Prepare garnish: With sharp knife, cut 1 carrot and 1 celery stalk crosswise into thirds; cut each third lengthwise into thin slices; then cut slices into matchstick-thin strips. In 2-quart saucepan over medium heat, melt 1 tablespoon butter or margarine; add carrot and celery strips and cook until vegetables are tender but not brown, stirring occasionally; remove saucepan from heat.

2. Dice remaining carrots and celery stalks. Dice onion and green pepper. In 5-quart Dutch oven over medium heat, melt 4 tablespoons butter or margarine; add diced vegetables and cook until vegetables are tender, stirring occasionally. Stir in 1 can chicken broth and shredded cheese. Over medium-low heat, heat until cheese is melted, stirring frequently.

3. In blender at medium speed, blend ¼ of cheese mixture at a time, until smooth; pour into large bowl. Return all blended mixture to Dutch oven; stir in milk and remaining broth. Over medium-low heat, heat soup until hot, stirring occasionally.

4. To serve, pour soup into large tureen; sprinkle with carrot and celery garnish (some garnish will sink). Makes 9 cups or eighteen ½-cup servings.

To do ahead:

Early in day or day ahead, prepare garnish as above in step 1; remove to small bowl; cover and refrigerate. Prepare soup mixture as in step 2. In step 3, pour blended mixture into medium bowl; cover and refrigerate. Just before serving, heat blended mixture with milk and remaining chicken broth and garnish as above.

COLONIAL PUDDING

- 5 tablespoons butter or margarine, softened
- 10 slices raisin bread with cinnamon
- 1 29-ounce can sliced pears
- 5½ cups milk
- ⅔ cup sugar
- 1½ teaspoons ground cinnamon
- 1 teaspoon salt
- 2 teaspoons vanilla extract
- 6 eggs
  boiling water

About 2 hours before serving or early in day:

1. Preheat broiler if manufacturer directs. Butter one side of raisin-bread slices; arrange slices, butter-side up, on cookie sheet. Broil about 2 minutes to toast the bread. Remove cookie sheet from oven; set aside. Turn oven control to 325°F.

2. Drain pears well; pat dry with paper towels; dice. Sprinkle pears in bottom of 13" by 9" baking dish. Arrange bread, overlapping slices slightly, on pears. In large bowl with fork, beat milk and next 5 ingredients until well mixed; pour over bread.

3. Set baking dish in 17½" by 11¼" roasting pan; place on oven rack. Fill roasting pan with boiling water to come halfway up sides of baking dish. Bake pudding 50 to 60 minutes until knife inserted in center comes out clean. Serve warm or refrigerate to serve cold later. Makes 16 servings.

Grandma's Classic Christmas Feast—Cheddar Cheese Soup, Turkey with Sausage Stuffing, Cranberry-Relish Apple Cups, Creamed Onions, Sweet Potato Bake, Pumpkin Butter, Steamed Fig Bread, Colonial Pudding and Carrot Cake.

TURKEY WITH SAUSAGE STUFFING

1   14- to 16-pound fresh or frozen (thawed) ready-to-stuff turkey
    salt
    water
1   16-ounce package pork-sausage meat
½   cup butter or margarine
4   large celery stalks, diced
1   large onion, diced
12 cups white-bread cubes (about 24 slices)
3   eggs
½   cup milk
½   cup minced parsley
1½ teaspoons rosemary
½   teaspoon pepper
    salad oil
    Gravy
    Cranberry-Relish Apple Cups for garnish
    parsley sprigs for garnish

About 6½ hours before serving:

1. Remove giblets and neck from turkey. Rinse turkey with running cold water and drain well; cover and refrigerate.

2. Prepare stuffing: In 2-quart saucepan over high heat, heat giblets, neck, ¼ teaspoon salt, and enough water to cover to boiling. Reduce heat to low; cover and simmer 1 hour or until giblets are tender. Drain, reserving broth. Pull meat from neck; discard bones; coarsely chop neck meat and giblets.

3. In 8-quart Dutch oven over medium heat, cook pork-sausage meat until browned; with slotted spoon, remove to medium bowl; set aside. In drippings in Dutch oven over medium heat, melt butter or margarine. Add celery and onion and cook until tender, stirring occasionally. Remove Dutch oven from heat; stir in neck meat, giblets, cooked sausage, bread cubes, eggs, milk, parsley, rosemary, and pepper; mix well.

4. Spoon some of stuffing lightly into neck cavity. (Do not pack stuffing; it expands during cooking.) Fold neck skin over stuffing; fasten neck skin to back with 1 or 2 skewers. With turkey breast-side up, lift wings up toward neck, then fold under back of turkey so they stay in place.

5. Spoon some stuffing lightly into body cavity. (Bake any leftover stuffing in covered, greased small casserole during last 40 minutes of roasting turkey.) Close by folding skin lightly over opening; skewer if necessary. Depending on brand of turkey, with string, tie legs and tail together; or push drumsticks under band of skin; or use stuffing clamp.

6. Place turkey, breast-side up, on rack in open roasting pan. Brush skin with salad oil. Insert meat thermometer into thickest part of meat between breast and thigh, being careful that pointed end of thermometer does not touch bone. Roast turkey in 325°F oven 4 to 4½ hours. Start checking for doneness during last hour of roasting.

7. When turkey turns golden brown, cover loosely with a "tent" of folded foil. Remove foil during last of roasting time and, with pastry brush, brush turkey generously with pan drippings for attractive sheen. Turkey is done when thermometer reaches 180° to 185°F and thickest part of drumstick feels soft when pressed with finger protected by paper towels.

8. When turkey is done, place on warm large platter; keep warm. Prepare Gravy.

9. To serve, arrange Cranberry-Relish Apple Cups and parsley sprigs around turkey on platter. Pass gravy in gravy boat. Makes 16 to 20 servings.

Gravy

Remove rack from roasting pan; pour pan drippings into a 4-cup measure or a medium bowl (set pan aside); let stand a few seconds until fat separates from meat juice. Skim ⅓ cup fat from drippings into 2-quart saucepan; skim off and discard any remaining fat. Add reserved giblet broth to roasting pan; stir until browned bits are loosened; add to meat juice in cup and enough *water* to make 4 cups.

Into fat in saucepan over medium heat, stir ⅓ *cup all-purpose flour* and *1 teaspoon* salt until blended; gradually stir in meat-juice mixture; cook, stirring, until mixture is thickened.

CRANBERRY-RELISH APPLE CUPS

2   large oranges
4   cups fresh or frozen cranberries
1¼ cups sugar
8   small red Delicious apples
    lemon juice

Early in day:

1. Coarsely chop oranges with their peels and cranberries; place in medium bowl. Stir in sugar; cover and set aside.

2. Cut off a thin slice from blossom end of each apple. Scoop out center of each apple, leaving ¼-inch-thick shells. Brush cut surface and inside of apples with lemon juice. Chop centers and blossom-end pieces; discard seeds. Add chopped apples to cranberry mixture. With sharp knife, trim rim of each apple into a scalloped pattern. Fill apple cups with some cranberry mixture; spoon remaining mixture into small bowl; cover and refrigerate until ready to serve with turkey. Makes 16 accompaniment servings.

CREAMED ONIONS

4   pounds small white onions
    water
½   cup butter or margarine
⅓   cup all-purpose flour
¾   teaspoon salt
1½ cups half-and-half
¼   cup cream sherry (optional)
    paprika

About 45 minutes before serving:

1. In 6-quart Dutch oven or saucepot over high heat, heat onions and 1 inch water to boiling. Reduce heat to medium-low; cover and cook 10 to 15 minutes until onions are fork-tender.

2. Drain onions, reserving ½ cup cooking liquid. In same Dutch oven over low heat, melt butter or margarine; stir in flour and salt until blended. Gradually stir in reserved onion liquid, half-and-half, and cream sherry; cook, stirring constantly, until mixture is thickened and smooth. Return onions to Dutch oven; heat through.

3. Spoon onions and cream sauce into serving bowl; sprinkle sauce with paprika. Makes 16 accompaniment servings.

SWEET POTATO BAKE

4	pounds sweet potatoes (12 medium)
	water
½	cup butter or margarine
¼	cup milk
1½	teaspoons salt
¼	teaspoon cracked pepper
1	8¼-ounce can crushed pineapple, well drained
3	tablespoons dark brown sugar

About 2 hours before serving:

1. In 6-quart Dutch oven or saucepot over high heat, heat unpeeled sweet potatoes and enough water to cover to boiling. Reduce heat to medium-low; cover and cook 30 minutes or until sweet potatoes are fork-tender; drain. Cool sweet potatoes until easy to handle; peel.

2. Preheat oven to 325°F. In large bowl with mixer at medium speed, beat sweet potatoes, butter, milk, salt, and pepper until smooth, about 3 minutes. Spoon mixture into 2-quart casserole; top with crushed pineapple and sprinkle with brown sugar. Bake casserole 45 minutes or until heated through. Makes 16 accompaniment servings.

CARROT CAKE

3¾	cups all-purpose flour
¾	cup packed brown sugar
1	tablespoon baking powder
1	teaspoon baking soda
¾	teaspoon salt
½	cup butter or margarine
1	6-ounce can pecan halves, chopped
4	eggs
¾	cup maple syrup
¾	cup orange juice
3	cups finely shredded carrots
	confectioners' sugar

About 4 hours before serving or day ahead:

1. Preheat oven to 350°F. Grease 10-inch Bundt or tube pan.

2. Into large bowl, measure flour, brown sugar, baking powder, baking soda, and salt. With pastry blender or two knives used scissor-fashion, cut in butter or margarine to resemble fine crumbs. Stir in chopped pecans.

3. In small bowl with fork, beat eggs slightly; stir in maple syrup and orange juice until well mixed. Stir egg mixture into flour mixture just until flour is moistened. Gently stir in carrots. Spoon batter evenly into pan.

4. Bake cake 50 minutes or until toothpick inserted in center comes out clean. Cool cake in pan on wire rack 10 minutes; remove from pan and cool completely on rack.

5. To serve, sprinkle cake with confectioners' sugar. Makes 16 servings.

PUMPKIN BUTTER

1	small lemon
1	16-ounce can pumpkin
½	cup apple juice
½	cup packed light brown sugar
½	teaspoon salt
¼	teaspoon ground ginger
⅛	teaspoon ground cinnamon
⅛	teaspoon ground allspice

About 4 hours before serving or up to 1 week ahead:

1. Grate lemon to make 1 teaspoon peel; squeeze to make 1 teaspoon juice. In 2-quart saucepan over medium-high heat, heat lemon peel and juice and remaining ingredients to boiling. Reduce heat to medium-low; cook 30 minutes, stirring often.

2. Spoon pumpkin mixture into small bowl; cover and refrigerate until well chilled, at least 3 hours. Serve with warm biscuits. Makes about 2½ cups.

STEAMED FIG BREAD

1¼	cups all-purpose flour
1¼	cups whole-wheat flour
¾	cup molasses
¾	cup buttermilk
3	tablespoons melted butter or margarine
1½	teaspoons baking soda
1½	teaspoons salt
1	egg
1	cup California walnuts, chopped
1	8-ounce package dried figs, chopped

Up to 3 days ahead:

1. Grease well two tall 1-pound coffee cans. Cut 2 sheets of foil, each 1 inch larger than opening of can to use as lids. Set aside.

2. In large bowl, mix all ingredients except walnuts and figs. Stir in nuts and figs. Spoon batter into cans; cover with foil; tie tightly with string.

3. Place metal trivet in deep 8-quart saucepot; pour in water to measure 2 inches. Set cans on trivet; over high heat, heat water to boiling. Reduce heat to low; cover saucepot and simmer 2 hours or until toothpick inserted through foil into center of bread comes out clean. Cool bread in cans on rack 5 minutes; loosen bread and invert onto rack to cool slightly. Serve warm or cool to serve later. Makes two loaves.

CRANBERRY TEA PUNCH

Frosted Cranberries for garnish
2   *32-ounce bottles cranberry-juice cocktail*
2   *cups brewed tea*
½   *cup sugar*
¼   *cup lemon juice*
½   *teaspoon ground cinnamon*
¼   *teaspoon ground cloves*
1   *small lemon, thinly sliced*
     lemon leaves for garnish

About 1½ hours before serving:
1. Prepare Frosted Cranberries; set aside.

About 15 minutes before serving:
2. In 4-quart saucepan over high heat, heat cranberry-juice cocktail and next 5 ingredients until sugar is dissolved and punch is hot, stirring occasionally.
3. To serve, pour punch into 4-quart heat-safe punch bowl. Float lemon slices on punch. Place punch bowl on large round tray. Arrange lemon leaves and Frosted Cranberries on tray around base of punch bowl. Makes about 10 cups or twenty ½-cup servings.

Frosted Cranberries
Rinse *2 cups fresh cranberries* with running cold water; gently pat dry with paper towels. In small bowl, place *1 cup sugar*. In another small bowl with fork, beat *1 egg white* until frothy. Dip cranberries, several at a time, into egg white; then toss with sugar to coat completely. Place frosted cranberries in 13″ by 9″ baking pan to dry, about 1 hour.

CHEER

COCONUT EGGNOG

12 eggs, separated
1 15- or 16-ounce can cream of coconut
1 3½-ounce container toasted coconut
    flakes
8 cups milk
1 cup heavy or whipping cream

About 2 hours before serving or early in day:

1. In large bowl with mixer at high speed, beat egg yolks and cream of coconut until thick and lemon-colored, about 10 minutes.

2. Reserve ¼ cup coconut flakes for garnish later. In food processor with knife blade attached or in blender at medium speed, blend remaining coconut and 1 cup milk until pureed. Pour pureed coconut mixture into yolk mixture; cover and refrigerate.

About 20 minutes before serving:

3. In chilled 5- to 6-quart punch bowl, mix egg-yolk mixture and remaining 7 cups milk until blended. In large bowl with mixer at high speed, beat egg whites until soft peaks form. In small bowl, using same beaters, with mixer at medium speed, beat heavy or whipping cream until stiff peaks form. With rubber spatula or wire whisk, gently fold beaten egg whites and whipped cream into egg-yolk mixture.

4. To serve, sprinkle reserved toasted coconut over eggnog. Makes about 18 cups or thirty-six ½-cup servings.

These "spirited" drinks are flavored with the fruits and spices of the season: Spiced Citrus Punch, Coconut Eggnog, Cranberry Tea Punch, Banana-Orange Nog, Rainbow Float, Mulled Cider, Frosty Mocha, Tomato Sip, Mock Sangria, Mint Cappuccino, Creamy Chocolate, Currant Punch. Recipes, pages 52-55.

CURRANT PUNCH

1   10-ounce jar red currant jelly
1   6-ounce can frozen grapefruit-juice
       concentrate
1   6-ounce can frozen lemonade
       concentrate
    water
1   28-ounce bottle lemon-lime soft
       drink, chilled
2   trays ice cubes

About 15 minutes before serving:

1. In small saucepan over medium heat, melt currant jelly; remove saucepan from heat.

2. In 4-quart punch bowl, mix grapefruit-juice and lemonade concentrates and enough water as labels direct. Stir in lemon-lime soft drink and melted currant jelly. Add ice cubes to punch. Makes about 11 cups or twenty-two ½-cups servings.

MINT CAPPUCCINO

4   cups water
½   cup instant espresso coffee powder
    sugar
4   cups milk
1   cup heavy or whipping cream
½   teaspoon vanilla extract
16 5-inch candy canes

About 30 minutes before serving:

1. In 3-quart saucepan over high heat, heat water, instant espresso, and 3 tablespoons sugar to boiling, stirring occasionally until sugar is dissolved. Add milk and cook over medium heat until very hot, but not boiling, stirring occasionally.

2. Meanwhile, in small bowl with portable mixer at medium speed, beat heavy or whipping cream, vanilla, and 1 tablespoon sugar until soft peaks form; spoon whipped cream into small serving bowl.

3. Remove saucepan from heat. With portable mixer, beat espresso mixture until foamy; pour into 3-quart heat-safe punch bowl.

4. To serve, place a candy cane in each cup of cappuccino (candy cane will melt in the hot cappuccino to add peppermint flavor). Let each person top cappuccino with some whipped cream. Makes about 8 cups or sixteen ½-cup servings.

MULLED CIDER

1   gallon apple cider
8   3½-inch-long cinnamon sticks
1½   teaspoons whole cloves
2   large oranges
2   medium red eating apples

About 30 minutes before serving:

1. In 5-quart saucepot over high heat, heat cider, cinnamon, and cloves to boiling. Reduce heat to low; cover; simmer 20 minutes.

2. Meanwhile, slice oranges and apples. Place orange and apple slices in 5-quart heat-safe punch bowl. Pour hot cider mixture over fruit slices. Makes about 16 cups or thirty-two ½-cup servings.

> Just a dash of Worcestershire adds zip to hot **mulled cider.**
> Use a crock pot as a punch bowl next time you are serving a warm beverage like cider or mulled wine. Just heat, turn crock pot on low; cover until ready to serve.

TOMATO SIP

1   large lime
1   24-ounce bottle Bloody Mary mix,
       chilled
1   10½-ounce can condensed consommé
1   tray ice cubes
    celery stalks for garnish

About 15 minutes before serving:

1. Thinly slice half of lime; sqeeze juice from remaining half. In 3-quart punch bowl, mix lime slices, lime juice, Bloody Mary mix, consommé, and ice cubes.

2. To serve, ladle punch into glasses. If you like, garnish each serving with a celery stalk. Makes 4½ cups or nine ½-cup servings.

RAINBOW FLOAT

1   12-ounce can frozen orange-juice
        concentrate
1   6-ounce can frozen grape-juice
        concentrate
     water
2   28-ounce bottles club soda, chilled
¼   cup lemon juice
½   gallon rainbow sherbet

About 15 minutes before serving:

1. In 4-quart punch bowl, mix orange- and grape-juice concentrates and enough water as labels direct. Add club soda and lemon juice. Cut sherbet into 24 chunks; add to punch mixture. Makes about 12 cups or twenty-four ½-cup servings.

MOCK SANGRIA

3   24-ounce bottles white grape juice,
       chilled
1   28-ounce bottle club soda, chilled
1   pint strawberries, hulled
1   8¾-ounce can sliced cling peaches,
       chilled and drained
1   8½- or 8¾-ounce can sliced pears,
       chilled and drained
1   8-to 8½-ounce can pineapple chunks,
       chilled and drained
1   large lemon, thinly sliced
1   tablespoon aromatic bitters
1   tray ice cubes

About 15 minutes before serving:

1. In 6-quart chilled punch bowl, combine all ingredients.

2. To serve, ladle juice mixture with some fruit into glasses. Serve with cocktail picks or teaspoons to eat fruit. Makes about 4 quarts or thirty-two ½-cup servings.

SPICED CITRUS PUNCH

    water
1/2 pound seedless green grapes
1/2 pound seedless red grapes
    about 8 kumquats with leaves or 8
      preserved kumquats
    Cinnamon Wreath for garnish
1/3 cup sugar
1/2 teaspoon ground cinnamon
1/4 teaspoon ground cloves
1   6-ounce can frozen limeade
      concentrate
1   6-ounce can frozen tangerine-juice
      concentrate
1   46-ounce can grapefruit juice, chilled
1   28-ounce bottle club soda, chilled
1   large pink grapefruit
1   large orange

Day ahead:

1. Prepare ice ring: Fill 5-cup ring mold with water to half inch below rim; freeze until firm. With kitchen shears, cut green and red grapes into small bunches; alternately arrange grapes on top of ice. Tuck kumquats and leaves here and there between grapes. Add water up to rim of mold, allowing some fruit to extend above water; freeze.

About 45 minutes before serving:

2. If you like, prepare Cinnamon Wreath; set aside.

3. In 1-quart saucepan over medium heat, heat sugar, cinnamon, cloves, and 1 cup water until sugar is dissolved. In 6-quart punch bowl, prepare limeade and tangerine-juice concentrates as labels direct; stir in sugar mixture, grapefruit juice, and club soda.

4. Peel and section grapefruit and orange. Cut sections into 1/2-inch pieces; discard seeds. Add cut-up fruit to punch.

5. To serve, place punch bowl on tray with Cinnamon Wreath. Unmold ice ring; add to punch, fruit-side up. Makes 20 cups or forty 1/2-cups servings.

Cinnamon Wreath
Arrange *holly leaves* in circle around inside edge of round tray large enough to hold 6-quart punch bowl. Cut *5 feet narrow red satin ribbon* into 12 pieces. Using *thirty-six*

2 1/2-inch-long cinnamon sticks, tie 1 piece of ribbon around 3 cinnamon sticks. Repeat with remaining ribbon and cinnamon sticks. Arrange cinnamon-stick bundles on holly leaves.

BANANA-ORANGE NOG

    sugar
2   bananas, peeled and sliced
4   eggs
4   cups orange juice
2   cups half-and-half
1/2 teaspoon vanilla extract
1/8 teaspoon ground cinnamon
    Fruit Kabobs for garnish

About 2 hours before serving or day ahead:

1. In large bowl, combine 2 tablespoons sugar with next 5 ingredients. Fill blender half full with mixture; cover and blend at high speed until pureed. Pour mixture into 3-quart punch bowl. Repeat with remaining banana mixture. Refrigerate at least 1 hour. Add more sugar to taste if you like. (Mixture can be refrigerated overnight.)

About 30 minutes before serving:

2. Prepare Fruit Kabobs. Sprinkle top of punch with cinnamon. Ladle punch into punch cups. Rest Fruit Kabob across top of each punch cup. Makes 8 cups or sixteen 1/2-cup servings.

Fruit Kabobs
Rinse and pat dry *16 small lemon leaves*. Cut *1 large banana*, peeled, crosswise into 16 slices. Cut *1 small orange* into 16 pieces. On each of *16 cocktail picks*, thread 1 lemon leaf, 1 piece orange, and 1 slice banana. Arrange kabobs on chilled platter.

FROSTY MOCHA

1/2 gallon chocolate ice cream, softened
8   cups coffee, chilled
1   pint half-and-half
1   teaspoon almond extract
1/8 teaspoon salt
1   square semisweet chocolate, grated
1/4 teaspoon ground cinnamon

About 20 minutes before serving:

1. In large bowl with mixer at low speed, beat ice cream and 3 cups coffee until smooth.

2. In chilled 5- to 6-quart punch bowl, stir ice cream mixture, half-and-half, almond extract, salt, and remaining 5 cups coffee until blended. Sprinkle top of punch with grated chocolate and cinnamon. (If you like, to keep punch chilled during serving, set punch bowl in a very large glass salad bowl filled half full with ice cubes.) Makes about 16 cups or thirty-two 1/2-cup servings.

CREAMY CHOCOLATE

12 squares unsweetened chocolate
4   cups milk
3   cups water
    sugar
1   cup heavy or whipping cream
1 1/2 teaspoons almond extract
1/4 cup nonmelting candy-covered
      chocolate candies

About 20 minutes before serving:

1. In heavy 4-quart saucepan over very low heat, melt chocolate, stirring often; gradually stir in milk, water, and 1 cup sugar. Cook over medium heat until sugar is dissolved and mixture is very hot, but not boiling, stirring constantly.

2. Meanwhile, in small bowl with mixer at medium speed, beat heavy or whipping cream, almond extract, and 1 tablespoon sugar until soft peaks form. Spoon whipped cream into small serving bowl.

3. To serve, pour hot mixture into heat-safe cups. Garnish each serving with a dollop of whipped cream and 3 chocolate candies. Make 8 cups or sixteen 1/2-cup servings.

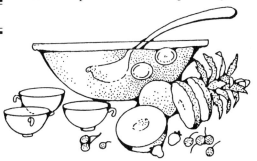

WINE-AND-CHEESE-TASTINGS

The next time you're thinking of having a get-together, make it a wine-and-cheese-tasting party. It's a wonderful—easy!—way to introduce guests, yourself, too, to some new (or old) vintages and varieties, and there's no limit to the number of people you can invite. The specifics for serving are all here. Use our chart, right, to help put together your "wine list"—we suggest cheeses to go along with each kind.

First, decide which type of tasting you want to have. For example, a first-course tasting, at the start of a dinner party, would concentrate on a few appetizer wines, such as sherry and vermouth. An after-the-meal or dessert tasting would feature sweet dessert wines—port, cream sherry. Or you might prefer a larger late-afternoon party, offering a more varied selection of wines, including table reds and whites and sparkling wines, though no more than eight should be offered at one time.

How much wine will you need? Serve one ounce of each appetizer or dessert wine; one to two ounces of all others. As a rule of thumb, you can figure on 1/3 to 1/2 a 24-ounce bottle of all wines combined, per person.

How much cheese? Provide about 1/4 pound of cheese per person, setting out no fewer than three varieties with flavors ranging from mild to sharp, textures from creamy to firm. Arrange with some unsalted crackers or crusty bread and fresh fruit for guests to nibble between wines.

The Party Plan: About two hours ahead chill white, rosé, and sparkling wines. Open red table wines to let them "breathe." Provide each guest with one wine glass. Set out a pitcher of water and a receptacle for rinsing glasses, a towel for drying them, between tastings. Then serve the wines, dry before sweet, white before red. Explain, as you go, how to "taste" like an expert: Once the wine is poured, hold it to the light to study its color, then swirl gently for a few seconds and inhale the "bouquet." Finally, sip, allowing wine to sit in your mouth for a moment before swallowing to get the full flavor. Take a bite of cheese only after you have had the first sip of wine.

Dry sherry, popular appetizer wine, pairs nicely with blue and Roquefort cheeses; also with sharp and extra-sharp Cheddars.

Try **Cabernet Sauvignon,** dry red table wine, with Brie and Camembert; also sharp Cheddar and blue cheeses.

Zinfandel, a fruity, medium-bodied red table wine, teams with Monterey Jack, Edam, longhorn, mellow Bel Paese, Port du Salut. With **Pinot Noir,** a Burgundy-type red table wine, offer Gorgonzola, Stilton, or blue, or a robust Cheddar.

Rosé, lightest in body and color of the red table wines, takes to mild cheeses such as brick, mozzarella, Muenster, Jarlsberg.

Pinot Chardonnay, dry and full-flavored white table wine, offsets the delicacy of Swiss and Gruyère, Gouda, Muenster.

Chenin Blanc, dry or semisweet white table wine, is good with Gouda, Edam, Swiss, Samsoe.

Chablis, dry or slightly sweet, is a fruity white table wine. Accompany with provolone or Swiss, robust Port du Salut, tangy Roquefort.

Pair **ruby** or **tawny port,** a sweet dessert wine, with Edam, Gouda, cream cheese, Cheddar, and Camembert.

Serve **cream sherry,** a sweet and rich dessert wine, with mild Neufchâtel or pungent Camembert; also with Edam, Gouda, Muenster.

Champagne—sparkling white or pink wine, ranging from dry to sweet in flavor—complements cream cheese, Brie.

Claret, medium-bodied, moderately dry red table wine, teams well with Double Gloucester, Stilton, Cheshire.

Try **Chianti,** strongly flavored, dry, fruity, and slightly tart red table wine, with feta, Gorgonzola, Port du Salut, fontina.

Riesling, a fruity, dry white table wine with a flowery fragrance, goes nicely with Muenster, Bonbel, Tilsit, Gouda, Gruyère.

Serve **Sauterne,** a white table wine, if dry or semisweet, with Edam, Emmentaler; if sweet (Haut Sauterne or Château Sauterne) with Boursault, Saga, Crema Dania.

The correct temperature for serving table wines:

White wines are served chilled to about 45° to 50°F, which takes about two hours in the refrigerator. Chilling them to a lower temperature greatly diminishes flavor. Always serve red wines at room temperature, about 60° to 70°F, to enjoy their aromatic qualities. Uncork about one hour before serving so the wine's bouquet develops fully.

For longer-lasting ice in holiday punches, freeze water in muffin tins or a ring mold. The larger the "cubes," the longer they'll last. Speaking of punch, a large frozen cluster of grapes makes a beatiful, colorful garnish that will keep punch cold—without diluting flavor!

DESSERT WINES

Wine served with dessert is an extra-elegant touch for the festive dinners of the season. The traditional dessert wines are sweet and full bodied. The classification "dessert wine" is based on alcohol content (18 to 20 percent) rather than sweetness. However, other wines, technically classified as "table wines" because they contain less alcohol, can also go with desserts—and may appeal to those who might prefer a lighter, lower-calorie beverage.

Traditional Favorites

Serve these favorite dessert wines at cool room temperature or well chilled:

Angelica—mild, fruity, and amber or straw colored—is the sweetest.

Cream Sherry is sweet and heavy, nut flavored, and rich golden in color.

Madeira is semisweet, nutty, and mellow, amber in color, with characteristic bouquet.

Marsala is a medium-bodied, deep amber wine resembling sherry but is sweeter and darker.

Muscatel is rich, flavorful, and robust, with typical Muscat grape flavor and aroma; gold to amber in color.

Port is sweet, heavy bodied, and rich tasting. Color is a deep red. *Tawny Port* is lighter in color and body. *White Port* is straw colored, sweeter than red Port.

Tokay is sweet with a nutty flavor, amber colored.

Lake Country Gold is fresh and fruity, with good body and clear, gold color.

Pink Catawba has fruity flavor—a bouquet characteristic of native Catawba grapes—and fresh pink color.

Riesling labeled "Late Harvest," from California, is sweet and rich with golden color.

Sauterne varies in sweetness. Ask your wine dealer for the sweet varieties of this full bodied, fragrant, golden wine.

Other Sweet Wines

These lighter wines should be served well chilled:

Ice Wine, produced in colder vineyards of Germany and of this country, comes from grapes that are frozen on the vine. It is sweet and fruity with a flowery aroma, pale gold color; alcohol content is 8.4 percent.

SPIRITED NOGS AND PUNCHES

SPIRITED COFFEE PUNCH

2 tablespoons instant-coffee powder or
*   granules*
2 tablespoons sugar
*   water*
3 pints vanilla ice cream
¾ cup orange-flavor liqueur
*   ground cinnamon*

About 40 minutes before serving:

1. In small saucepan over medium heat, heat instant coffee, sugar, and ¼ cup water until coffee and sugar are dissolved; stir in 3¾ cups very cold water. Refrigerate.

2. Meanwhile, remove vanilla ice cream from freezer; let stand at room temperature to soften sligthly, about 30 minutes.

3. In chilled 3-quart punch bowl with wire whisk or rubber spatula, stir coffee mixture, orange-flavor liqueur, and softened vanilla ice cream until blended. Sprinkle top of punch with cinnamon. Makes 9 cups or eighteen ½-cup servings.

HOLIDAY CHAMPAGNE PUNCH

*   water*
1 pint strawberries
1 pound seedless green grapes
8 to 10 small nontoxic leaves
2 cups orange juice
¼ cup black-currant- or black-
*   raspberry-flavor liqueur*
3 tablespoons sugar
1 28-to 32-ounce bottle club soda,
*   chilled*
1 750 ml. bottle (4/5 quart)
*   champagne or sparkling white*
*   wine, chilled*

Day ahead:

1. Prepare ice ring: Fill 5-cup ring mold with ¼ inch water; freeze until firm. Reserve 8 strawberries; slice remaining strawberries. On ice in ring mold, arrange one-half sliced strawberries, ½ cup grapes, and enough water to just cover fruit (so fruit does not float). Freeze until firm. Repeat with remaining strawberry slices, another ½ cup grapes, and enough water to cover fruit; freeze until firm.

2. With kitchen shears, cut remaining grapes into small bunches; alternately arrange grape bunches and reserved whole strawberries in ring mold; tuck leaves here and there between grapes and strawberries. Add water up to rim of mold, allowing some fruit to extend above water; freeze until firm.

About 15 minutes before serving:

3. In shallow 5-quart punch bowl, large enough to hold ice ring, combine orange juice, black-currant liqueur, and sugar. Gently stir in chilled club soda and champagne.

4. To serve, unmold ice ring; add to punch, fruit-side up. Makes about 10 cups or about twenty ½-cup servings.

TOASTED ALMOND EGGNOG

6 eggs, separated
⅓ cup sugar
½ teaspoon salt
¾ cup almond-flavor liqueur
½ 3½-ounce can sliced blanched
*   almonds (½ cup)*
3 cups milk
1 cup heavy or whipping cream

About 2 hours before serving or early in day:

1. In large bowl with mixer at low speed, beat egg yolks, sugar, and salt until well blended. At high speed, beat egg-yolk mixture until thick and lemon-colored, about 15 minutes, frequently scraping bowl with rubber spatula. One tablespoon at a time, beat in almond-flavor liqueur.

(Egg-yolk mixture will curdle if liqueur is beaten in too quickly.) Cover bowl; refrigerate mixture until well chilled.

2. Meanwhile, in 10-inch skillet over medium heat, cook sliced almonds until lightly browned on both sides, shaking skillet frequently.

About 20 minutes before serving:

3. In chilled 3-quart punch bowl, stir egg-yolk mixture and milk until blended. In large bowl with mixer at high speed, beat egg whites until soft peaks form. In small bowl, using same beaters, with mixer at medium speed, beat heavy or whipping cream until stiff peaks form. With rubber spatula or wire whisk, gently fold egg whites and whipped cream into egg-yolk mixture just until blended.

4. To serve, sprinkle toasted almonds over top of eggnog. Makes 8 cups or sixteen ½-cup servings.

It's **eggnog** time and many of us wouldn't dream of using anything other than freshly grated nutmeg to top off this holiday favorite. Just a dusting of this pungent spice will do. But other holiday recipes call for a specific amount. So here's a handy fact: One whole nutmeg will yield about one tablespoon "ground". And should you have some leftover eggnog, remember that you can refrigerate or freeze it to use later as a delicious dessert sauce on fruit, pudding, ice cream, or cake.

To make **eggnog** really special, decorate it with dollops of whipped cream garnished with "holly"—strips of citron or angelica for leaves, bits of maraschino or candied red cherry for berries. The dollops can be made in advance. Just drop them on a cookie sheet and freeze; remove with spatula, then place in a freezer container with waxed paper between layers. They'll quickly defrost as they float on the eggnog.

For safety's sake, be sure your holiday **eggnog** stays cold. You can simply place the filled punch bowl in a larger bowl filled with ice. Or freeze some of the eggnog into cubes or a mold and add to the punch when serving. It will keep the punch "chilled" but won't dilute it the way ordinary ice cubes would.

ADD A LIQUEUR!

Liqueurs, once reserved for after-dinner sipping, have joined the ranks of spices, herbs, extracts, and wines as flavoring ingredients. Their vast range of tastes gives the adventurous cook an almost unlimited choice for adding new dimensions to dishes.

What are liqueurs?

Liqueurs, or cordials, are sweet alcoholic beverages made by adding sugar, flavoring, and sometimes coloring to a base of distilled spirits. The base may be neutral spirits (such as ethyl alcohol), brandy, rum, gin, or other spirit. Sugar content must be at least 2½ percent by weight, and many liqueurs contain more. Flavorings include fruits, nuts, seeds, herbs, bark, roots, spices, flowers, tea, coffee. In some, a single flavor predominates, as in crème de cacao (chocolate) and kummel (caraway seed). Others are made with a blend of flavors, such as coffee amaretto (coffee and almond); and Chartreuse, said to contain 130 different plants in its formula. Growing in popularity are blends of a liqueur with real cream, such as Irish Cream.

Liqueur colors go from crystal clear (white crème de menthe) to brilliant blue (blue Curaçao), with all shades of the spectrum in between; consistency, from water-thin (Cointreau) to syrupy (amaretto) to creamy (Irish Cream).

Add new flavor to foods

Liqueur flavors are concentrated, so start with a small amount—a dash or two, or a teaspoon—and taste until you reach the desired flavor level. When cooked in a mixture, the alcohol evaporates but the inimitable flavor remains. (Tip: If you use liqueurs only in cooking, buy them in "miniatures" instead of larger bottles.) Here, ideas for using some favorite liqueurs. Substitute others if you like, or ask a knowledgeable wine dealer for some suggesions.

●For delightful **almond** flavor, use *amaretto* or *creme de noyaux.* Use instead of vanilla extract in butter-cream frosting, cooked chocolate pudding, bread or rice pudding. Add to egg mixture for French toast.

●Some of the **anise**-flavored liqueurs are *anisette, sambuca, ouzo.* Use a dash on buttered carrots, peas, spinach, broccoli, green beans; in vinaigrette dressing.

●*Kummel* and *aquavit* are **caraway** flavored. Add a little to cream sauce for cooked onions, gravy for pork chops or roasts, cheese-soufflé mixture, hot buttered cauliflower, sour cream marinade for cucumbers.

●*Crème de cacao* has a rich **chocolate** taste. There are also blends such as *chocolate-mint, chocolate-cherry, chocolate-orange.* Use in tapioca cream; to flavor pecan pie, creampuff filling, hot coffee.

●*Crème de menthe* and *peppermint schnapps* boast refreshing **mint** flavor. Add a dash to hot buttered peas or spinach. Brush over leg of lamb before roasting. Use as flavoring in chocolate sauces, desserts.

●For **orange** flavor, use *Triple Sec, Curaçao, Cointreau, Grand Marnier*—a dash in buttered hot carrots, beets, corn. Stir a little into baked beans, raisin sauce for ham, mashed sweet potatoes or winter squash.

●Try any of the **fruit**-flavored brandies or liqueurs in barbecue sauce for chicken or spareribs; or use as glaze for roasting ham, lamb, pork, or poultry.

WASSAIL BOWL

2 quarts apple cider or apple juice
3 3½-inch-long cinnamon sticks
2 teaspoons whole cloves
2 teaspoons whole allspice
1 orange for garnish
1 lemon for garnish
   whole cloves for garnish
1 6-ounce can frozen orange-juice concentrate
1 6-ounce can lemonade concentrate
1 750 ml. bottle (4/5 quart) dry white wine
4 cups water
¾ cup packed brown sugar

About 30 minutes before serving:

1. In 5-quart saucepot over high heat, heat apple cider, cinnamon, cloves, and allspice to boiling. Reduce heat to low; cover and simmer 15 minutes.

2. Meanwhile, slice orange and lemon. Place one lemon slice on each orange slice; secure in center with 1 or 2 whole cloves. Place orange-and-lemon-slice garnish in heat-safe punch bowl; set aside.

3. Add frozen orange-juice concentrate, lemonade concentrate, white wine, water, and brown sugar to cider mixture; over high heat, heat to boiling. Pour hot cider mixture over fruit slices in bowl. Makes 16 cups or thirty-two ½-cup servings.

PEACH FIZZ

1 6-ounce can frozen limeade concentrate
1 3-ounce package peach-flavor gelatin
1 29-ounce can sliced cling peaches in heavy syrup, chilled
2 tablespoons lime juice
2 10- or 12-ounce bottles tonic water, chilled
   lime slices for garnish

About 1½ hours before serving:

1. In 3-quart pitcher, prepare limeade concentrate as label directs. Measure 1 cup reconstituted limeade into 1-quart saucepan; over high heat, heat to boiling. Remove saucepan from heat. Stir peach-flavor gelatin into hot limeade, stirring until gelatin is completely dissolved. Stir gelatin mixture into limeade in pitcher.

2. Fill blender with peaches and their syrup; cover and blend at high speed until peaches are pureed. Stir pureed peaches and lime juice into limeade mixture. Refrigerate 1 hour or until well chilled.

3. To serve, stir tonic water into limeade mixture. Garnish with lime slices. Makes 9 cups or twelve ¾-cup servings.

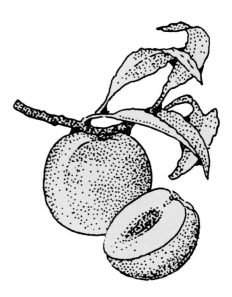

III.
TRADITIONAL FAVORITES MADE EASY AND LIGHT

Once in a while, the Christmas Cook (whether it's Grandma, Dad or Mother) needs a little inspiration. When the family has its heart set on turkey, try a light and savory vegetable stuffing instead of the traditional. Do you want to splurge on Filet Mignon and not spend hours in the kitchen? Here is a simple Beef Tenderloin recipe using four flavored butters. Make any one or all four. If you've promised to think thin this year, this chapter offers a selection of lighter holiday recipes including lower calorie egg nog and mincemeat pie. And if you prefer to be chatting with the guests instead of checking the roast, here is an assortment of favorite recipes prepared in the microwave to reduce cooking time.

Roast Turkey with Savory Vegetable Stuffing- blend of zucchini, red pepper strips, bean sprouts a carrots. Great new zest for the bird: crushed fen seeds, mixed with a bit of salt, oil, rubbed into skin before roasting.

ROAST TURKEY WITH SAVORY VEGETABLE STUFFING

Savory Vegetable Stuffing
1 *12-pound fresh or frozen (thawed) ready-to-stuff turkey*
½ *teaspoon fennel seeds, crushed*
    salad oil
    salt
12 *medium-sized potatoes (about 4 pounds)*
    water
⅓ *cup all-purpose flour*
1 *tablespoon soy sauce*

About 6 hours before serving:

1. Prepare Savory Vegetable Stuffing; set aside.

2. Remove giblets and neck from turkey; set aside. Rinse turkey with running cold water; drain well.

3. Spoon some stuffing lightly into neck cavity. Fold neck skin over stuffing; fasten neck skin to back with 1 or 2 skewers. With turkey breast-side up, lift wings up toward neck, then fold under back of turkey so they stay in place.

4. Spoon stuffing lightly into body cavity. (Bake any leftover stuffing in covered, greased small casserole during last 40 minutes of roasting turkey.) Close by folding skin lightly over opening; skewer closed if necessary. Depending on brand of turkey, with string, tie legs and tail together; or push drumsticks under band of skin; or use stuffing clamp.

5. Place turkey, breast-side up, on small rack in large open roasting pan. In small plate, mix fennel seeds with 1 tablespoon salad oil and 1 teaspoon salt. With hands, rub fennel-seed mixture over turkey. Insert meat thermometer into thickest part of thigh next to body, being careful that pointed end of thermometer does not touch bone. Roast turkey in 325°F oven about 4 hours. Start checking for doneness last hour of roasting.

6. After roasting turkey 1½ hours, peel potatoes. Cut potatoes into halves or quarters if they are large. Remove roasting pan from oven; arrange potatoes around turkey in pan. Return pan to oven and continue roasting turkey and potatoes, turning potatoes occasionally to coat with pan drippings.

7. While turkey is roasting, prepare giblets and neck to use in gravy: In 3-quart saucepan over high heat, heat giblets, neck, and enough water to cover to boiling. Reduce heat to low; cover and simmer 1 hour or until giblets are tender. Drain, reserving broth. Pull meat from neck; discard bones. Coarsely chop neck meat and giblets; refrigerate.

8. When turkey turns golden brown, cover loosely with a tent of folded foil. Remove foil during last of roasting time and, with pastry brush, brush turkey generously with pan drippings for attractive sheen. Turkey is done when thigh temperature on thermometer reaches 180° to 185°F and thickest part of drumstick feels soft when pressed with fingers protected by paper towels.

9. When turkey is done, place on warm large platter; arrange potatoes on platter with turkey; keep warm. Prepare giblet gravy: Remove rack from roasting pan. Pour pan drippings into a 4-cup measure or medium bowl (set pan aside); let drippings stand a few seconds until fat separates from meat juice. Skim ⅓ cup fat from drippings into 2-quart saucepan; skim off and discard remaining fat. Add reserved giblet broth to roasting pan; stir until brown bits are loosened; add to meat juice in cup and add enough water to make 4 cups.

10. Into fat in saucepan over medium heat, stir flour and 1 teaspoon salt until blended.

Gradually stir in meat-juice mixture and soy sauce; cook, stirring constantly, until mixture thickens slightly and is smooth. Stir in reserved giblets and neck meat; cook until heated through. Pour gravy into gravy boat. Serve gravy with turkey. Makes 12 servings.

Savory Vegetable Stuffing

Cut *4 medium-sized zucchini* (about 8 ounces each) into 3" by ¼" strips. In large bowl, mix zucchini and *1 teaspoon salt*; cover and let stand at room temperature 30 minutes.

Meanwhile, cut *4 medium-sized celery stalks* into 3" by ⅛" strips. Cut *2 medium-sized onions* into ¼-inch-thick wedges. Cut *1 medium-sized red pepper* into thin strips. Grate *1 large carrot*. In 10-inch skillet over medium heat, heat *4 tablespoons butter* or margarine until hot; add celery and onions and cook until tender, stirring occasionally.

Tip bowl over sink and press zucchini with hand to drain off liquid. Into drained zucchini in bowl, stir onion mixture, red pepper, carrot, *three 14- to 16-ounce cans bean sprouts*, drained *¼ cup chopped parsley*, *1 tablespoon soy sauce, 2 teaspoons salt*, and ½ teaspoon pepper.

Great Garnishes For The Turkey

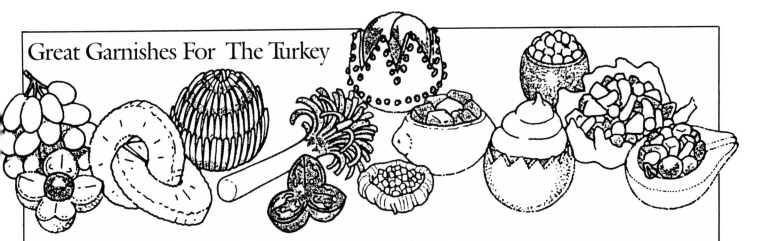

A sampling of garnishes (from left): grape cluster, kumquat flower, double pineapple rings, orange-peel "mum," green-onion frill, tomato clover, orange crown, festive fruit and vegetable cups.

When a gloriously roasted turkey is the star of your holiday dinner, set it off with a simple yet beautiful garnish like the ones we suggest below.

Except for the greens, which go on at the last minute, these garnishes should be made early in the day, covered, and refrigerated until time to use. When arranging on turkey platter, remember that the carver must have elbow room to work, so make sure the garnish is easily removable, either to the dinner plates or to a special plate.

Greens
Simple **greens**—parsley, watercress, celery leaves, curly endive (chicory)—dress up the platter, can be moved aside readily when it's time to carve. Just before serving, arrange one or several small bunches on the platter, or surround the bird with them.

Greens plus: Any of the greens above can serve also as a bed for colorful additions: fresh or preserved kumquats, carrot curls, radish roses, celery fans, pickled whole or sliced crab apples, cherry tomatoes, canned peach or apricot halves, a scattering of fresh cranberries or pomegranate seeds, ripe or stuffed green olives, or some of the garnishes that follow.

Tomato "clovers": Cut each cherry tomato from blossom end almost to, but not quite through, stem end, into three wedges. Spread wedges apart; set tomato on greens.

Garland of grapes: Alternate small bunches of red and green grapes around bird. If you like, tuck in pecan halves and/or whole natural almonds here and there.

Kumquat flowers: Cut twice through stem end of fresh or preserved kumquat to form 4 petals: press a candied cherry into center. Place on greens, singly or in clusters of three.

Double pineapple rings: For each garnish, use 2 canned-pineapple slices. Cut through one side of one ring; slip other pineapple ring through cut. Set on greens.

Green-onion frills: Cut off all but 3 inches green tops from green onions. Shred tops down to white part. Place onions in iced water; cover and refrigerate; tops will curl. Arrange in clusters on greens.

Orange-peel "mum": For each "mum," slice top from one orange, about one-fourth of the way down. Scoop out pulp (save for salad or dessert next day). Then, with kitchen shears, carefully snip orange shell from top rim down about three-fourths of the way; repeat this snipping at ¼-inch intervals, forming a fringe; if you wish, trim top of each strip in the fringe so it tapers to a sharp point. Repeat this with a second orange; then nest one orange fringe in the other. Set on greens.

Orange crown: Slice about ½ inch from both top and bottom of a large orange. Scoop out orange pulp (save for salad or dessert next day). From top, cut 6 wedges down to one-third from bottom to form a 6-pointed crown. From 1 tablespoon whole cloves, cut off part of stems, leaving cloves about ⅜-inch long; stud peel with cloves around points and around bottom of peel. For "velvet," tuck small red cabbage leaf in center of crown. Set directly on turkey; surround turkey with greens.

Festive fruit or vegetable cups.
Lemon-cranberry: For each serving, slice about ¼ off top of large lemon and a sliver from bottom so lemon stands level. Scoop out insides (press pulp through strainer to release juice for use in recipes, drinks). Fill lemon cup with cubes of canned jellied cranberry sauce, heaping cubes in cup. Set on greens.

Apple-cranberry: For each serving, cut off top of apple that stands straight. Scoop out center of apple, leaving ¼-inch-thick shell. Brush cut surface and inside of apple with lemon juice. Chop centers and top pieces; discard seeds; mix chopped apple with favorite cranberry relish. With sharp knife, trim rim of apple into a scalloped pattern; fill apple cup with fruit mixture. Set on greens.

Mixed fruit: Fill canned-fruit halves with a little mixed candied fruit that has been marinated in white grape juice or white wine. Set on greens.

Fig-nut: Cut off stems from dried Calimyrna figs. With finger, gently press stem end into center of each fig to make a cup; fill cup with coarsely broken nuts or whole preserved kumquat. Set on greens.

Sweet-potato oranges: With small sharp knife, make zigzag cuts all around center of orange; separate halves. Scoop out pulp (save for salad or dessert next day); cover shells and refrigerate. Just before serving, place hot mashed sweet potatoes in decorating bag with large rosette tube; pipe mixture into orange shells. Or, spoon seasoned hot mashed butternut squash or pumpkin into shells; sprinkle with slivered almonds.

Cabbage and corn relish: For each serving, spoon favorite corn relish into small red cabbage (or Bibb-lettuce leaf).

Beets and peas: Cut slice from bottoms of cooked medium whole beets (so beets will stand level) and hollow out beets (easy with melon baller), leaving ¼-inch-thick shells. Just before serving, heat beets; fill with drained hot cooked peas.

Mushroom-limas: Sauté large fresh mushroom caps in butter; fill with hot cooked baby lima beans.

CELEBRATION FILET MIGNON

¼ pound medium mushrooms
1 large or 2 medium tomatoes
*   butter or margarine*
1 large onion, cut into ¾-inch-thick
*   slices*
4 beef loin tenderloin steaks, each cut 1
*   inch thick*
½ cup water
2 tablespoons prepared mustard
4 teaspoons capers, drained
*   watercress sprigs for garnish*

About 45 minutes before serving:

1. If you like, flute mushrooms. Set aside.

2. Cut four thick center slices from tomatoes; reserve any leftover tomatoes to use in salad another day. In 10-inch skillet over medium heat, in 1 teaspoon hot butter or margarine, cook tomato slices until heated through. Remove to warm large platter.

3. Meanwhile, in 12-inch skillet over medium heat, in 2 tablespoons hot butter or margarine, cook onion until tender, stirring occasionally. Remove to bowl. In drippings remaining in skillet over medium-high heat, cook mushrooms and beef loin tenderloin steaks about 5 minutes for medium or until of desired doneness, turning steaks once. Remove steaks and mushrooms to platter, placing one steak on each tomato slice; keep warm.

4. Into drippings remaining in skillet, stir water, mustard, and capers; over medium heat, cook until mixture boils and thickens slightly, stirring constantly. Return onions to skillet; heat through. Pour sauce over and around steaks. Garnish platter with watercress sprigs. Makes 4 servings.

Celebration Filet Mignon: Luscious melt-in-your-mouth steaks on sweet tomato slices with fluted mushrooms, in a mustard-and-caper-laced onion sauce.

BEEF TENDERLOIN WITH FLAVORED BUTTERS

*   Herb, Roquefort, Wine, and Lemon*
*   Butters*
2 1½-pound beef tenderloin roasts
*   (large end)*
*   salt*
*   pepper*
*   parsley sprigs or holly sprigs for*
*   garnish*

Early in day:

1. Prepare Herb, Roquefort, Wine, and Lemon Butters. (Refrigerate leftover butters to use within one week on broiled steaks, hamburgers, fish fillets, or broiler-fryers.)

About 40 minutes before serving:

2. Preheat broiler if manufacturer directs. Sprinkle beef tenderloin roasts lightly with salt and pepper. Place both pieces of meat on rack in broiling pan; broil 30 minutes for rare or until of desired doneness, turning meat once.

3. To serve, unmold all four butter molds onto a small wooden board or chilled plate. Cut meat into thick slices; arrange on warm platter; garnish with parsley sprigs. Let each guest select and spread butter on meat slices. Makes 10 servings.

Herb Butter

In small bowl with mixer at low speed, beat *½ cup butter* or margarine, softened, *2 teaspoons fresh or frozen chopped chives, ½ teaspoon dill weed,* and *⅛ teaspoon salt* until well blended. Spoon mixture into a 4-ounce butter mold or small custard cup. Cover and refrigerate until well chilled, at least 1½ hours.

Roquefort Butter

In small bowl with mixer at low speed, beat *½ cup butter* or margarine, softened, *3 ounces Roquefort* or blue cheese, crumbled, and *⅛ teaspoon caraway seeds* until well blended. Spoon mixture into a 4-ounce butter mold or small custard cup. Cover and refrigerate until well chilled, at least 1½ hours.

Wine Butter

In small bowl with mixer at low speed, beat *½ cup butter* or margarine, softened, *2 tablespoons dry red wine, 2 teaspoons minced parsley, ⅛ teaspoon cracked black pepper,* and *⅛ teaspoon salt* until well blended. Spoon mixture into a 4-ounce butter mold or small custard cup. Cover and refrigerate until well chilled, at least 1½ hours.

Lemon Butter

From *1 medium lemon,* grate ½ teaspoon peel and squeeze 1 tablespoon lemon juice. In small bowl with mixer at low speed, beat *½ cup butter* or margarine, softened, lemon peel, lemon juice, *2 teaspoons minced parsley, ⅛ teaspoon salt,* and *⅛ teaspoon ground red pepper* until well blended. Spoon mixture into a 4-ounce butter mold or small custard cup. Cover and refrigerate until well chilled, at least 1½ hours.

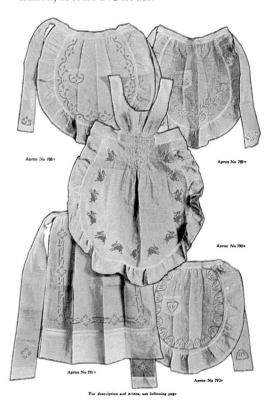

Good Housekeeping   December 1909

SUNDAY LEG OF LAMB WITH CRISPY POTATO FRILLS

salad oil
1 *small celery stalk, minced*
½ *small onion, minced*
¼ *pound pork-sausage meat*
1 *slice white bread*
¼ *cup slivered almonds, finely chopped*
¼ *cup chopped parsley*
2 *tablespoons milk*
½ *teaspoon grated lemon peel*
1 *egg*
 salt
1 *4½-pound lamb leg shank half (round leg bone removed from large end to make a pocket)*
⅛ *teaspoon pepper*
3 *large potatoes (1½ pounds)*
1 *cup dry white wine*
1 *cup water*
1 *tablespoon tomato paste*
 Poached Apples

About 3¼ hours before serving:

1. In 2-quart saucepan over medium heat, in 1 tablespoon hot salad oil, cook celery, onion, and sausage until sausage is well browned and vegetables are tender, stirring to break up sausage. Remove saucepan from heat.

2. Into sausage mixture, tear bread into small pieces; stir in almonds, parsley, milk, lemon peel, egg, and ¼ teaspoon salt. Spoon stuffing mixture into pocket in lamb leg. Skewer opening closed.

3. Place lamb, fat-side up, on rack in open roasting pan. In cup, mix pepper, 1 tablespoon salad oil, and ½ teaspoon salt; rub mixture over lamb. Insert meat thermometer into center of lamb. Roast in 325°F oven about 2½ hours or until thermometer reaches 160°F for medium (30 to 35 minutes per pound) or until of desired doneness.

4. Meanwhile, prepare Potato Frills: With vegetable peeler, peel potatoes. Then, using same peeler, peel ½-inch-wide, paper-thin strips from potatoes, dropping strips into large bowl of water mixed with 1 teaspoon salt as you work.

5. In 12-inch skillet over medium heat, heat 1 inch salad oil to 400°F. Remove one handful of potato strips from water and pat dry with paper towels. Drop strips into hot salad oil and fry until crisp and golden, about 2 minutes. With slotted spoon, remove potato strips to more paper towels to drain. Repeat with remaining potato strips. Since potato strips are not served hot, it is not necessary to keep them warm after frying.

6. After roasting lamb 1½ hours, in bowl, mix white wine, water, and tomato paste; pour mixture over lamb. Continue roasting lamb, basting occasionally with pan liquid.

7. Prepare Poached Apples.

8. When lamb is done, place on warm large platter; let stand 15 minutes for easier carving. Meanwhile, strain pan liquid into 1-quart saucepan; skim off excess fat. Over medium heat, heat sauce to boiling. Pour sauce into gravy boat.

9. To serve, remove skewers from lamb; cut lamb with stuffing into thin slices. Serve with potato frills and apples. Pass sauce in gravy boat. Makes 10 servings.

Poached Apples
In 4-quart saucepan over high heat, heat *4 cups water, 1 cup sugar,* and *1 tablespoon vanilla extract* to boiling. Add *5 small red cooking apples* (about 1 pound); heat to boiling. Reduce heat to low; cover and simmer about 5 minutes or until apples are just tender, occasionally basting apples with cooking liquid.

BUFFET SALMON WITH THREE SAUCES

7 *cups water*
1 *cup dry white wine*
2 *medium celery stalks, sliced*
1 *medium onion, sliced*
1 *tablespoon salt*
½ *teaspoon peppercorns*
1 *envelope chicken-flavor bouillon*
1 *6-pound whole salmon or striped bass, dressed, with head and tail on*
 Confetti Sauce, Mustard Sauce, and Green Mayonnaise
3 *eggs*
3 *medium tomatoes*
3 *lemons*
 parsley sprigs for garnish

Early in day or day ahead:

1. In 26-inch fish poacher, over high heat, heat first 7 ingredients to boiling. The poacher will require 2 heating units. (If you don't have a poacher, use a 12-inch skillet. Cut fish crosswise in half; cook one piece of fish at a time. To serve, reassemble fish on large platter to make a whole fish.)

2. Rinse salmon under running cold water. Place salmon on poaching rack; lower rack with salmon into boiling liquid in fish poacher; over high heat, heat to boiling. Reduce heat to low; cover and simmer 30 minutes or until fish flakes easily when tested with a fork. Remove rack from poacher. With two pancake turners, place salmon on large platter; cover and refrigerate until well chilled.

3. Meanwhile, prepare Confetti Sauce, Mustard Sauce, and Green Mayonnaise; cover and refrigerate. Hard-cook eggs; refrigerate.

4. To serve, with knife or kitchen shears, carefully cut skin around top half of salmon; remove and discard skin. Slice tomatoes, lemons, and hard-cooked eggs; arrange on platter with salmon. Garnish with parsley sprigs. Serve with all three sauces. Makes 12 servings.

Confetti Sauce
Drain and reserve ½ cup liquid from *one 16-ounce jar pickled mixed vegetables;* dice pickled mixed vegetables. In large bowl with fork, combine reserved liquid, *½ cup olive or salad oil, 4 teaspoons tarragon vinegar,* and *½ teaspoon salt* until well blended. Stir in diced vegetables; refrigerate until well chilled.

Mustard Sauce
In blender at medium speed or in food processor with knife blade attached, blend *½ cup mustard, ½ cup olive or salad oil, 2 tablespoons sugar, 3 tablespoons dry white wine, 1 tablespoon sour cream,* and *¼ teaspoon salt* until blended. Stir in *1 teaspoon minced fresh dill* or *¼ teaspoon dill weed,* and *1 teaspoon minced parsley;* refrigerate until chilled.

Green Mayonnaise
In blender at medium speed or in food processor with knife blade attached, blend *1 cup mayonnaise, 2 tablespoons chopped parsley, 2 teaspoons tarragon vinegar, ¼ teaspoon salt,* and *1 green onion,* cut up, until smooth stopping blender occasionally and scraping container with rubber spatula.

PRUNE-PEAR STUFFED PORK LOIN

½   12-ounce package pitted prunes
     (about ½ cup)
½   12-ounce package dried pears (about
     ½ cup)
     water
1   3-pound boneless pork top loin roast
     (single)
¼   teaspoon pepper
     salt

About 3 hours before serving:

1. In 1-quart saucepan over medium heat, heat prunes, pears, and ½-cup water to boiling; remove saucepan from heat; let stand 30 minutes. Drain fruit well.

2. With pork loin roast fat-side up, cut a 1-inch deep slit lengthwise along center top of roast, being careful not to cut all the way through ends, to form a deep "pocket". Pack prunes and pears firmly into pocket.

3. Sprinkle roast with pepper and 1 teaspoon salt. Place roast, fat-side up, on rack in open roasting pan. Insert meat thermometer into center of roast, being careful that pointed end of thermometer does not touch fruit. Roast in 325°F oven 1½ to 1¾ hours until thermometer reaches 170°F (about 30 to 35 minutes per pound).

4. When pork roast is done, place on warm large platter; let pork roast stand 15 minutes for easier carving.

5. Meanwhile, prepare gravy: Remove rack from roasting pan; pour drippings into 2-cup measure or medium bowl (set pan aside); let stand a few seconds until fat separates from meat juices. Return 3 tablespoons fat from drippings to roasting pan; skim off and discard any remaining fat from drippings. (If roast is very lean and does not have enough fat, add salad oil to make up 3 tablespoons.) Add enough water to meat juices to make 1½ cups. Into fat in roasting pan over low heat, stir flour until blended; gradually stir in meat-juice mixture and cook, stirring, until gravy thickens slightly and brown bits are loosened from pan. Add ½ teaspoon salt. Pour gravy into gravy boat.

6. To serve, arrange roast on platter. Serve with gravy. Makes 10 servings.

GLAZED PORK SHOULDER ROLLS WITH CRANBERRY CORN BREAD

2   3-pound smoked pork shoulder rolls
1   small onion, cut in half
6   peppercorns
     water
     Cranberry Corn Bread
⅔   cup white grape juice
3   tablespoons sugar
2   teaspoons cornstarch
½   teaspoon salt
¼   teaspoon ground ginger
⅛   teaspoon ground cloves
     watercress sprigs for garnish

About 2½ hours before serving:

1. Prepare smoked pork shoulder rolls; Leave stockinette casing on rolls during simmering so rolls will keep their shape. In 8-quart saucepot over high heat, heat pork rolls, onion, peppercorns, and enough water to cover to boiling. Reduce heat to low; cover; simmer 1½ hours or until pork is fork-tender.

2. After cooking pork rolls 1 hour, preheat oven to 425°F and prepare Cranberry Corn Bread.

3. When pork rolls are done, cool until easy to handle. Meanwhile, prepare glaze: In 2-quart saucepan over medium heat, heat grape juice and remaining ingredients except watercress to boiling; boil 1 minute stirring often, until glaze thickens; remove from heat.

4. When corn bread is done, remove from oven but do not turn oven off. Carefully remove casings from pork rolls; arrange in small open roasting pan. Brush rolls with some glaze; bake in 425°F oven 20 minutes or until heated through, brushing occasionally with glaze.

5. To serve, cut Cranberry Corn Bread into 12 pieces. Cut pork rolls into slices. Arrange corn bread and pork rolls on large platter. Garnish with watercress. Makes 12 servings.

Cranberry Corn Bread
Grease 13″ by 9″ baking pan. In large bowl, with fork, mix *2 cups all-purpose flour, 1½ cups yellow cornmeal, ⅓ cup sugar, 4 teaspoons baking powder, 1 teaspoon salt, and ¾ teaspoon baking soda.* In medium bowl, with fork, beat *one 8-ounce container sour cream, ½ cup milk, ½ cup butter* , melted, and *2 eggs* until blended. Pour mixture all at once into flour mixture, stirring just until flour is moistened. Gently fold in *1 cup cranberries,* coarsely chopped; spoon evenly into prepared pan. Bake 25 minutes or until toothpick inserted in center comes out clean. Cool bread in pan on rack 10 minutes. Remove from pan.

Good Housekeeping   December 1950

SAUSAGE-STUFFED VEAL WITH SAFFRON RICE

1   *pound hot Italian-sausage links*
    water
2   *eggs*
¾   *cup fresh bread crumbs*
1   *4-ounce jar diced pimento, drained*
¼   *pound green beans, trimmed*
    salt
1   *4-pound rolled boneless veal leg sirloin*
    roast
1   *8-ounce package thick-sliced bacon*
2   *cups regular long-grain rice*
½   *teaspoon crushed saffron threads*
3   *tablespoons all-purpose flour*
    watercress sprigs for garnish

About 3 hours before serving:

1. In 10-inch skillet over medium heat, heat sausages and ¼ cup water to boiling. Cover; simmer 5 minutes. Remove cover and continue cooking, turning sausages frequently, until water evaporates and sausages are well browned, about 20 minutes. Remove sausages to paper towels to drain. Finely chop sausages. In medium bowl, combine chopped sausages with eggs, bread crumbs, and pimento.

2. Meanwhile, in 1-quart saucepan over high heat, heat whole green beans, ½ teaspoon salt, and 1 inch water to boiling. Reduce heat to low; cover and simmer 5 to 10 minutes until beans are fork-tender; drain.

3. Untie veal sirloin roast; place fat-side down, on work surface. To make veal evenly thick, with sharp knife held parallel to the cutting surface, cut off horizontal slices from thick parts of veal. Press the cut-off slices, where needed, along edges of veal roast to make about a 12″ by 10″ rectangle. Then, if necessary, pound veal with dull edge of French knife or meat mallet to make about 1-inch evenly thick throughout.

4. Spoon sausage mixture onto veal; place green beans parallel to short side, here and there on sausage mixture. Starting at a narrow end, carefully roll veal, jelly-roll fashion; fasten with skewers. Place veal roast seam-side down; wrap roast with bacon slices. With string, tie veal roast at about 2-inch intervals.

5. Place roast on rack in open roasting pan. Insert meat thermometer into center of roast. Roast in 325°F oven 2 hours or until meat is tender and meat thermometer reaches 170°F.

6. About 30 minutes before veal is done, prepare rice as label directs, adding saffron.

7. When roast is done, remove strings and skewers; place roast on warm platter. Remove rack from pan. Skim 3 tablespoons fat from drippings into 1-quart saucepan; skim off and discard any remaining fat. Stir pan juices until brown bits are loosened from pan; pour pan juices into 2-cup measure; add water to make 2 cups.

8. Into fat in saucepan over medium heat, stir flour and ½ teaspoon salt until blended; gradually stir in meat-juice mixture; cook, stirring constantly, until thickened.

9. To serve, arrange veal roast and saffron rice on warm large platter. Garnish platter with watercress sprigs. Pass gravy to serve with veal. Makes 12 servings.

SPICED PEACH AND CRANBERRY RELISH

1 12-ounce package cranberries (about 3 cups)
1 cup water
1 cup sugar
1 teaspoon lemon juice
½ teaspoon ground allspice
1 16-ounce can sliced cling peaches

About 2 hours before serving or up to 2 days ahead:
1. In 2-quart saucepan over high heat, heat cranberries, water, sugar, lemon juice, and allspice to boiling. Reduce heat to medium; cook 5 to 10 minutes until cranberries pop and sugar is dissolved, stirring occasionally. Spoon cranberry mixture into bowl; cover and refrigerate at least 1½ hours or until chilled.
2. To serve, drain peaches; cut into bite-sized chunks; gently stir into cranberry mixture. Makes about 4 cups.

CRANBERRY CHUTNEY

2 12-ounce packages fresh or frozen cranberries (about 6 cups)
1 medium red cooking apple, diced
2½ cups packed brown sugar
½ cup diced pitted prunes
½ cup water
½ cup cider vinegar
¼ cup minced preserved ginger
1 tablespoon grated orange peel
2 teaspoons salt
1 teaspoon ground allspice

About 4 hours before serving or up to 1 week ahead:
1. In 5-quart saucepot or Dutch oven over medium-high heat, heat all ingredients to boiling, stirring occasionally. Reduce heat to low; cover and simmer until thickened,

about 15 minutes, stirring occasionally. Spoon chutney into large bowl; cover and refrigerate. Makes about 6 cups.

FESTIVE WHITE AND WILD RICE

½ cup wild rice
   water
   butter or margarine
1 small onion, diced
1 chicken-flavor bouillon cube
1 cup regular long-grain rice
½ teaspoon salt
⅛ teaspoon pepper

About 1¼ hours before serving:
1. Wash wild rice well; drain. In 2-quart saucepan over high heat, heat 1 cup water to boiling; stir in wild rice. Reduce heat to low; cover and simmer 45 minutes or until rice is tender and all liquid is absorbed.
2. About 30 minutes before wild rice is done, in 4-quart saucepan over medium heat, in 2 tablespoons hot butter or margarine, cook onion until tender, stirring occasionally. Add bouillon and 2 cups water; over high heat, heat to boiling; stir in regular long-grain rice. Reduce heat to low; cover and simmer 20 minutes or until rice is tender and all liquid is absorbed.
3. Stir wild rice into rice mixture in 2-quart saucepan; stir in salt, pepper, and 2 tablespoons butter or margarine until butter is melted. Makes 6 servings.

BRAISED HEARTS OF CELERY

2 large bunches celery
   water
1 medium onion, chopped
2 chicken-flavor bouillon cubes or envelopes
3 tablespoons butter or margarine
¾ teaspoon oregano leaves
½ teaspoon salt
1 2-ounce jar diced pimentos, drained

About 30 minutes before serving:
1. Remove outer rows of celery ribs; trim root ends. Cut tops and leaves from celery 6 to 8 inches from root ends. (Save outer ribs, tops, and leaves for soup or salad another day.) Cut each bunch of celery lengthwise into quarters.
2. In 12-inch skillet over high heat, in 1 inch boiling water, heat celery, onion, and bouillon to boiling. Reduce heat to medium; cover and cook 15 minutes or until celery is fork-tender; drain. Stir in butter and remaining ingredients. Makes 8 servings.

CRANBERRY-GINGER RELISH

2 12-ounce packages cranberries (about 6 cups)
1 15¼- to 20-ounce can chunk pineapple in juice
2 cups packed brown sugar
½ cup dark seedless raisins
1 tablespoon minced preserved ginger
1 teaspoon salt
½ teaspoon ground cinnamon

About 30 minutes before serving or day ahead:
1. In 5-quart Dutch oven or saucepot over high heat, heat all ingredients to boiling, stirring occasionally. Reduce heat to low; cover and simmer 15 minutes or until cranberries pop and mixture thickens slightly. Serve relish warm. Or, cover and refrigerate to serve cold later. Makes about 6 cups.

To Cook Cranberry-Ginger Relish In Microwave Oven
In 4-quart casserole, combine all ingredients. Cover with casserole lid. Cook on High 25 minutes or until cranberries pop and mixture thickens slightly, stirring every 5 minutes.

For
Beginners
or
Experts

Cleveland's Baking Powder

OLD FAVORITES MADE LIGHT

Holiday Dinner

This special holiday menu is drawn from recipes in Christmas à la Carte (Chapter I) which have been adapted for low calorie dining.

VELVETY PUMPKIN BISQUE

(50 calories per serving)

1	16-ounce can pumpkin
1	cup water
1	tablespoon minced green onion
2	teaspoons brown sugar
1/2	teaspoon salt
1/8	teaspoon white pepper
1/8	teaspoon ground cinnamon
2	chicken-flavor bouillon cubes or envelopes
2	cups skimmed milk
6	lemon slices for garnish
	minced parsley for garnish

About 30 minutes before serving:

1. In 3-quart saucepan over medium heat, heat first 8 ingredients to boiling. Reduce heat to low; cover and simmer 15 minutes, stirring occasionally. Stir in milk; heat through.

2. To serve, ladle soup into soup bowls; garnish each serving with a lemon slice and some minced parsley. Makes 5 cups or 6 servings.

HOLIDAY ROCK CORNISH HENS

(680 calories per servings)

2	tablespoons butter or margarine
1/2	pound mushrooms, sliced
2	celery stalks, diced
1	small onion, diced
1 1/2	cups white-bread cubes (3 slices)
	salt
	pepper
3	1 1/2-pound fresh or frozen (thawed) Rock Cornish hens
	salad oil
	paprika
	Gingered Peaches
	watercress sprigs for garnish

About 3 hours before serving:

1. Prepare stuffing: In 10-inch skillet over medium heat, in hot butter or margarine, cook mushrooms, celery, and onion until vegetables are tender, stirring occasionally. Remove skillet from heat. Stir in bread cubes, 1/4 teaspoon salt, and dash pepper.

2. Remove excess fat from Rock Cornish hens; refrigerate giblets and necks to use another day. Rinse hens with cold water; pat dry with paper towels.

3. Spoon stuffing into body cavity of each hen. Fold neck skin to back; lift wing up toward neck, then fold under back. With string, tie legs, tail of each hen together. Place hens, breast-side up, on rack in open roasting pan.

4. Brush hens lightly with salad oil; lightly sprinkle with salt, pepper, and paprika. Roast hens in 350°F oven about 1 1/4 hours, brushing occasionally with drippings in pan. Hens are done when legs can be moved up and down easily, or when two-tined fork is inserted between leg and body cavity and juices that escape are not pink.

5. When hens are done, discard strings. With sharp knife, cut each hen in half. Place hens on warm large platter; keep warm. Prepare Gingered Peaches.

6. To serve, with slotted spoon, arrange peaches on platter with hens. Garnish with watercress. Makes 6 servings.

Gingered Peaches
In 2-quart saucepan over medium heat, stir *one 16-ounce can sliced cling peaches* with their juice and *2 teaspoons slivered preserved ginger*. Cook until peaches are heated through, stirring occasionally.

BROCCOLI "PUFF"

(60 calories per serving)

2	eggs, beaten
3/4	cup skimmed milk
2	tablespoons crumbled cooked bacon
1/2	teaspoon salt
1	10-ounce package frozen chopped broccoli, thawed and patted dry

About 1 hour before serving:

1. Preheat oven to 350° F. In greased 1-quart casserole, stir together eggs, milk, bacon, and salt. Stir in broccoli. Bake in oven 45 minutes or until toothpick inserted in center comes out clean. Makes 6 accompaniment servings.

CRUNCHY ONION TWISTS

(10 calories each)

½ cup all-purpose flour
¼ cup yellow cornmeal
¼ teaspoon salt
2 tablespoons shortening
2 tablespoons instant minced onions
cold water

Early in day or day ahead:

1. In medium bowl, mix flour, cornmeal, and salt. With pastry blender, cut in shortening until mixture resembles coarse crumbs. With fork stir in onions and 3 tablespoons water. With hands, shape dough into a ball. (If mixture is too dry, add more water, a teaspoon at a time, until moist enough to hold together.)

2. Preheat oven to 425°F. On lightly floured surface with lightly floured rolling pin, roll dough into 12″ by 8″ rectangle. Cut dough into 4″ by ½″ strips. Remove each strip; holding ends, make twist by turning ends in opposite directions. Arrange twists on cookie sheet; press ends to sheet to prevent curling.

3. Bake twists 6 to 8 minutes until golden. Remove twists to wire racks to cool. Store in tightly covered container. Serve as breadsticks. Makes 4 dozen.

ORANGE AND AVOCADO SALAD

(110 calories per serving)

3 tablespoons orange juice
1 tablespoon lemon juice
1 tablespoon olive or salad oil
1½ teaspoons sugar
½ teaspoon salt
3 large oranges, peeled and sectioned
½ small avocado, peeled and sliced
½ medium head romaine lettuce
½ large head Boston lettuce

Early in day:

1. In large bowl, mix first five ingredients. Stir in oranges and avocado; cover and refrigerate.

2. Into plastic bag, tear lettuce into bite-size pieces; seal and refrigerate.

3. To serve, into fruit mixture, add lettuce. Gently toss to mix well. Makes 6 accompaniment servings.

ORANGE CREAM PUNCH

(90 calories per serving)

2 medium oranges
2 eggs, separated
2 tablespoons sugar
3 tablespoons orange-flavor liqueur
¾ cup skimmed milk
½ cup frozen whipped topping, thawed
ground cinnamon for garnish

Early in day:

1. Grate ½ teaspoon peel and squeeze juice from oranges (about ¾ cup). Wrap peel with plastic wrap; reserve for garnish.

2. In large bowl with wire whisk, beat egg yolks and sugar, until sugar is dissolved; beat in orange juice, orange-flavor liqueur, skimmed milk, and whipped topping until well blended. Cover and refrigerate until well chilled.

3. To serve, in small bowl with mixer at high speed, beat egg whites until soft peaks form. With rubber spatula or wire whisk, gently fold egg whites into yolk mixture just until blended. Pour into 1-quart chilled glass bowl. Sprinkle cinnamon and reserved orange peel over punch. Makes 3⅔ cups or 6 servings.

ESPRESSO NUT MOUSSE

(150 calories per serving)

⅓ cup California walnuts
1½ cups skimmed milk
sugar
4½ teaspoons instant espresso-coffee powder
1 envelope unflavored gelatin
⅛ teaspoon salt
2 egg whites, at room temperature
1¼ cups frozen whipped topping, thawed

About 5 hours before serving or day ahead:

1. In blender at medium speed, finely grind walnuts.

2. In 1-quart saucepan, mix ¾ cup skimmed milk, 2 tablespoons sugar, and instant-espresso coffee powder; sprinkle gelatin evenly over mixture; over medium-low heat, cook, stirring constantly, until gelatin is completely dissolved. In medium bowl, mix gelatin mixture, walnuts, salt, and remaining ¾ cup skimmed milk. Refrigerate until mixture mounds when dropped from a spoon, about 45 minutes, stirring occasionally.

3. In small bowl with mixer at high speed, beat egg whites until soft peaks form. Beating at high speed, gradually sprinkle in 2 tablespoons sugar, beating until sugar is completely dissolved. (Whites should stand in stiff, glossy peaks.)

4. With rubber spatula or wire whisk, fold beaten egg whites and 1 cup whipped topping into walnut mixture until blended. Spoon mixture into six 6-ounce wine or dessert glasses; refrigerate until set, about 2½ hours.

5. To serve, garnish tops of mousse with remaining ¼ cup whipped topping. Makes 6 servings.

NO-SALT MUSTARD

(25 calories per teaspoon)

2/3   cup salad oil
2/3   cup corn syrup
2/3   cup dry mustard
1/2   cup white wine vinegar
1/8   teaspoon ground allspice
1   small garlic clove, cut in half

About 15 minutes before serving or up to
2 weeks ahead:
1. In blender at medium speed or in food
processor with knife blade attached, blend
all ingredients until smooth and well
blended. Store mustard in tightly covered
jars in the refrigerator to use up within 2
weeks. Stir before serving. Makes 2 cups.

NO SALT
HERB-AND-SPICE MIX

(5 calories per teaspoon)

3   tablespoons savory
2   teaspoons whole black peppercorns
1   teaspoon fennel seeds
1   teaspoon ground ginger
1/8   teaspoon garlic powder

Up to 1 month ahead:
1. In small bowl, stir all ingredients until
mixed. Spoon into pepper mill. Use to
sprinkle on chicken, fish, or pork before
cooking. Or serve at table to sprinkle over
vegetables or salad. Makes 1/4 cup.

For Gift Giving
Spoon mixture into clear glass or Lucite
pepper mill. If you like, attach card listing
the ingredients.

CALORIE-WISE
HERB SALAD DRESSING

(35 calories per tablespoon)

1   cup red wine vinegar
2/3   cup water
1/2   cup salad oil
1   tablespoon basil
1   tablespoon chervil
2   tablespoons honey
1 1/2   teaspoons dry mustard
3/4   teaspoon salt
1/2   teaspoon pepper

About 10 minutes before serving or up to
1 week ahead:
1. In small bowl with wire whisk or fork,
mix all ingredients until well blended.
Store salad dressing in tightly covered jar
or cruet in refrigerator to use up within 1
week. Mix well again just before using.
Serve on tossed green salad, sliced tomatoes, or cooked broccoli. Makes about 2 1/4
cups.

For Gift Giving
Fill cruet with salad dressing. If you like,
write storing, serving suggestions, and
calories on gift card.

MINCEMEAT PIE

(355 calories per serving without whipped cream)

2   large cooking apples, cored and diced
2   medium ripe pears, cored and diced
1 1/4   cups dark seedless raisins
1/2   cup packed brown sugar
2   tablespoons lemon juice
1/2   teaspoon ground cloves
1/2   teaspoon ground cinnamon
1/8   teaspoon salt
1 1/2   cups California walnuts, chopped
1/4   cup brandy (optional)
     Crumb Crust
     whipped cream, for garnish

Day ahead:
1. In heavy 3-quart saucepan, combine apples and next 7 ingredients. Over medium
heat, heat apple mixture to boiling. Reduce
heat to low; cover and simmer 15 minutes,
stirring occasionally. Remove saucepan
from heat; stir in walnuts and brandy.
Cover and refrigerate overnight to blend
flavors.
2. Preheat oven to 375°F. Prepare Crumb
Crust. Bake crust 5 minutes; remove from
oven. Firmly press mincemeat mixture into
crust. Bake 45 minutes. Cool pie on wire
rack; refrigerate until chilled, about 2
hours. To serve, garnish pie with whipped
cream. Makes 10 servings.

Crumb Crust
In blender or food procesoor with knife
blade attached, blend 5 *cups oven-toasted rice
cereal* to make 2 1/2 cups crumbs. In small
saucepan over low heat, melt *6 tablespoons
butter or margarine*. In 9-inch pie plate, mix
2 tablespoons sugar with cereal crumbs and
melted butter or margarine, then press
mixture onto bottom and side of pie plate.

APPETIZERS & SNACKS

These recipes were developed in 600- to 700-watt microwave ovens. If your oven is slower or faster, adjust cooking times accordingly.

FESTIVE CRAB-STUFFED MUSHROOMS

24	medium mushrooms
4	green onions, sliced
1	medium red pepper, diced
1	6½-ounce can crabmeat, drained
½	cup blanched almonds, chopped
½	cup mayonnaise
2	tablespoons dry sherry
½	teaspoon salt

About 20 minutes before serving:

1. Remove stems from mushrooms; chop stems. Set aside mushroom caps.

2. In 2-quart casserole or bowl, place mushroom stems, green onions, and red pepper; cover with casserole lid or large plate. Cook on High 2½ to 3 minutes until mushroom stems are tender, stirring after 1½ minutes. Stir in crabmeat and remaining ingredients except mushroom caps. Fill caps with mixture.

3. Line large platter with sheet of paper towel; arrange caps in double circle. Cook on High 5 to 6 minutes until hot, turning dish ¼ turn after 3 minutes. Makes 24.

RAISIN-BRAN MUFFINS

1	cup water
3	cups bran cereal with raisins
½	cup butter or margarine
1½	cups sugar
2	eggs
2½	cups all-purpose flour
2	teaspoons baking soda
2	cups buttermilk

About 25 minutes for up to 6 muffins, 50 minutes for all 42 muffins before serving:

1. Line microwave cupcake pan with paper liners. In a large bowl measure water. Cook on High 2 to 3 minutes until boiling. Add bran cereal. Stir until cereal is moistened. Add butter or margarine and let mixture stand 5 to 6 minutes until cereal is softened. With wire whisk, stir in sugar and eggs, beating until well mixed. Blend in flour, baking soda, and buttermilk.

2. Spoon batter into desired number of paper-lined cups, filling half full. Remaining batter may be stored in refrigerator for up to 6 weeks.

3. Cook 2 muffins on High for 1 minute, 4 muffins for 1½ to 2 minutes, or 6 muffins for 2 to 3 minutes. (Muffins will be flat, they do not "peak.") Let stand 5 minutes. Makes 42 muffins.

NIBBLES FOR A CROWD

2	12-ounce cans mixed nuts
1	12-ounce package bite-sized shredded wheat
1	12-ounce package bite-sized crispy rice squares
1	11-ounce bag pretzel nuggets
1	7-ounce package toasted oat cereal
1	tablespoon seasoned salt
1	teaspoon garlic powder
2	cups salad oil
2	tablespoons Worcestershire

About 50 minutes before serving:

1. In large bowl, place half of each of the first 7 ingredients. Cover bowl and shake until well mixed. Stir together half each of the oil and Worcestershire; sprinkle over cereal mixture while stirring cereal. Cook on High 9 to 10 minutes until hot and no longer glistening with oil, stirring every 2 minutes.

2. Repeat with remaining half of ingredients. Let stand about 20 minutes before serving. Makes 4 quarts.

PIZZA SNACKS

1	pound ground beef
1	16-ounce package hot sausage
1	16-ounce package mozzarella cheese, cut into small chunks
2	6-ounce cans tomato paste
1	cup minced parsley
1	tablespoon oregano leaves
1	teaspoon Worcestershire
½	teaspoon garlic powder
2	8-ounce loaves party rye or thinly-sliced French bread

About 30 minutes before serving:

1. In 3-quart casserole, mix ground beef and sausage. Cook on High 6 to 8 minutes until thoroughly cooked, stirring every 2 minutes. Drain. Add cheese and remaining ingredients except bread; cook on High 2 to 3 minutes until cheese melts, stirring every minute.

2. Spread heaping tablespoon of mixture on each slice of bread. Arrange half on large platter; heat on High 2 to 3 minutes. Repeat with second half. Serve immediately. Makes 70.

For **even heating,** arrange appetizers such as meatballs, stuffed mushrooms, canapés in a double or single circle on microwave-safe cooking/serving platter.

Most **cheeses** taste best served at room temperature, so take the chill off refrigerated cheese by warming in microwave oven. One minute on Medium makes 8-ounce wedge of Brie just begin to ooze and brings out nutty flavor of 8 ounces of Swiss.

Quick **canapés:** Spread canned or fresh ham, chicken or shrimp salad on crackers; top with shredded cheese. Arrange 12 on a platter; heat on High about 60 seconds to melt cheese.

Easy hot **snack:** Spoon ½ to 1 tablespoon canned filling (sloppy-joe sauce with meat, chicken à la king) into a Parker House roll. Cover with paper towel and heat on High 10 seconds per roll.

To **crisp** pretzels, chips, popcorn, heat on High 30 to 45 seconds for medium-size bowl-full. Let stand a minute.

FRUIT-GLAZED HAM

5   pound canned ham
¼   cup water
    Cranberry or Peach or Raisin Sauce

About 40 minutes before serving:

1. Slice ham crosswise into ¼-inch-thick slices. Fan slices out on a roasting rack in oblong baking dish. Add water. Cover with vented plastic wrap. Cook on Medium 4 to 5 minutes per pound until heated through, rotating dish ½ turn after half the cooking time. Let stand, covered, 10 minutes.

2. Meanwhile, prepare Cranberry or Peach or Raisin Sauce. Pour over ham slices placed on serving platter. Let stand a few minutes to set. Makes 18 servings.

Cranberry Sauce

Blend ¼ cup apple juice with 1 tablespoon cornstarch in a 1-quart glass measure or bowl. Add one 8-ounce can whole-berry cranberry sauce. Cook on High for 3 to 4 minutes until thickened, stirring once during cooking time.

Peach Sauce

Blend ½ cup water with 2 tablespoons cornstarch in a 1-quart glass measure or bowl. Add one 16-ounce jar peach preserves and ¼ teaspoon allspice. Cook on High for 3 to 5 minutes until thickened and clear, stirring once during cooking.

Raisin Sauce

Combine ½ cup dark seedless raisins and ½ cup orange juice in a 1-quart glass measure or bowl. Cook on High for 1 minute. Stir in ½ cup orange juice blended with 3 tablespoons light brown sugar, 1 tablespoon cornstarch, 1 teaspoon prepared mustard, ⅛ teaspoon each ground cloves and nutmeg. Cook on High for 4 to 5 minutes until thickened, stirring once during cooking.

SHRIMP AND SCALLOPS WITH ARTICHOKES

1¼   pounds medium-sized shrimp
     salt
3   tablespoons dry sherry
1¼   pounds sea scallops
2   9-ounce packages frozen artichoke
     hearts
½   cup water
¼   cup prepared mustard
3   tablespoons lemon juice
2   tablespoons cider vinegar
1   teaspoon sugar
¼   teaspoon pepper
⅔   cup salad oil
1   medium-sized head romaine lettuce
½   cup pitted ripe olives, each cut in half
1   2-ounce jar sliced pimentos, drained

1. Shell and devein shrimp. Place shrimp and 1 teaspoon salt in 3-quart casserole or bowl, leaving center of casserole empty; cover with casserole lid or large plate. Cook on High 4 minutes or just until shrimp turn pink, stirring after 2 minutes. With slotted spoon, remove shrimp to large bowl; stir in sherry. Discard liquid.

2. In same casserole, place scallops and 1 teaspoon salt, leaving center of casserole empty. Cover and cook on High 4 to 5 minutes just until scallops turn opaque, stirring after 3 minutes. With slotted spoon, remove scallops to bowl with shrimp. Discard liquid.

3. In same casserole, combine artichokes and water. Cover and cook on High 12 to 15 minutes until artichokes are tender, stirring every 5 minutes. Drain.

4. With rubber spatula, stir artichoke hearts, mustard, lemon juice, vinegar, sugar, pepper, salad oil, and 1 teaspoon salt into shrimp mixture until blended. Cover bowl and refrigerate 1 hour or until ready to serve.

5. To serve, line large platter with lettuce leaves. Add olives to shrimp mixture; spoon mixture onto lettuce. Garnish with sliced pimentos. Makes 16 first-couse servings.

ORANGE-GLAZED BEETS

3   pounds small beets with tops or 3 16-
    ounce cans or jars small whole beets
    salt
    water
2   medium-sized oranges
1   10- to 12-ounce jar orange
    marmalade
1   tablespoon cornstarch
1   tablespoon prepared mustard

Day ahead:

1. Cut off stems and leaves from beets. (If using canned beets, drain and follow recipe in steps 3 through 5 only.) Wash beets and leaves well with running cold water; discard stems. If beets are large, cut in halves or quarters. Wrap leaves with plastic wrap and refrigerate for garnish.

2. In 4-quart casserole or bowl, combine beets, ½ cup water, and 1 teaspoon salt; cover with casserole lid or large plate. Cook on High 20 minutes or until beets are tender, stirring every 5 minutes. Drain; peel.

3. From one orange, grate 1 tablespoon peel and squeeze ½ cup juice. Wrap 2 teaspoons orange peel with plastic wrap and refrigerate for garnish.

4. In same casserole, mix orange marmalade, cornstarch, mustard, orange juice, remaining 1 teaspoon orange peel, and ¼ teaspoon salt. Cover and cook on High 5 minutes, stirring after 3 minutes, and every minute thereafter. Add beets. Cover and cook on High 3 to 5 minutes until beets are heated through. Cover and refrigerate.

5. To serve, slice remaining orange. Arrange orange slices and reserved beet greens if any on large platter. Spoon beets and sauce onto platter. Sprinkle with reserved orange peel. Makes 10 accompaniment servings.

APPLE-DATE STEAMED PUDDING

1	8-ounce package pitted dates
1/2	cup cranberry-juice cocktail or apple cider
3/4	cup sugar
1/2	cup butter or margarine, softened
4	eggs
2	cups all-purpose flour
2	teaspoons baking powder
1/2	teaspoon ground cinnamon
1/4	teaspoon ground cloves
1/4	teaspoon salt
1	large cooking apple (about 8 ounces), peeled, cored and coarsely chopped
3/4	cup California walnuts, chopped Custard Sauce red and green candied cherries for garnish

1. Heavily grease deep 2½-quart bowl; set aside.

2. In blender at medium speed or food processor with knife blade attached, blend dates and cranberry-juice cocktail until smooth; set aside.

3. In large bowl with mixer at medium speed, beat sugar and butter or margarine until light and fluffy. Add eggs, next 5 ingredients, date mixture, and ¼ cup water. Beat at low speed until blended. Increase speed to medium; beat 1 minute, occasionally scraping bowl with rubber spatula. With rubber spatula, gently fold in chopped apple and walnuts. Spoon pudding mixture into prepared bowl; cover bowl with vented plastic wrap.

4. Cook pudding on Low 10 minutes. Rotate bowl ¼ turn; cook on High 8 to 9 minutes, rotating bowl ¼ turn every 4 minutes until toothpick inserted in center of pudding comes out clean.

5. When pudding is done, cool in bowl on wire rack 10 minutes. Meanwhile, prepare Custard Sauce.

6. Carefully loosen pudding with metal spatula and invert onto warm platter.

7. Garnish pudding with red and green candied cherries. Serve pudding warm with warm sauce. Make 12 servings.

Custard Sauce

In 2-quart bowl with wire whisk, mix *1½ cups milk, 2 tablespoons sugar,* and *¼ teaspoon salt.* Cook on High 3 minutes or until milk is steaming. In small bowl, beat *4 egg yolks* slightly. Gradually beat in small amount of hot milk. Pour yolk mixture back into hot milk mixture, beating rapidly to prevent lumping. Cook on Medium 2 to 3 minutes until mixture thickens slightly and coats the back of a spoon, stirring briskly every minute. Beat in *½ teaspoon vanilla extract.*

CRANBERRY-ORANGE COFFEE CAKE

2	cups all-purpose flour
3/4	cup milk
1/2	cup sugar
1/2	cup butter or margarine, softened
2	teaspoons baking powder
2	teaspoons ground cinnamon
1/2	teaspoon salt
2	eggs
1	14-ounce jar cranberry-orange sauce
1/2	cup pecans or California walnuts, finely chopped

About 50 minutes before serving:

1. In large bowl with mixer at medium speed, beat flour and next 7 ingredients until well-blended, about 2 minutes, scraping bowl often with rubber spatula. Pour batter into 10-inch cake dish or deep-dish pie plate. Spoon cranberry-orange sauce over outer edge of batter; with knife or spatula, spread sauce evenly in two-inch-wide band. Then, gently spread some of sauce from inside edge of band to lightly cover center of batter. Sprinkle evenly with nuts.

2. Place dish on rack or inverted custard cup in microwave oven. Cook on Medium 20 to 22 minutes until toothpick inserted in center of cake comes out clean, turning dish ¼ turn every 6 minutes. Let stand on solid surface at least 20 minutes or until completely cool before serving. Makes 10 servings.

CHOCOLATE SWIRL CHEESECAKE

2	tablespoons butter
1/2	cup chocolate-wafer crumbs (10-12 wafers)
	sugar
3	eggs
1	8-ounce container sour cream
1	8-ounce container cottage cheese
1	8-ounce package cream cheese, at room temperature
5	teaspoons cornstarch
1/2	teaspoon lemon juice
1	square semisweet chocolate
1/2	teaspoon ground cinnamon

Early in day:

1. In 8-inch round cake pan, melt butter on High about 1 minute. Stir in crumbs and 1 tablespoon sugar. Press mixture over pan bottom. Cook on High 1½ minutes, turning dish ¼ turn every 30 seconds.

2. In blender or food processor, blend eggs, sour cream, cottage cheese, cream cheese, cornstarch, lemon juice, and 1 cup sugar on high speed until smooth. (Stop occasionally to scrape down sides with rubber spatula.) Pour cheese mixture into 3-quart bowl. Cook on Medium 12 to 15 minutes, stirring with whisk every 3 minutes, until very thick. Pour into prepared shell.

3. In small bowl, melt chocolate on High about 2 minutes. Stir in cinnamon. Drizzle chocolate over cheesecake. With knife, cut halfway through batter and swirl to marbleize. Cook on High 4 minutes. Cool, then refrigerate several hours before serving. Makes 12 servings.

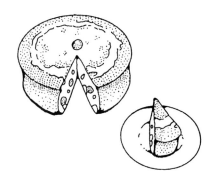

Cake mixes using oil and recipes high in fat and sugar generally do best in a microwave oven.

For more **even cooking,** use ring molds and straight-edged baking dishes for cakes. If you use a loaf pan for bread, shape a 2-inch-wide strip of foil to shield the ends, extending 1 inch over batter so bread doesn't overcook. Remove halfway through cooking time.

To make sure **cake cooks more uniformly,** elevate cake dish on a microwave-oven rack or inverted bowl or pie plate.

Test cake or bread for **doneness** by inserting toothpick in center; it should come out clean. If baking dish is glass, lift up and check bottom to make sure there are no wet, unbaked areas.

Microwave-cooked **cakes** and quick breads appear slightly glossy or "wet" on top just after removing from oven, but will dry as cake cooks during standing time.

PUMPKIN BREAD RING

1/3	*cup dried currants*
1/3	*cup pitted dates, chopped*
1 1/2	*cups all-purpose flour*
1	*cup canned pumpkin*
1/2	*cup packed brown sugar*
1/2	*cup buttermilk (or use 1/2 cup milk mixed with 1 1/2 teaspoons cider vinegar)*
1/3	*cup salad oil*
1	*teaspoon baking soda*
1/2	*teaspoon ground nutmeg*
1/2	*teaspoon ground allspice*
1/2	*teaspoon ground ginger*
1	*egg*

About 1 hour before serving or day ahead:
1. Grease 5-cup ring mold. In small bowl, combine currants and dates; press evenly in bottom of mold; set mold aside.

2. In large bowl with mixer at medium speed, beat flour and remaining ingredients until well-blended, about 2 minutes, scraping bowl often with rubber spatula. Pour batter over fruit in mold; spread evenly. Cook on Medium 20 minutes or until toothpick inserted in center of bread comes out clean, turning mold 1/4 turn every 5 minutes. Let stand on solid surface 20 minutes; unmold. Serve warm. Or, refrigerate to serve cold later. Makes 12 servings.

SWEET-POTATO PIE

1	*9-inch cooked piecrust*
2	*medium-sized sweet potatoes (about 1 pound)*
1/2	*cup water*
2	*cups half-and-half*
2	*eggs*
1	*cup packed brown sugar*
1	*teaspoon vanilla extract*
1	*teaspoon ground cinnamon*
1/2	*teaspoon ground ginger*
1/4	*teaspoon ground cloves*

About 4 hours before serving or early in the day:

1. Prepare piecrust. Set aside.

2. Peel sweet potatoes and cut into 1-inch pieces. In 2-quart casserole, place sweet potatoes and water. Cover and cook on High 12 to 15 minutes until potatoes are tender, stirring every 5 minutes.

3. In blender or food processor with knife blade attached, blend half-and-half, eggs, brown sugar, vanilla, cinnamon, ginger, cloves, and reserved sweet potatoes until smooth; stop blender or food processor occasionally to scrape down sides with rubber spatula.

4. Pour mixture into same 2-quart casserole. Cook on High 5 to 6 minutes until mixture thickens, stirring every 2 minutes.

5. Pour sweet-potato mixture into piecrust. Cook on High 2 minutes. Refrigerate until set, about 4 hours. Makes 8 servings.

Pastry shell and filling should be cooked separately first. This prevents the crust from getting soggy, allows filling to be stirred for even cooking results.

Pastry shells cooked in a microwave oven come out more tender, flaky. Start with your favorite pastry-crust recipe—no special recipe is needed. With fork, prick crust all around sides and across bottom, especially where sides and bottom meet. Cook pastry on High 5 to 7 minutes, turning dish halfway after 3 minutes. Crust will not brown, but will appear blistered, dry, and opaque when done.

To give **crusts** a more traditional **golden-brown** color, try the following: Add a teaspoon of vanilla extract to cold water in preparing a recipe for a dessert shell. Or, mix together a teaspoon of melted butter with a 1/4 teaspoon of cinnamon, brown sugar, molasses, or cocoa; brush on rim of pastry before cooking. Add a teaspoon of bottled sauce for gravy when making meat pie or quiche.

Crumb crusts are easy to make and require no browning. Simply melt 3 to 4 tablespoons butter in 9-inch glass pie plate. Mix in 2 tablespoons brown or granulated sugar and 1 1/2 to 2 cups of one of the following: vanilla or chocolate wafers, gingersnap cookies, or graham crackers. Press in bottom and on sides of pie plate. Cook on High 1 1/2 to 2 minutes, rotating dish halfway through cooking.

To make a **top crust,** try a crumb topping; or pastry strips sprinkled with cinnamon and sugar, baked separately on High for a few minutes, then placed on top of pie. Or, for a festive touch, cut dough with a cookie cutter.

Frozen pie shells can also be cooked in the microwave oven. Simply remove from foil container and place in glass, plastic, or paper pie plate to defrost in microwave oven or at room temperature. When soft, press to shape of pie plate. Prick and cook as directed above.

COCONUTTY CREAM PIE

1   9-inch cooked piecrust
¼   cup sliced almonds
1   cup shredded coconut
⅓   cup sugar
¼   cup all-purpose flour
1½   cups milk
3   eggs, slightly beaten
¾   teaspoon almond extract

About 4 hours before serving or early in the day:

1. Prepare piecrust. Set aside.

2. In small bowl, place almonds and ½ cup coconut. Cook on High 2 to 2½ minutes until evenly browned, stirring every 30 seconds. Set mixture aside.

3. In 3-quart bowl, combine sugar, flour, and milk. Cook on High until mixture boils about 6 minutes, stirring every 2 minutes.

4. In small bowl, with fork, beat eggs slightly. Stir small amount of hot milk mixture into eggs. Slowly pour egg mixture back into milk mixture, stirring rapidly to prevent lumping. Cook mixture on High about 30 seconds until thickened. Stir in almond extract and remaining coconut. Pour mixture into prepared piecrust. Sprinkle with toasted coconut mixture. Refrigerate until set, about 4 hours. Makes 8 servings.

COFFEE-WALNUT FUDGE

3   cups sugar
1   cup half-and-half
3   tablespoons light corn syrup
¼   teaspoon salt
1   tablespoon instant coffee powder
2   teaspoons hot water
4   tablespoons butter or margarine
¼   teaspoon vanilla extract
1   cup California walnuts, coarsely
        chopped

About 1½ hours before serving or day ahead:

1. In 5-quart glass or glass-ceramic casserole, combine first four ingredients. Cook on High 5 to 7 minutes, until mixture comes to a full boil, stirring occasionally.

2. Set **microwave-safe candy thermometer** in place. Continue to cook on High 7 to 10 minutes or until temperature reaches 240°F, or soft-ball stage (when a small amount of mixture dropped into a bowl of cold water forms a soft ball that flattens on removal from water).

3. Dissolve coffee in hot water. Add coffee mixture, butter, and vanilla to hot candy mixture, but **do not stir.** Cool without stirring to 110°F, or until outside of casserole feels lukewarm. Meanwhile, lightly butter an 8-inch square baking pan.

4. When mixture is cool, with wooden spoon, beat until fudge becomes thick and begins to lose its gloss. Stir in nuts. Pour fudge into prepared pan. (Do not scrape casserole; mixture on side may be sugary.) Chill. When firm; cut into 6 strips, then cut each strip crosswise into 6 pieces. Makes about 2 pounds of fudge or 36 pieces.

DOUBLE-CHOCOLATE PEANUT BRITTLE

1   cup sugar
½   cup light corn syrup
1   6½-ounce can salted peanuts (about
        1¼ cups)
3   tablespoons cocoa
1   teaspoon butter or margarine
1   teaspoon vanilla extract
1   teaspoon baking soda
½   cup semisweet chocolate pieces

About 1½ hours before serving:

1. Lightly grease cookie sheet; set aside.

2. In 2-quart glass or glass-ceramic casserole, combine sugar and corn syrup. Cook on High 4 minutes. With wooden spoon, stir in peanuts. Cook on High 3 to 5 minutes, until peanuts are lightly browned.

3. Stir in cocoa, butter, and vanilla. Set **microwave-safe candy thermometer** in place. Continue to cook on High 2 to 3 minutes until temperature reaches 300°F, or hard-crack stage (when a small amout of mixture dropped into a bowl of very cold water forms hard and brittle threads).

4. Blend in baking soda and stir until mixture is foamy. Immediately pour onto prepared cookie sheet and spread into ¼-inch thickness.

5. Sprinkle hot peanut brittle with chocolate pieces. As pieces begin to melt, spread chocolate evenly over candy. Refrigerate until set. Break into pieces before serving. Makes about 1 pound.

Packaged in a pretty container, **homemade candy** makes a great gift or sweet treat for holiday entertaining. And with a microwave oven, it doesn't take a lot of time from a busy schedule. Candy cooks quickly, more uniformly than on a rangetop, so there's hardly any need to stir.

Because **candy-making** ingredients reach high temperatures, they tend to boil up, so it's important to cook in a **container** that's at least twice the volume of the ingredients, and can tolerate high temperatures, such as glass or glass-ceramic.

For best results when making candy, be sure to monitor temperature carefully. For the most accurate reading, use a specially designed **microwave-safe candy thermometer.** A conventional candy thermometer cannot be placed in the candy mixture while it's cooking in the microwave oven.

To test candy temperature without a microwave-safe candy thermometer, use the **cold water test:** Simply drop a teaspoon of the candy mixture into a cup of very cold water. Let stand 1 minute; then check with fingers to see if candy has reached stage of firmness called for in the recipe.

To soften stuck-on candy residue for easier **clean-up,** fill the sticky containers with warm tap water, placing any microwave-safe utensils, such as a wooden spoon, into the container too. Heat in microwave oven a few minutes, then wash.

IV. GIFTS FROM HAND, HEART AND HEARTH

Christmas is a time for feasting but it is also a time for giving, and if " 'tis better to give than to receive" is your motto, here are fifty gift ideas to help you live up to it. These gifts are all personal statements, as each one will be cooked, baked, stitched, knitted or cut out by you. Some are simple enough for a child to make; some take more patience and care. There are take-alongs and send-alongs, sweets and savories, last-minutes and low-calories, with tips on how to mail your home-baked treats as well as a glorious display of how to present gifts with outsides as precious as the treasures within.

This little girl in the kitchen explains it all—from her dishtowel-ruffled pinafore to the dainty doll to the Christmas cookies she's about to cut out. These are the treasures of Christmas giving. Instructions to make pinafore and doll on pages 92-93.

CRISP CHINESE FRIED WALNUTS

6   cups water
4   cups California walnuts
½   cup sugar
    salad oil
    salt

About 1½ hours before serving or up to 2 weeks ahead:

1. In 4-quart saucepan over high heat, heat water to boiling; add walnuts and heat to boiling; cook 1 minute. Rinse walnuts under running hot water; drain. Wash saucepan and dry well.

2. In large bowl with rubber spatula, gently stir warm walnuts with sugar until sugar is dissolved. (If necessary, let mixture stand 5 minutes to dissolve sugar.)

3. Meanwhile, in same saucepan over medium heat, heat about 1 inch salad oil to 350°F. on deep-fat thermometer (or heat oil according to manufacturer's directions in deep-fat fryer set at 350°F.). With slotted spoon, add about half of walnuts to oil; fry 5 minutes or until golden, stirring often.

4. With slotted spoon, place walnuts in coarse sieve over bowl to drain; sprinkle very lightly with salt; toss lightly to keep walnuts from sticking together. Transfer to paper towels to cool. Fry remaining walnuts. Store walnuts in tightly covered container to use up within two weeks. Makes 4 cups.

ALMOND CRUNCH

5   4½-ounce cans blanched whole almonds (4½ cups), finely chopped
1¾   cups sugar
⅓   cup sugar
⅓   cup light corn syrup
¼   cup water
1   cup butter or margarine
     Chocolate Glaze

About 2 hours before serving or up to 1 week ahead:

1. Preheat oven to 375°F. In 15½″by 10½″ jelly-roll pan, toast chopped almonds until lightly browned, about 30 minutes, stirring occasionally.

2. In heavy 2-quart saucepan over medium heat, heat sugar, corn syrup, and water to boiling, stirring constantly. Stir in butter or margarine. Set candy thermometer in place and continue cooking, stirring frequently, until temperature reaches 300°F. or hard-crack stage (when small amount of mixture dropped into very cold water separates into threads that are hard but not brittle), about 20 minutes.

3. Remove saucepan from heat; stir in 1½ cups chopped and toasted almonds. Immediately pour mixture evenly into ungreased 15½″ by 10½″ jelly-roll pan. Cool slightly in pan on wire rack, about 3 minutes. With knife, cut candy lengthwise into 7 strips, then cut each strip crosswise into 10 pieces. Cool candy completely; remove from pan, then break into squares along cut lines.

4. Place remaining almonds in pie plate. Line jelly-roll pan with waxed paper. Prepare Chocolate Glaze. With fork, dip candy pieces, one at a time, into chocolate mixture until coated, scraping any excess chocolate across rim of pan; then coat completely with almonds. Arrange candies, in single layer, on waxed-paper-lined jelly-roll pan; refrigerate 20 to 25 minutes until chocolate is set. Store candy in single layer in tightly covered container to use up within 1 week. Makes about 2 pounds, 70 pieces.

Chocolate Glaze

In 1-quart saucepan over low heat, heat 3 squares semisweet chocolate, 3 squares unsweetened chocolate, 6 tablespoons butter or margarine (¾ stick), and 4½ teaspoons light corn syrup until melted and smooth, stirring occasionally. Remove saucepan from heat. With wooden spoon, beat mixture until cool but still pourable.

CARAMELS

1   cup sugar
1   cup heavy or whipping cream
3   tablespoons light corn syrup
2   tablespoons butter or margarine
1   teaspoon vanilla extract
    plastic wrap

About 1¾ hours before serving or up to 2 weeks ahead:

1. Grease 8″ by 8″ baking pan. In heavy 2-quart saucepan over medium heat, heat all ingredients except plastic wrap to boiling and until sugar is completely dissolved, stirring frequently. Carefully set candy thermometer in place and continue cooking, stirring frequently, until temperature reaches 245°F. or firm-ball stage (when a small amount of mixture dropped into a bowl of very cold water forms a firm ball that does not flatten on removal from water), about 30 minutes.

2. Pour caramel mixture into prepared pan. Cool in pan on wire rack 30 minutes. With knife, cut candy into thirty-two 4″ by ½″ pieces; cool completely, about 45 minutes longer. Wrap each caramel in plastic wrap. Store in tightly covered container to use up within 2 weeks. Makes about 1 pound.

CANDIED GRAPEFRUIT PEELS

4   *large grapefruits*
    water
½   *cup light corn syrup*
    sugar
1   *3-ounce package lemon-flavor gelatin*

Day ahead or up to 2 weeks ahead:

1. With sharp knife, score peel of each grapefruit into quarters; pull from fruit. (Reserve fruit to use in salad.) Trim off as much white membrane from peel as possible; cut peel into long, thin strips. You should have about 4 cups firmly packed peel.

2. In 4-quart saucepan over high heat, heat peels and 8 cups water to boiling; boil 15 minutes. Drain; rinse. With 8 more cups water, boil peels 15 minutes again; drain.

3. In same saucepan over high heat, heat corn syrup, 1¾ cups sugar, and 1½ cups water until boiling and sugar is dissolved, stirring frequently. Gently stir in peels. Reduce heat to medium-low; cook until most of the syrup has been absorbed, about 40 minutes, stirring occasionally.

4. Remove saucepan from heat; gently stir in gelatin until dissolved; cool 10 minutes. (Mixture will be thin and sticky.) On waxed paper, place 1 cup sugar. Lightly roll peels, a few at a time, in sugar; place in single layer on wire racks. Let peels dry overnight or about 12 hours. Store in tightly covered containers. Makes about 1½ pounds.

Candied Orange Peels
Prepare as above but substitute grapefruit with *10 large oranges*.

SWEET PRALINES

2   *cups sugar*
¾   *cup evaporated milk*
3   *tablespoons light corn syrup*
    dash baking soda
2   *tablespoons orange juice*
1½ *cups pecan halves*

About 2 hours before serving or up to 2 weeks ahead:

1. Line a large cookie sheet with waxed paper; set aside.

2. In heavy 3-quart saucepan over medium heat, heat sugar, evaporated milk, corn syrup, and baking soda to boiling, stirring constantly, until mixture boils and sugar is dissolved. Set candy thermometer in place. Reduce heat to low and continue cooking, stirring frequently, until temperature reaches 234°F. or soft-ball stage (when small amount of mixture dropped into very cold water forms a soft ball that flattens on removal from water).

3. Quickly stir in orange juice and pecans; cook 5 minutes longer, stirring often. Remove pan from heat; beat 2 to 3 minutes until mixture just begins to lose its gloss.

4. Working quickly, drop mixture by heaping tablepoonfuls, 2 inches apart, on waxed-paper-lined cookie sheets. (Mixture will spread into 3-inch circles.) Let Pralines stand 30 minutes or until cool before removing from waxed paper. Store in tightly covered container to use within 2 weeks.

2	4½-ounce cans blanchea whole almonds (2 cups)
1½	tablespoons butter or margarine
1	tablespoon curry powder
1½	teaspoons salt

About 1½ hours before serving or up to 1 week ahead:

1. Preheat oven to 375°F. In 15½" by 10½" jelly-roll pan, place all ingredients. Toast almond mixture in oven 15 minutes, stirring occasionally. Cool almonds completely in pan on wire rack. Store almonds in tightly covered container to use up within one week. Makes 2 cups.

COCOA NUTS

3	4½-ounce cans blanched whole almonds
½	cup light corn syrup
2	tablespoons butter or margarine sugar
½	teaspoon vanilla extract
⅓	cup cocoa
¼	teaspoon salt

SNAP-CRACKLE POPCORN AND NUTS

16	cups popped corn (about ¾ cup popcorn)
1½	cups pecans
1½	cups California walnuts
1	cup packed brown sugar
½	cup butter or margarine
½	cup light corn syrup
½	teaspoon salt
½	teaspoon vanilla extract

About 2 hours before serving or up to 1 week ahead:

1. Preheat oven to 250°F. Place popped corn, pecans, and walnuts in large open roasting pan (17¼" by 11½"); set aside.

2. Prepare caramel coating: In heavy 2-quart saucepan over medium heat, heat brown sugar, butter or margarine, corn syrup, and salt to boiling; boil 5 minutes, stirring frequently. Remove saucepan from heat; stir in vanilla extract.

3. Pour hot sugar mixture over popped-corn mixture, stirring to coat well. Bake popped-corn mixture 1 hour, stirring occasionally.

4. Spoon caramel-covered popcorn mixture into another large roasting pan or onto waxed paper to cool, stirring occasionally to separate. Store popcorn mixture in tightly covered containers to use up within 1 week. Makes about 21 cups.

To Cook Caramel Coating In Microwave Oven
In deep 2-quart bowl, combine brown sugar, butter or margarine, corn syrup, and salt. Cook on High 7 minutes or until mixture boils and thickens, stirring after 4 minutes; stir vanilla extract into mixture.

pan; keep remaining almonds warm. With fork, toss almonds in cocoa mixture to coat evenly.

4. Push coated almonds to one end of pan. Repeat adding almonds to cocoa mixture until all the almonds are coated with cocoa mixture. (If corn-syrup mixture hardens on almonds, and cocoa will not adhere, cook almonds on Medium 30 to 60 seconds until mixture is sticky; stir almonds before adding to cocoa mixture.) Cool almonds in jelly-roll pan on wire rack.

MELTAWAY MOCHA TRUFFLES

1	*12-ounce package semisweet-chocolate or milk-chocolate pieces*
¾	*cup sweetened condensed milk*
1	*tablespoon instant espresso coffee powder*
2	*tablespoons coffee-flavor liqueur*
⅛	*teaspoon salt*
	cocoa

About 2 hours before serving or up to 2 weeks ahead:

1. In double boiler over hot, *not boiling*, water (or in heavy 2-quart saucepan over low heat), melt chocolate pieces, stirring occasionally. Stir in sweetened condensed milk, espresso coffee powder, coffee-flavor liqueur, and salt until well mixed. Refrigerate mixture about 30 minutes or until easy to shape.

2. With hands dusted with cocoa, shape a rounded teaspoon chocolate mixture into a ball. Roll ball immediately in more cocoa. Repeat with remaining mixture. Store in covered container to use up within 2 weeks. Makes about 50 candies.

About 2½ hours before serving or up to 1 week ahead:

1. Preheat oven to 350°F. Place almonds in 13″ by 9″ baking pan; bake 15 minutes or until almonds are lightly toasted, stirring occasionally.

2. In 2-quart saucepan over medium heat, heat corn syrup, butter or margarine, and ⅓ cup sugar to boiling, stirring frequently; boil 5 minutes without stirring. Remove saucepan from heat; stir in vanilla extract. Pour hot corn-syrup mixture over almonds in pan, stirring almonds to coat completely.

3. Turn oven control to 250°F. Bake almonds 45 minutes longer, stirring occasionally.

4. Meanwhile, in small bowl, stir cocoa, salt, and ¼ cup sugar. Spread cocoa mixture in 15½″ by 10½″ jelly-roll pan. When almonds are done, with spoon, remove some almonds to cocoa mixture in jelly-roll pan; return remaining almonds in pan to oven to keep warm. With fork, toss almonds in cocoa mixture to coat evenly.

5. Push coated almonds to one end of pan.

Repeat, adding more almonds to cocoa mixture until all the almonds are coated with cocoa mixture. Cool almonds in jelly-roll pan on wire rack. Store cocoa-covered almonds in tightly covered container to use up within 1 week. Makes about 2½ cups.

To Cook Cocoa Nuts In Microwave Oven

1. In 1½ quart bowl, place almonds. Cook, uncovered, on High 5 minutes or just until almonds are very lightly toasted, stirring every 2 minutes. Pour almonds into 13″ by 9″ baking dish; set aside.

2. In 4-cup glass measuring cup, combine corn syrup, butter or margarine, and ⅓ cup sugar. Cook, uncovered, on High 5 minutes, stirring after 2 minutes; stir in vanilla extract. Pour hot syrup over almonds, stirring to coat completely. Cook syrup-coated almonds, uncovered, on Medium 15 minutes, stirring almonds every 5 minutes.

3. Meanwhile, in small bowl, stir cocoa, salt, and ¼ cup sugar. Spread cocoa mixture in 15½″ by 10½″ jelly-roll pan. When almonds are done, with spoon, remove some almonds to cocoa mixture in jelly-roll

Here, tips for handling dough.

Bar cookies: Spread dough evenly in pan so cookies will have uniform texture.

Drop cookies: Scoop up uniform amounts of dough and drop about 2 inches apart on cookie sheet. Use a small spatula to shape and round them.

Refrigerator cookies: Slice roll thinly and evenly so cookies will be uniform and crisp.

Molded cookies: Chill dough so it will be firm enough to shape. Work with a small amount at a time and keep the rest refrigerated.

Pressed cookies: Follow manufacturer's directions for using cookie press. Chill dough only if recipe directs.

Rolled cookies: If dough seems too soft, don't add flour—refrigerate it until cold and firm. Roll a small amount of dough at a time (keep rest refrigerated) on floured pastry cloth so too much flour isn't worked into dough. Cut with floured cookie cutter or knife. Press trimmings together, reroll, and cut.

When baking cookies, have oven preheated to correct temperature before putting cookies in. Cookies bake quickly, so test doneness at end of minimum baking time. If cookies feel set and dry, they are done.

The best ways to cool cookies: Remove from oven; if cookies are small, with pancake turner, remove them at once from cookie sheet to wire racks to cool (they continue to bake on the hot cookie sheet); cool large cookies a few minutes before removing from cookie sheet unless recipe directs otherwise. Don't overlap or place cookies on top of each other—they will become soggy. Slightly cool bar cookies in pan before cutting into pieces; they'll be crumbly if cut while too warm.

Always make sure cookies are completely cooled before storing in containers.

Maple Meltaways, Braided Herb Breads, Cheddar Straws, Pickled Celery Stalks, and Sweet Christmas Wreath Bread. Recipes on pages 88-89.

MAPLE MELTAWAYS

2   cups all-purpose flour
1   cup butter or margarine, softened
3/4 cup sugar
1½ teaspoons maple-flavor extract
¼   teaspoon salt
    about ⅔ cup pecan halves

About 1¼ hours before serving or up to 2 weeks ahead:

1. Into large bowl, measure flour, softened butter or margarine, sugar, maple-flavor extract, and salt. With mixer at low speed, beat ingredients until blended, occasionally scraping bowl with rubber spatula. Increase speed to medium; beat until light and fluffy.

2. Preheat oven to 350°F. Drop dough by rounded teaspoonfuls, about 1 inch apart, onto ungreased cookie sheet. Gently press a pecan half into top of each cookie. Bake 12 minutes or until cookies are lightly browned. Cool cookies slightly on cookie sheet, then with pancake turner, carefully loosen cookies and remove to wire rack to cool completely. Repeat with remaining dough and pecans. Store cookies in tightly covered container to use up within 2 weeks. Makes about 4 dozen.

LITTLE BRAIDED HERB BREADS

½   cup sugar
2   teaspoons salt
3   packages active dry yeast
    about 6½ cups all-purpose flour
1   cup milk
½   cup water
6   tablespoons butter or margarine
3   eggs
¼   cup grated Parmesan cheese
1½ teaspoons thyme leaves

About 4½ hours before serving or day ahead:

1. In large bowl, combine sugar, salt, yeast, and 2 cups flour. In 2-quart saucepan over low heat, heat milk, water, and butter or margarine until very warm (120° to 130°F.). (Butter or margarine does not need to melt completely.)

2. With mixer at low speed, gradually beat liquid into dry ingredients until just blended. Increase speed to medium; beat 2 minutes, occasionally scraping bowl with rubber spatula. Beat in eggs, Parmesan cheese, thyme, and 1 cup flour to make a thick batter; continue beating 2 minutes, scraping bowl often. With wooden spoon, stir in 3 cups flour to make a soft dough.

3. Turn dough onto lightly floured surface and knead until smooth and elastic, about 10 minutes, working in more flour while kneading (about ½ cup). Shape dough into a ball and place in greased large bowl, turning dough over so that top is greased. Cover with towel and let rise in warm place (80° to 85°F.), away from draft, until doubled, about 1 hour. (Dough is doubled when two fingers pressed lightly into dough leave a dent.)

4. Grease six 5¾" by 3¼" loaf pans. When dough is ready, punch down dough; turn onto lightly floured surface; cover with bowl and let rest for 15 minutes for easier shaping.

5. Cut dough into nine equal pieces. With floured hands, roll one dough piece into an 18-inch-long rope. Repeat with two more dough pieces. Place three ropes side by side and loosely braid, beginning in the middle and working toward each end. (Braid should be about 12 inches long.) Cut braid crosswise in half. Pinch cut ends; tuck ends under to seal to make two small braided loaves. Place each loaf, seam-side down, in a prepared pan. Repeat with remaining dough. Cover with towel and let rise in warm place until doubled, about 30 minutes. (Dough is doubled when one finger very lightly pressed against dough leaves a dent.)

6. Preheat oven to 400°F. Bake loaves 15 minutes or until golden and loaves sound hollow when lightly tapped with fingers. Remove from pans immediately; cool on wire racks. Makes 6 loaves, each 4 servings.

CHEDDAR STRAWS

2   cups all-purpose flour
½   teaspoon salt
    ground red pepper
1   cup butter or margarine
8   ounces Cheddar cheese, shredded
½   cup iced water

Early in day or up to 1 week ahead:

1. In large bowl with fork, combine flour, salt, and ¼ teaspoon ground red pepper. With pastry blender or two knives used scissor-fashion, cut in butter or margarine until mixture resembles coarse crumbs.

2. With fork, stir in cheese and water just until mixture forms a soft dough and leaves side of bowl. On lightly floured surface with floured hands, pat dough into 6" by 6" square. Wrap dough with plastic wrap and chill in freezer for 30 minutes for easier handling.

3. On lightly floured surface, roll chilled dough into 18" by 8" rectangle. Starting from one 8-inch end, fold one-third of dough over middle one-third; fold opposite one-third over both to make 8" by 6" rectangle.

4. Repeat rolling and folding as in step 3. Wrap in plastic wrap; freeze 30 minutes again.

5. Remove dough from freezer; roll and fold as above in step 3 again. Then, roll dough into 18" by 12" rectangle. Sprinkle dough rectangle lightly with ground red pepper; cut lengthwise in half. Cut each half crosswise into thirty-six 6" by ½" strips.

6. Place strips, ½ inch apart, on ungreased large cookie sheets, twisting each strip twice and pressing ends to cookie sheet. (This prevents strips from uncurling during baking.)

7. Meanwhile, preheat oven to 375°F. Bake cheese straws 15 minutes or until golden. Remove cheese straws from cookie sheets; cool completely on wire racks. Store in tightly covered container to use up within 1 week. Makes 6 dozen.

PICKLED CELERY STALKS

2¼ cups white vinegar
2¼ cups sugar
1 teaspoon mustard seeds
1 teaspoon ground ginger
¼ teaspoon cracked black pepper
4 3-inch-long cinnamon sticks
3 medium bunches celery

Day ahead or up to 1 week ahead:

1. In 2-quart saucepan, combine vinegar, sugar, mustard seeds, ginger, pepper, and cinnamon; over high heat, heat to boiling. Reduce heat to low; cover and simmer 5 minutes to blend flavors. Refrigerate liquid until chilled.

2. Meanwhile, cut off root ends and leaves to separate celery stalks. With vegetable peeler, peel tough stringy fiber from celery stalks. Then cut each stalk crosswise in half; if any stalk is too large, you may also want to cut lengthwise in half.

3. Place celery in large bowl; pour vinegar mixture over celery; cover and refrigerate at least 24 hours. Drain celery before serving. Serve sliced as pickles with sandwiches or cold meats. Makes about 5 cups.

SWEET CHRISTMAS WREATH BREAD

1 cup sugar
1 teaspoon salt
2 packages active dry yeast
  about 9 cups all-purpose flour
2 cups milk
1 cup butter or margarine
3 eggs
1 tablespoon grated lemon peel
1 teaspoon almond extract
¼ cup slivered blanched almonds

About 4½ hours before serving or day ahead:

1. In large bowl, combine sugar, salt, yeast, and 2½ cups flour. In 1-quart saucepan over low heat, heat milk and butter or margarine until very warm (120° to 130°F.). (Butter or margarine does not need to melt completely.)

2. With mixer at low speed, gradually beat liquid into dry ingredients just until blended. Increase speed to medium; beat 2 minutes, occasionally scraping bowl with rubber spatula.

3. Reserve 1 egg white for brushing top of loaves. To mixture in large bowl, gradually beat in egg yolk, remaining 2 eggs, lemon peel, almond extract, and 2 cups flour to make a thick batter; continue beating 2 minutes, scraping bowl often. With wooden spoon, stir in 3¾ cups flour to make a soft dough.

4. Turn dough onto well-floured surface and knead until smooth and elastic, about 10 minutes, working in more flour while kneading (about ¾ cup). Shape dough into a ball and place in greased large bowl, turning dough over so that top is greased. Cover with towel and let rise in warm place (80° to 85°F.), away from draft, until doubled, about 1 hour. (Dough is doubled when two fingers pressed lightly into dough leave a dent.)

5. Punch down dough. Turn dough onto lightly floured surface; cut dough into six equal pieces; cover with towel and let rest for 15 minutes for easier shaping. Grease two large cookie sheets.

6. On floured surface with hands, roll one piece dough into a 24-inch-long rope. Repeat with two more pieces of dough. Place 3 ropes side by side and loosely braid, beginning in the middle and working toward each end. Place braid on a cookie sheet and shape into a ring; join ends and pinch to seal so ring holds together. Repeat with remaining dough pieces. Cover breads with towels and let dough rise in warm place until doubled, about 1 hour. (Dough is doubled when one finger very lightly pressed against dough leaves a dent.)

7. Preheat oven to 350°F. In cup with fork, beat reserved egg white. With pastry brush, brush loaves with egg white; top with almonds. Place cookie sheets with loaves on 2 oven racks; bake 15 minutes. Switch cookie sheets between upper and lower racks so both loaves brown evenly; bake about 20 to 25 minutes longer until golden and loaves sound hollow when lightly tapped with finger. (If loaves start to brown too quickly, cover loosely with foil.) Remove loaves from cookie sheets and cool on wire racks. Makes two loaves, each 16 servings.

To Freeze And Serve Up To 1 Month Later
When loaves are cool, wrap each loaf tightly with foil or freezer wrap; seal; label; and freeze. To thaw, remove wrap; let bread stand at room temperature 2 hours.

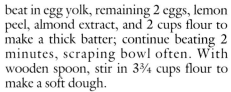

How To Mail Home-Baked Treats

A package of homemade goodies in the mail is sure to be a hit with friends and family during the holidays. To be sure cookies, candies, cakes, and other treats from your kitchen arrive on time and in best condition, follow these tips:

Choose foods that are "good travelers"—that can stand up to the holiday mailing rush.

Wrap, package, and mail your treats as soon as you can after they are made and cooled.

Use a container just slightly larger than the contents: a strong cardboard box, plastic or metal food container with tight-fitting lid.

Line the container with waxed paper or plastic wrap, and place a thick cushion of crumpled waxed paper on the bottom.

Pack cookies in pairs, back to back, with waxed paper in between; wrap in plastic wrap, foil, or waxed paper or wrap individually. Wrap pieces of candy individually. Wrap breads, fruitcakes, steamed puddings, with foil or plastic wrap.

Place heaviest items on bottom and arrange layers with waxed-paper cushions in between. Top with more waxed paper; seal securely with freezer, adhesive, or plastic tape. Place your address and the receiver's address on container.

Wrap container in sturdy brown paper and seal with package-sealing tape. Using waterproof ink, label package with mailing address and return address; cover addresses with clear tape.

Add correct postage. Check with your post office for the best and speediest way to mail your gifts.

SWEET-AND-SOUR RELISH

9   medium-sized onions (about 3
      pounds)
1   medium-sized green pepper
1   medium-sized red pepper
2   bay leaves
8   whole cloves
½   teaspoon whole peppercorns
½   teaspoon crushed red pepper
      cheesecloth
      string
¾   cup light corn syrup
½   cup sugar
½   cup white vinegar
1½ teaspoons salt
1½ teaspoons dry mustard
½   teaspoon celery seeds

Early in day or up to 2 weeks ahead:

1. Thinly slice onions. Cut green and red pepper into thin strips.

2. Break bay leaves into several pieces. Wrap bay leaves, cloves, peppercorns, and crushed red pepper in piece of double-thickness cheesecloth. Tie spice bag with string.

3. In 5-quart saucepot over medium heat, heat corn syrup, sugar, vinegar, salt, dry mustard, celery seeds, and spice bag to boiling, stirring occasionally. Reduce heat to low; simmer, uncovered, 5 minutes, stirring occasionally.

4. Stir in onions and peppers; over high heat, heat to boiling. Reduce heat to low; cover and simmer 15 minutes or until onions and peppers are tender. Discard spice bag. Store relish in tightly covered jars in the refrigerator to use up within 2 weeks. Serve relish with roast pork, fried fish, hamburgers, frankfurters, baked ham. Makes about 5½ cups.

CARAWAY HORSERADISH MUSTARD

½   cup Dijon mustard
2   teaspoons caraway seeds, crushed
1½ teaspoons prepared white horseradish

About 10 minutes before serving or up to 2 weeks ahead:

1. In small bowl with spoon, mix all ingredients until well blended. Cover and refrigerate mustard to use up within 2 weeks. Makes about ¾ cup.

ZUCCHINI PICKLES

6   8-ounce freezer-safe, dishwasher-safe
      containers with tight-fitting lids
      boiling water
7   small zucchini (about 4 ounces each)
4   small onions
1   large red pepper
1   medium-sized green pepper
      salt
2   teapoons dill weed
¼   teaspoon pepper
1¾ cups white vinegar
1   cup light corn syrup
½   cup sugar

1. Prepare containers and lids: Use only containers 1 pint or less in size. Check containers to be sure there are no nicks, cracks, or sharp edges. Wash containers and lids in hot soapy water; rinse well. Carefully and slowly pour boiling water inside and out of containers and lids; invert on dish rack or clean cloth towel, away from draft, to drain dry. Or, wash containers and lids in dishwasher with very hot rinse cycle (150°F. or higher) and leave in dishwasher until ready to fill.

2. Thinly slice zucchini and onions. Cut red and green pepper into matchstick-thin strips.

3. In large bowl, stir zucchini, onions, and 4½ teaspoons salt; toss to mix well. Cover and let stand at room temperature 2 hours. In medium bowl, stir red pepper, green pepper, and 1½ teaspoons salt. Cover and let stand at room temperature 2 hours. Tipping container over sink, press zucchini mixture with hand to drain liquid. (Do not rinse.) Repeat with pepper mixture.

4. In same large bowl, combine drained vegetables with dill weed and pepper. In 4-quart saucepan over medium heat, heat vinegar, corn syrup, and sugar to boiling, stirring constantly, until sugar is dissolved. Add vegetable mixture to vinegar mixture in saucepan; over high heat, heat to boiling. Reduce heat to medium; cook vegetables mixture 2 minutes, stirring constantly. Remove saucepan from heat.

5. With slotted spoon, spoon vegetables into containers to within ½ inch from top. Then ladle vinegar mixture to just cover vegetables. Cover containers with lids. Let stand at room temperature until cool. Store in freezer to use up within 6 months. Thaw pickles in refrigerator. Store pickles in refrigerator to use up within 2 weeks after thawing. Makes about six 8-ounce containers.

GINGERED ORANGE MUSTARD

½   cup Dijon mustard
⅓   cup orange marmalade
½   teaspoon ground ginger
1½ teaspoons Worcestershire

About 10 minutes before serving or up to 2 weeks ahead:

1. In small bowl with spoon, mix all ingredients until well blended. Cover and refrigerate mustard to use up within 2 weeks. Makes about ¾ cup.

For Gift Giving
If you like, give mustard in pretty ceramic or glass mustard jar.

CHOCOLATE-DIPPED ORANGES

(35 calories per piece)

Arrange orange sections on a colorful enamel tray and wrap tightly in plastic wrap.

About 1½ hours before serving or early in day:

1. In double boiler over hot, *not boiling,* water, heat *¾ cup semisweet-chocolate pieces* and *1 tablespoon shortening* until chocolate is melted and mixture is smooth, stirring frequently.

2. Meanwhile, peel *3 medium oranges;* separate oranges into sections. Place *1 cup sugar-frosted cornflakes cereal* on one-half 12-inch-long piece of waxed paper; fold waxed paper over to cover cereal. With palm of hand, crush cereal.

3. When chocolate is melted, hold 1 piece of orange at a time and dip into chocolate, leaving about two-thirds of orange uncovered. Shake off excess chocolate or gently scrape one side of orange across rim of double boiler, being careful not to scrape too much chocolate from orange; dip chocolate-covered end into crushed cereal, then place on another piece of waxed paper. Cover with plastic wrap. Serve the same day for freshest texture. About 30 pieces.

ZUCCHINI-CARROT LOAVES

(100 calories per slice)

This recipe makes two gift loaves. Wrap them individually in foil or plastic wrap; then place each on a cutting board with a serrated knife.

3	cups all-purpose flour
¾	cup sugar
½	cup California walnuts, chopped
4½	teaspoons baking powder
1	teaspoon salt
4	eggs
½	cup salad oil
2	cups shredded zucchini
2	cups shredded carrots
¾	teaspoon grated lemon peel

About 2 hours before serving or up to 3 days ahead:

1. Preheat oven to 350°F. Grease two 8½" by 4½" loaf pans. In large bowl with fork, mix flour, sugar, walnuts, baking powder, and salt. In medium bowl with fork, beat eggs slightly; stir in oil, zucchini, carrots, and lemon peel; stir vegetable mixture into flour mixture just until flour is moistened; spread batter evenly in pans.

2. Bake breads 55 minutes or until toothpick inserted in center comes out clean. Cool in pans on wire racks 10 minutes; remove from pans. Serve bread warm or cool completely to serve cold. Makes two loaves or 16 slices per loaf.

BRAN-OATMEAL COOKIES

(35 calories per cookie)

Place these chewy tidbits in a pretty apothecary jar or decorative cookie canister.

1	cup shreds of wheat bran cereal
½	cup all-purpose flour
½	cup quick-cooking oats, uncooked
½	cup packed light brown sugar
⅓	cup shortening
½	teaspoon salt
½	teaspoon baking soda
½	teaspoon ground ginger
½	teaspoon ground cinnamon
½	teaspoon ground cloves
½	teaspoon grated lemon peel
½	teaspoon vanilla extract
1	egg

About 3 hours before serving or up to 2 weeks ahead:

1. Into large bowl, measure all ingredients. With mixer at low speed, beat ingredients until well blended, scraping bowl with rubber spatula. Preheat oven to 375°F. Drop dough by level ½ tablespoons, about 2 inches apart, onto ungreased cookie sheets. Bake 12 minutes or until golden. With metal spatula, remove cookies to wire racks to cool. Store in tightly covered container to use up within 2 weeks. Makes about 4 dozen cookies.

SPICED FRUIT

(75 calories per serving)

A glass compote is the perfect way to present this flavorful fruit mixture. Wrap it in clear plastic, tucking a small cinnamon stick into a bow around the stem.

1	11-ounce can mandarin-orange sections
2	medium cooking apples
2	ripe medium pears
½	cup water
1	teaspoon grated lemon peel
½	teaspoon whole cloves
3	3-inch-long cinnamon sticks
2	tablespoons shredded coconut

About 1 hours before serving or up to 5 days ahead:

1. Drain mandarin-orange sections, reserving syrup. Core and peel apples; cut apples crosswise into ½-inch rings. Core and peel pears; cut pears crosswise into ½-inch rings.

2. In 12-inch skillet over high heat, heat apples, pears, water, lemon peel, cloves, cinnamon sticks, and reserved syrup to boiling. Reduce heat to low; cover and simmer until tender but firm, 3 to 6 minutes, removing slices as they are done to medium bowl. Discard cloves and cinnamon sticks; pour liquid over slices in bowl. Add coconut and mandarin-orange sections; gently toss. Serve warm or cover and refrigerate to serve chilled. Makes about 4 cups or 8 servings.

❧ GIFTS FROM THE HAND AND HEART ❧

LITTLE GIRL'S PINAFORE

Materials

Three 20″ by 30″ red-and-white windowpane-check linen dish towels; ⅛ yd. lightweight white cotton for lining; Simplicity Pattern #7197; six-strand embroidery floss (8.7-yd. skein): 1 skein each Shaded Blue, Dark Blue, Medium Blue, Leaf Green, Apple Green, Dark Green, Yellow and Red; dressmaker's tracing paper.

To Make

Enlarge embroidery diagrams. Bodice front and back, waistband and ruffle are cut from one towel. Be very careful! to place pieces as close together as possible. Centering pattern piece and placing straight edge of ruffle ⅜″ from one long edge of towel, cut first ruffle. Turn pattern over and cut second ruffle from other long edge. Using pattern piece as a guide to length, cut waistband 2″ wide (slightly narrower than pattern piece). From remainder of towel, cut bodice front and back, matching checks. For skirt front, cut off border on one long edge of one towel, 2½″ from edge; cut off short borders. For skirt backs, cut off borders as for front, cut towel in half crosswise. With dressmaker's tracing paper, trace designs to center of bodice front and to skirt front just above bottom border. Following diagrams and photograph for colors and stitches and using 3 strands of floss throughout, embroider designs. Stitch back seam of skirt to within 3″ of cut edge; do not press seam open. Stitch side seams; press open. Stitch under ¼″ on back opening edges. Turn right back opening to inside on seamline; baste. Gather top edge of skirt. Right sides together, pin waistband to skirt, matching center fronts and placing open edge of skirt ⅝″ in from ends of waistband. Pull up gathers to fit; stitch. Trim seam and press toward band. From lining fabric, cut bodice front and backs and waistband facing. Complete pinafore following pattern guide sheet. Hem skirt to desired length.

DAINTY DOLLY

Materials

One 20″ by 30″ red-and-white windowpane-check dish towel; ½ yd. 45″-wide unbleached muslin; ¼ yd. each red and white cotton fabric; scrap of black fabric; 1 yd. each ¾″-wide and ⅜″-wide red grosgrain ribbon; 1 lb. polyester-fiber-fill; six-strand embroidery floss: small amounts each Red, Brown and Blue; 4-oz. skein Yellow knitting-worsted-weight yarn; white and red sewing thread; 8″ white bias tape; 12″ red bias tape; 1½ yds. ¼″-wide white elastic; 2½ yds. ½″-wide preruffled lace; dressmaker's tracing paper; 2 small snap fasteners.

To Make

Use ¼″ seams. Enlarge patterns. Trace 2 bodies onto unbleached muslin; do not cut out. Trace face to one body. Using 3 strands of floss throughout, outline eyes with Brown outline stitch; fill in irises with Blue outline stitch. Outline, then fill in mouth with Red outline stitch. Work 2 Brown French knots for nose. Cut out muslin bodies; cut 4 black shoes. Turning under ¼″ at tops of shoes, baste to right side of feet. Right sides in, stitch bodies together, leaving 3″ opening at one side for turning. Clip curves, turn and stuff head, arms and legs first, then stuff body. Slipstitch opening. **Hair:** Cut approximately ninety 16″-long strands of yarn. Place white bias tape at midpoint of yarn, spreading yarn across tape evenly; stitch yarn to tape. Stitch tape across top of head along seam. Pull yarn back over tape leaving a few strands for bangs. Trim bangs and turn them under to form loops; stitch. Spread yarn to cover head; at center back, turn section of yarn under at base of head; stitch in place. Braid remaining yarn at sides; tie with 12″ lengths of narrow ribbon. Tack braids in place. **Dress:** Placing center line on fold, cut skirt and bodice front from red fabric. Cut 2 sleeves and 2 bodice backs from red. Right sides in, stitch front to back at shoulders. Turn under ¼″ at sleeve edges; sew lace to edge of sleeves on right side. Cut 2 pieces of elastic

the length of the wrist measurement. Stretching elastic to fit, stitch to wrong side of sleeves, ½″ from edge. Right sides together, baste sleeves to bodice, easing in fullness. Stitch; press seam toward sleeves. Cut a length of red bias tape to fit around neckline of dress. Open out tape; right sides together, pin to neckline. Stitch; turn tape to inside and top-stitch in place. Sew lace to neck edge. Stitch side seams of bodice. Gather top edge of skirt. Right sides together, pin skirt to bodice, drawing up gathers to fit; stitch. Right sides together, baste center back seam; stitch to within 5″ below neck. Press seam open; remove basting. Turn under raw edges and stitch. Sew on snap. Turn up and sew hem. **Pants:** Cut 2 pants sections from white cotton. Turn under ¼″ at bottom edge; stitch lace to edge on right side. Cut 2 lengths of elastic the length of ankle measurement. Stretching elastic to fit, stitch to wrong side of pants legs. Right sides in, stitch front seam and back seam. Press seams open, then stitch crotch seam. Turn under ¼″ at waist; then turn under ½″ to form casing. Stitch close to lower fold, leaving an opening for elastic. Cut elastic to fit waist; insert into casing. Stitch ends of elastic together and close opening. **Pinafore:** Cut skirt with bottom edge on one long edge of towel. Cut bodice front and back and 9″ circle for bonnet from center of towel. From remaining long border, cut two 2″ by 10″ strips for ruffles. Piecing fabric as needed, cut a 1¼″ by 13″ strip of bias binding. Right sides in, stitch front to back at shoulders and sides. Gather one long edge of each ruffle. Turn under ⅛″, then ⅛″ again on all remaining edges of ruffle; stitch. Right sides together, pin ruffles to armholes, adjusting gathers to fit; stitch. Gather top edge of skirt. Right sides in, pin skirt to bodice, adjusting gathers to fit. Stitch. Turn under ⅛″, then ⅛″ again on back edge; stitch. Bind neck edge with bias strip. Sew on snap. For bonnet, turn under ¼″ on raw edge of circle; stitch lace over edge. Cut a 14″ length of elastic. Stretching to fit, stitch ½″ from edge on wrong side. Place bonnet on head; tack in place.

ENLARGING DESIGNS: Use a piece of tracing paper or wrapping paper large enough to accommodate design. Starting with a perfect right angle at one corner, mark paper in same number of 1″ squares as indicated on pattern, or use large sheets of Light Blue graph paper with 1″ markings; or special paper with grid for enlarging patterns. Copy design square by square.

OR, have design photostated to full size according to scale under chart (check your Classified Directory for photostat service). This process, however, may be expensive.

OR, use a pantograph (available through art supply stores)—a mechanical device that will reduce or enlarge pictures and drawings.

TRANSFERRING THE DESIGN: Either method can be used. Trace enlarged design to fabric using dressmaker's tracing paper and a pencil.

OR, make a punched pattern by tracing design on heavy paper, then punching holes along the lines using a pin or unthreaded sewing machine. Sand back of paper to remove rough edges of holes. Place cornstarch or powdered chalk in center of a piece of cotton fabric; tie corners together to make a little sack. Pat and rub sack over the holes so that the powder goes through to the fabric. Remove pattern and connect dots using a pencil.

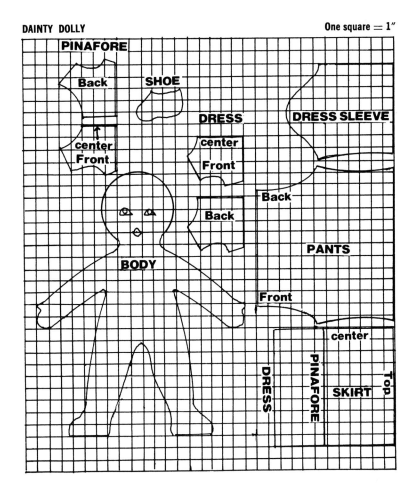

DAINTY DOLLY — One square = 1″

LITTLE GIRL'S PINAFORE

Skirt — One square = 1″

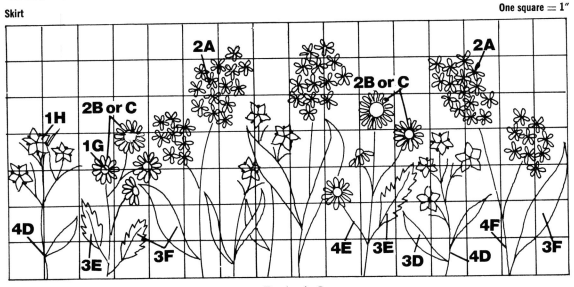

Bodice — One square = 1″

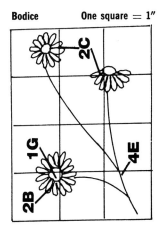

1—Satin Stitch	A—Shaded Blues	E—Apple Green
2—Lazy-Daisy Stitch	B—Dark Blue	F—Dark Green
3—Long-&-Short Stitch	C—Medium Blue	G—Yellow
4—Split Stitch	D—Leaf Green	H—Red

DUMP TRUCK

Materials
Cotton or cotton-blend fabrics: 1 yd. Blue denim, ⅔ yd. Yellow; felt: two 9″ by 12″ pieces White, scrap Black; matching threads; two 7″ Yellow zippers; polyester stuffing; Black Velcro: ⅔ yd. 1″-wide and a 2″ by 3″ piece; 2 coat-size snap fasteners; two 1″ buttons.

To Cut Pieces
From Red cut two cab sides and one plow bracket following diagram; cut two 5″ by 13″ truck bodies, two 2½″ by 13″ truck body sides, two 2½″ by 5″ truck ends, two 3″ by 5″ cab fronts, one 3″ by 5″ cab top, one 4″ by 5″ cab bottom, and one 5″ by 5″ cab back. From Blue denim cut twelve 4″ diameter tires and six 2½″ by 15½″ tire treads. From Yellow cut dumper side, bottom, and plow following diagram. From White felt cut two side windows following diagram; cut 1″ by 3″ front window, two 1″ diameter headlights, and six 2″ diameter hubcaps. Cut one 1″ by 3″ Black felt radiator grill.

To Assemble
Use ⅝″ seams and sew pieces together right side in unless otherwise indicated.

Dumper and Body
Right sides together, fold dumper side piece in half lengthwise. Stitch shorter ends; turn right side out and press. Topstitch 8″ from each short end through all thicknesses to form 3 pockets. Stuff each pocket firmly; wrong sides together, sew raw edges together. Pin one edge of each open zipper face down on dumper side piece at raw edge, with bottom of one zipper at A and other at D (zippers will close towards center). Using a zipper foot, stitch zipper edges in place. Right sides together, pin dumper side piece between dumper bottom pieces matching A to A, B to B, etc., and keeping loose zipper edges free. Using zipper foot, stitch through all thicknesses pivoting at B and C. Clip corners; turn right side out. Turn raw ends of dumper bottoms to inside along seamline and slip-stitch opening, keeping loose zipper edges free. Stitch 2″ by 3″ Velcro piece on right side at one short end of truck body

close to seamline. Pin one free zipper length, right side up, to either long side of truck body with bottom ends of zippers at opposite end from Velcro. Using zipper foot, stitch in place. Close zippers. Dumper assembly should open away from Velcro. Stitch 11″ length of Velcro to each right side of truck body side. Cut matching strip into six 1″ by 3″ lengths. Matching shorter edges, stitch truck body sides to truck ends forming a continuous circle. Press seams open. Using zipper foot, stitch truck side and end piece to truck body matching corners of body to side and end seamlines and keeping dumper free of stitching. Open zippers; stitch remaining truck body piece to body sides and end piece leaving an opening in rear for turning. Trim corners, turn, stuff and slip-stitch opening.

Cab
Stitch cab windows to cab sides, front window to one cab front and grill to other cab front. Sew headlights to cab front above grill, overlapping grill but not touching seamline. Stitch cab fronts together along one long edge with window above grill. Stitch remaining half of 2″ by 3″ Velcro to center of right side cab bottom. Stitch cab top to upper edge of cab front; cab bottom to lower edge of front. Stitch cab back to remaining edge of cab top. Press seams open. Matching seamlines to corners, stitch cab sides in place; turn right side out through opening at back bottom. Stuff and slipstitch opening. Attach cab to Velcro on truck body.

Tires
Center and stitch hub cups to right side of 6 tires for fronts. Center and stitch one 1″ by 3″ Velcro strip to right side of 6 remaining tires for backs. Right sides in, baste short ends of each tire tread together to form a circle. Stitch a tread around each front, then around each back. Remove basting. Turn right side out through opening in tread. Stuff and slip-stitch opening.

Plow and Plow Bracket
Stitch plow pieces together leaving one short edge open for turning. Trim corners, turn right side out. Press under seam allowance on open edge. Topstitch two diagonal lines opposite the open end, see diagram. Stuff corners firmly; topstitch across end joining the diagonal lines. topstitch two long lines on top and bottom of

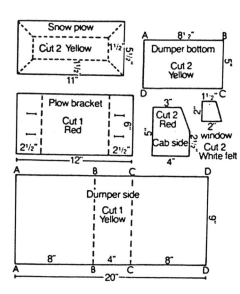

plow. Stuff sides and center using a pencil to insert stuffing. Topstitch remaining diagonal lines and line joining them. Stuff end; slip-stitch opening. Right sides together, fold plow bracket in half lengthwise, stitch edges leaving one short end open for turning. Clip corners, turn right side out. Make buttonhole at closed end of bracket; using pencil, stuff around buttonhole to stitching line. Topstitch along nearest stitching line. Stuff between stitching lines; topstitch remaining stitching line. Make remaining buttonhole, stuff around it and slip-stitch opening. Sew a button to front of each side of truck. Sew snaps evenly in center of bracket and at corresponding spot on plow. Snap plow to bracket; button bracket to truck; attach tires to truck sides along Velcro.

WOOLLY LITTLE LAMB

Materials

3/8 yd. 60″-wide synthetic sherpa fabric; 3/8 yd. 60″-wide Light Brown wool tweed; scraps Red, Brown, Beige, and White felt; 9″ by 12″ piece Green felt; 1 yd. each Brown and Red crewel yarn; 1 yd. Black carpet thread; 1¼ yds. 1″-wide Red satin ribbon; polyester stuffing; 6″ by 12″ piece quilt batting; Red, Green, and Off-White thread; white glue.

To Make

Use ½″ seams. Enlarge pattern. Reversing pattern for second body side, cut 2 body sides and 1 underbody from sherpa. From wool tweed, cut 1 face top, 2 face sides, 8 legs, and 4 ears. Transfer facial features to right side of fabric, remaining marks to wrong side. Cut 2 ears from quilt batting. Cut 6 Green felt holly leaves. From felt scraps, cut 2 White eyes, 2 Brown pupils, 2 Beige eyelids, and five 1″-diameter Red felt berries. Right sides in, stitch face sides together along curved edge marked with large ○'s. Stay-stitch double-curved top edge of face top; clip to inner point between curves. Right sides together, matching ○'s, stitch face top to straight edge of face sides. Baste quilt batting to wrong side of two ears. Right sides in, stitch backed ears to plain ears along curved edges, leaving remaining edge open. Clip curves and corners; trim seam allowance; turn right-side out. Fold ear along broken lines; baste along raw edges. Matching raw edges, with folded edges toward face, baste ears to face just below side seams. Right sides in, stitch body sides together along back and front, leaving straight edge and edge between large ○'s open. Clip to inner point below tail. Right sides together, matching ○'s, stitch face to curved opening of body. Right sides together, matching ●'s, stitch underbody to body sides, leaving a 5″ opening along one side. Turn right-side out; stuff face and body firmly; slip-stitch opening. Stitch darts in legs. Right sides in, stitch legs together in pairs leaving straight edge open. Trim seam allowance; clip curves. Turn right-side out. Press under seam allowance on top edge. Stuff legs firmly; slip-stitch securely to body as in-

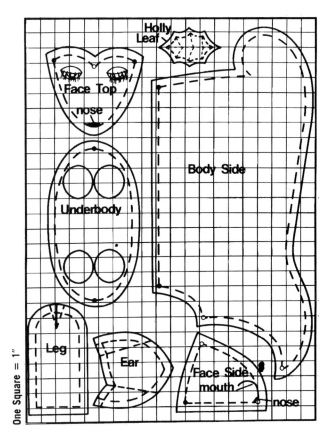

dicated on pattern. Tack legs together between each pair ½″ below body. Fold a 3″ length of carpet thread in half; insert fold in large needle. Gently pull needle and loop through eyelid at first point indicated along straight edge. Remove needle; pull ends of thread through loops to form knot; trim ends to about 5/8″. Repeat for each lash. Glue pupil and eyelids to eyes; glue eyes to face. Embroider Brown satin-stitch nose, Red stem-stitch mouth. Right sides in, using ¼″ seams, stitch holly leaves together in pairs leaving a small opening on one edge. Clip curves and corners; turn right-side out. Stuff each leaf lightly; slip-stitch opening. Hand-quilt along broken lines on leaves. By hand, make a row of small gathering stitches around edge of each Red berry. Gather edge and knot thread securely. Tack 1 or 2 berries to each holly leaf. Tie Red ribbon bow around sheep's neck; tack leaves around bow.

SANTA FAMILY PORTRAITS

Materials For Salt Dough

¼ cup salt; ⅜ cup hot water; 1 cup all-purpose flour; evaporated milk.

Materials For Decoration

Acrylic paints; small paintbrush; white glue; quick-setting epoxy glue; clear acrylic spray; light brown broad-tip felt marker; black fine-tip felt marker; pen with black India ink; 1" by 2" piece clear acetate; 3" length ½"-wide White preruffled lace edging; floral appliqué.

Materials For Assembly

⅛ yd. 72"-wide green felt; 1 yd. ¼"-wide gold braid; ¾ yd. 2"-wide red velvet ribbon; 3 yds. narrow yellow piping; 3 yds. gold jumbo rickrack; 3 yds. gold baby rickrack; 2½"-diameter wooden curtain ring; 9" by 12" stiff cardboard; sewing thread.

Cutting And Baking—General Directions

Mix salt, hot water, and flour in a large bowl. On a floured breadboard, knead dough for 7 to 10 minutes until it is smooth and the consistency of biscuit dough. If dough is too dry, add a few drops of water; if too sticky, add more flour. If dough is not used immediately, store in a plastic bag and refrigerate. Roll out dough to desired thickness on a well-floured cookie sheet. Place patterns on dough, allowing at least 1½" between them; cut around them with a sharp paring knife. Lift away excess dough; smooth edges with moist knife. Prick piece all over with a fine needle. Cover each piece with plastic wrap immediately after cutting to prevent its drying out. To make three-dimensional figures, moisten underneath piece, then lightly press top piece in place. Preheat oven to 300°F. Uncover pieces and bake until they are hard—about 1½ to 2 hours. Pieces will warp and distort as they bake, but this merely adds to their primitive look. Cool pieces on a wire rack.

Frames

Roll dough to ¼" thickness; cut out frames. With finger, smooth top edges of frames to round them as in the photograph. Bake frames, basting with evaporated milk 20 minutes before they are done.

Figures

Roll dough to ⅛" thickness. Cut and assemble pieces; bake, basting Rudolph's antlers and ears with evaporated milk.

Santa

With the flat side of knife, slightly flatten face and top of hat, leaving hatband raised. Slightly flatten two ⅛"-diameter balls; attach for cheeks. Attach beard; draw lines with toothpick. Attach moustache and eyebrows; attach balls of dough for nose, eyes, hat pompon, and buttons. Flatten arm and hand, leaving sleeve cuff raised. Depress bowl of pipe with end of ⅛" dowel; flatten hand around pipe. Do not attach arm—it will be baked separately.

Rudolf

Attach head to neck. Smooth edges of head to round jaw. Attach small balls of dough for nose and necklace.

Mrs. Santa

Flatten face and top of hat, leaving hatband raised. Attach lower part of face; smooth edges to round the face. Attach balls of dough for hair, eyes, nose, and hat pompon. Attach sleeves; score at shoulders for "gathers." Make small depression in mouth area; sharpen corners of mouth with sharp stick.

Decorating And Assembling

When pieces are done check to see if figures fit into frame. Sand or file sides and bottom of figures if necessary. Paint Santa and Mrs. Claus white, Rudolph's body brown. Do not paint Rudolph's antlers and ears. Let dry. Paint details as in photograph, giving white sections a second coat. Glue on Santa's hand. Glue lace edging at Mrs. Claus's neck; glue on floral appliqué brooch. With India ink, draw eyeglasses on acetate; cut out and glue to Mrs. Claus's face. When pieces are dry, spray front and back of frames and figures with acrylic spray to prevent molding. Stain curtain ring with brown marker; spray with acrylic spray. Let dry. Glue gold braid around inside of frames and outside of curtain ring. For each frame, cut cardboard backing ⅛"

smaller all around than frame. Glue felt to one side of backing; glue backing to frame. To make frames stronger, mix a small amount of epoxy; place a dab at 4 points on back of each frame over backing and edge of frame. Let dry. With white glue, glue figures into frames. Cut a 1½-yd. strip of felt. Glue yellow piping along each long edge on wrong side so that piping extends beyond edge; glue baby rickrack to back of piping so that points extend beyond edge. Glue felt strip to center of red ribbon. Glue jumbo rickrack along each side of ribbon on back so that points extend beyond edge. Insert one end of ribbon through curtain ring; turn under ends and sew to back of ribbon. Cut off ribbon 23" below ring; cut end into a point. Glue frames to ribbon.

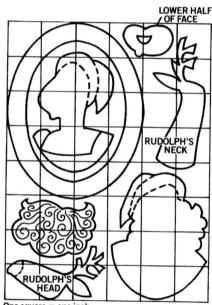

LOWER HALF OF FACE

RUDOLPH'S NECK

RUDOLPH'S HEAD

One square = one inch

Full size

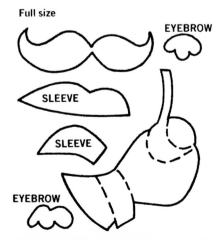

EYEBROW

SLEEVE

SLEEVE

EYEBROW

General Instructions For Rugs

For the foundation, use a piece of heavy, not-too-closely-woven burlap or monk's cloth, 3" bigger on each edge than the finished rug.

Transferring Design

Enlarge the design and transfer it to the foundation in either of the following ways: With a hot-iron transfer pencil, go over the design lines on the back of the pattern. Place the pattern, right-side up, on the fabric; press it with a hot iron. **OR,** place a piece of net over the design and go over the lines with an indelible felt-tip marker. Pin net to fabric and go over lines again.

Binding Fabric

By machine, stitch 2 rows of straight stitching or 1 row of zigzag stitching around, about ½" from the outer edge of the design. Holding the foundation fabric right-side up over your knee, lay 1½"- to 2"-wide cotton twill tape just inside the edge of the design; turn back about ¾" at the end. Sew the tape in place by hand, sewing about ⅛" from outer edge of tape with ⅛"-long running stitches; take a backstitch every few stitches to secure. Ease tape around corners, making a backstitch at the corner. Lap the end 1½" over the beginning and cut off the excess tape.

Placing Fabric In Frame

There are many elaborate frames available for hooking, but a simple rectangular frame made from artist's stretcher strips can be used to hold the fabric taut. Attach the fabric to the frame with thumbtacks, making a pleat in the fabric so that the tack goes through 3 layers. The frame does not have to be as large as the design—the fabric can be moved as you work.

Choosing Fabrics

Wool is the most commonly used fabric for rug hooking. Wool and synthetic blends can be used if the percentage of synthetic fiber is low. Tweeds, checks, paisleys, and prints are all suitable for primitive hooking. Instead of the fine shading seen in some types of hooked rugs, primitive rugs often mix different textured and patterned fabrics of the same color at random in a motif. Because of the wide variety of fabrics used

in a rug, hooking is a wonderful way to use scraps left over from sewing projects and old clothes. It will take approximately 1 pound of fabric to hook a square foot.

Preparing Fabrics

Make sure all fabrics are clean. The strips should be cut on the lengthwise grain, although they may be cut on the crosswise grain if necessary. First, cut or tear the fabrics into 3" by 12" strips, then cut the strips the width desired—for primitive rugs, this will usually be ¼" to ½" wide.

Hooking the Rug

Use a 5"-long straight rug hook. Hold the fabric strip in your left hand under the foundation fabric; hold the hook in your right hand with the forefinger extended along the shaft. Holding the hook at a 45° angle with the hook up, insert the hook into the fabric, going between the threads. Catch the end of the strip and pull it through. Insert the hook 2 or 3 threads away, catch the strip and pull through a loop, rolling the hook away from you to release the fabric (Fig. 1). Continue pulling up loops until the strip is complete; pull the end to the right side. Start the next strip in the same hole. Be careful not to have your loops too close together or the rug will buckle. Begin hooking in the center of the rug. First, outline the center motif, working just inside the design line. Hook any details, then fill in the motif. Repeat for each motif. Hook a row of the background color around each motif following its contours. The background can be filled in one of several ways. It can be hooked in straight lines across the rug; you can continue following the contours of the motifs; or you can hook wavy lines, circles, or "S" shapes across the background. Work the background all the way to the binding, working one row parallel to the binding around the rug.

Finishing The Rug

Trim strip ends to height of loops. Cut excess fabric at the machine stitching. Fold the binding to the back and blind stitch in place. Place the rug upside down on the floor; place a wet towel over it and steam press. Turn the rug right-side up and steam it again, stretching it into shape. Allow the rug to dry overnight.

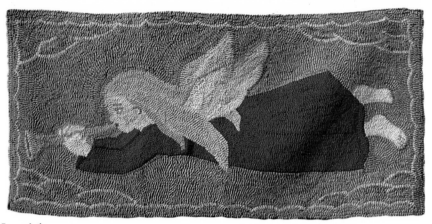

Materials

43″ by 24″ piece of foundation fabric; fabrics for hooking: Cranberry, Dark Cranberry, and Dark Rust for dress, Light Gold and Medium Gold for hair, Brassy Gold and Rust for trumpet, Peach, Cream, Light Rose Beige, and Rose Beige for face, hands, and feet, Blue, White, Rose, and Camel for features, Light Celery, Medium Light Celery, Medium Celery, and Dark Celery for wings, Tan for background, Light and Dark Celery for Border; 5″ straight rug hook.

To Make

Following General Instructions, enlarge design and transfer it to the foundation fabric. Mount the foundation in a frame. Cut the strips for the angel ⅛″ wide; cut the strips for the background, clouds, and border ¼″ wide. Outline dress in Dark Rust; work details in Dark Rust and Dark Cranberry; fill in with Cranberry. Outline top of lower wing with Dark Celery; work details in Medium Light Celery; and fill in

with Light Celery. Outline and work details of upper wing with Medium Celery; fill in with Medium Light Celery. Outline upper hand with Rose Beige; fill in with Light Rose Beige. Work remainder of angel as specified. Outline clouds and border with Light Celery. Following contour of angel, fill in background with Tan. Fill in clouds and border with Dark Celery.

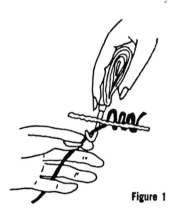

Figure 1

1 square = 2 inches

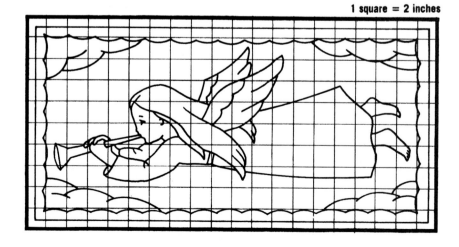

CROCHETED MOCCASINS

Instructions are for Small (5-7½). Changes for Medium (8-10) are in ( ).

Materials

Worsted weight yarn (3½-oz. skein): 1 each Beige (A), Red (B), small amounts Burgundy (C), Cranberry (D), and Emerald Green (E); size G crochet hook or size for gauge.

Gauge

4 sc = 1″; 4 rows = 2″.

To Make
Sole

With A, ch 5. **Row 1:** Sc in 2nd ch from hook and in each ch across, ch 1, turn on this and every row—4 sc. **Row 2:** 2 sc in first sc, sc to last sc, 2 sc in last sc—6 sc. **Row 3:** Rep Row 2—8 sc. **Rows 4 and 5:** Sc in each sc. **Row 6:** Rep Row 2—10 sc. **Row 7:** Sc in each sc. **Rows 8 and 9:** Rep Rows 6 and 7—12 sc. **Medium Only—Row 10:** Rep Row 2—14 sc. **All size—Rows 10-13 (11-14):** Work even. **Row 14 (15):** Draw up a lp in first sc, draw up a lp in next sc, yo and draw through all 3 lps on hook—dec made, sc to within last 2 sts, dec over last 2 sts—10 (12) sc. **Rows 15 and 16 (16 and 17):** Work even. **Row 17 (18):** Rep Row 14 (15)—8(10) sc. **Rows 18-22 (19-24):** Work even. **Row 23 (25):** Rep Row 14 (15)—6 (8) sc. **Rows 24-34 (26-37):** Work even. **Medium Only—Row 38:** Dec 1 st at each end—6 sc. **All Sizes—Rows 35 and 36 (39 and 40):** Rep Row 14 (15) twice—2 sc. Do not fasten off. Ch 1, work 74 (80) sc around edge of Sole, join with sl st in first sc; fasten off.

SIDE

Rnd 1: Attach C in back loop of any sc at heel on Sole; ch 1, sc in same sc. Working in back lps, sc in each sc around; join to first sc; fasten off. **Rnd 2:** Right-side facing, attach D, ch 1, draw up a lp in same sc, drop D to wrong side of work, yo with B and draw through both lps; † draw up a lp in next st, drop B to wrong side of work, yo with D and draw through both lps on hook*, with D, rep between *'s; rep from † around; insert hook through first sc, draw E through both lps. **Rnd 3:** Ch 1, sc in each sc; join to first sc, changing to D. **Rnd 4;** Rep Rnd 2; join and fasten off. **Rnd 5:** Attach C, ch 1 and sc in each sc; join and fasten off.

VAMP

With B, ch 4. **Row 1:** Sc in 2nd ch from hook and in each ch across, ch 1, turn on this and all rows—3 sc. **Row 2:** 2 sc in first sc, sc in next sc, 2 sc in last sc—5 sc. **Row 3:** Work even. **Row 4:** 2 sc in first sc, sc to end, 2 sc in last sc—7 sc. **Rows 5 and 6:** Work even. **Rows 7-9:** Rep Rows 4-6. **Medium Only—Row 10:** Rep Row 4. **Rows 10-18 (11-20):** Work even; do not fasten off. Ch 1, being careful to keep work flat, sc in end of rows, across starting ch and in ends of rows along other side; fasten off.

Finishing

Matching center fronts, pin Vamp into moccasin. From outside, with C, working through both lps of sts, join with sl st; fasten off.

Edging

Rnd 1: Right-side facing, attach B at right-hand corner of Vamp, ch 1, sc around back of moccasin and across Vamp, dec 1 st at each side of Vamp; join with sl st. **Rnds 2-5:** Sc in each sc, dec'g at corners; join and fasten off. Make second moccasin the same.

CROCHETED BOOTS

Directions are for Men's size Medium—11½"sole. Changes for Men's size Large—12½" sole are in ().

Materials

Worsted weight yarn (4-oz. skeins): 2 skeins Lt. Brown, 1 skein each Red and Dk Brown; size 1 crochet hook or size for gauge.

Gauge

3 sc = 1"; 7 rows = 2".

To Make

Note: Use yarn double throughout.
Sole
With Dk Brown ch 26 (29). **Rnd 1:** Mark last ch worked. Sc in 2nd and each ch across—25 (28) sc. Work 2 more sc in last ch and mark first of these with contrasting thread. Sc in each st on opposite side of ch—24 (27) sc; join; ch 1; turn. **Rnd 2:** Sc in first sc and mark this st; 2 sc in next st, sc in next 23 (26) sc, 2 sc in next sc, sc in next sc and mark this st, sc in next 23 (26) sc, 2 sc in next sc; join; ch 1; turn.

Rnds 3-6: Work as for Rnd 2, inc 1 sc each side of marked center scs—4 sc inc on each rnd. End last rnd, ch 1, **do not turn. Rnd 7:** Working in back lp only, sc in each sc around; cut off Dk Brown, join Red. **Rnd 8:** Working in both lps, work 1 rnd even with Red. Fasten off Red.

Instep Piece

With Lt. Brown, ch 8 (9). **Row 1:** Sc in second and each ch across; ch 1; turn. **Row 2:** Sc in 7 (8) sc; ch 1; turn. **Row 3:** Sc in each sc, inc 1 sc in last st; ch 1; turn. **Row 4:** Rep Row 3—9 (10) sts. **Rows 5-12:** Work even on 9 (10) sts. Ch 1; turn. **Rows 13-16:** Work to within last 2 sts; work 2 tog (dec); ch 1; turn. **Row 17:** Work 2 tog; sc in next st; work 2 tog; ch 1 turn. **Row 18:** Work 2 tog; sc in next sc; ch 1; turn. **Row 19:** Work 2 tog; sc around entire instep. Break off.

Attach Instep Piece

Center first row of instep piece at toe; pin in place. Join Red at side at beg of dec. Sl st instep to sole; continue with sc along top of instep with 3 sc in point at top. Join Lt. Brown at center back. Sc in each sc along side, inc or dec if necessary to total 21(23) sts; ch 7 loosely for instep and join at opposite side; sc in sts on this side to total 21 (23), ch 1, turn. Mark first and last sts of ch-7. Sc to within 2 sts of marked st; work the 2 sts tog; sc in 7 instep chs; work 2 sts tog; sc in each st to center back; join with sl st; ch 1; turn. Continue in this manner, dec 2 sts each side of instep until 13 (15) sts rem on each side. Break off Lt. Brown; join Red. Work even in sc as follows; 1 rnd Red, 5 rnds Dk Brown, 1 rnd Red—do not cut off Red. Fold Red strand to double; ch 14 for loop and fasten end at inside.

Materials For 2

45"-wide cotton or cotton-blend fabrics: ¼ yd. Gold calico, ⅛ yd. Brown calico; 12" by 18" piece terry fabric; 18" by 24" piece quilt batting; Gold thread; four ¼"diameter Black ball buttons.

To Make

Enlarge pattern; trace separate pattern for ear, adding ¼" seam allowance around. For each pig, cut 2 Gold bodies, 2 batting bodies, 1 terry body, 4 Brown ears, and a 1" by 4½" Brown strip for tail. Right sides in, stitch ears together in pairs leaving straight edge open. Notch curves; turn right-side out. Turn in seam allowance on straight edge; topstitch around curved edges. Pin an ear to right side of each Gold body; topstitch along straight edge. Fold long edges of tail strip to center; fold strip in half lengthwise. Stitch close to edge. Bring ends of strip together to form loop. Matching raw edges, baste loop to right side of a Gold body at marks. Baste batting to wrong side of each Gold body; baste terry to wrong side of one body. Right sides in, stitch bodies together leaving an opening for turning. Trim batting and terry close to stitching; notch seam allowance. Turn right-side out and slip-stitch opening. Topstitch around pig ¼" from edge. Sewing through all layers, sew button eyes in place.

One Square = 1"

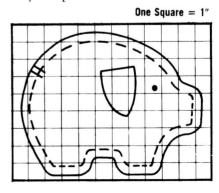

DARLING DUO KNITTED DOLLS

Approximately 20" tall

Materials For Both
Knitting-worsted-weight-yarn: 4 ozs. White (A), 1 oz. each Gold (B), Dark Pink (C), Medium Pink (D), Light Purple (E), Dark Purple (F), Orange (G), and Turquoise (H); scrap of Red; size 8 knitting needles or size for gauge; size F crochet hook; Felt: 16" square Magenta, 12" square Turquoise; sewing thread to match felt; 6 small buttons; 2 snap fasteners; polyester stuffing; yarn needle.

Gauge
9 sts = 2"; 5 rows = 1".

Note: All knitted pieces are worked in stockinette stitch (k 1 row, p 1 row) unless otherwise indicated.

Girl Doll

Leg (Make 2)
Starting at foot, with B cast on 20 sts; work 2 rows. **Dec Row 1:** K 8, k 2 tog twice, k 8. P 1 row. **Dec Row 2:** K 7, k 2 tog twice, k 7. P 1 row. **Dec Row 3:** K 6, k 2 tog twice, k 6. Work even on 14 sts for 5 more rows B, *2 rows C, 4 rows B; rep from * twice. With B, work 4 rows k 1, p 1 ribbing for top of sock. Fasten off B and C. Join A and continue in St st for 4". Bind off.

Body
Starting at bottom, with B cast on 30 sts; work for 2½"; fasten off B. With A, continue for 4"; bind off.

Arm (Make 2)
Starting at shoulder, with A, cast on 12 sts. Work even for 5½"; end with p row. **Wrist Dec Row:** *K 2, k 2 tog; rep from * twice. Work even on 9 sts for 1½"; bind off.

One Square = 1"

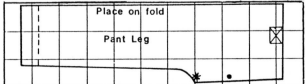

Pant Leg / Place on fold

Head
With A, cast on 12 sts; work even for ½"; end with p row. **Inc Row 1:** *K 3, inc 1 st in next st; rep from * 3 times—16 sts. P 1 row. **Inc Row 2:** *K 4, inc 1 st in next st; rep from * 3 times—30 sts. P 1 row. **Inc Row 3:** *K 5, inc 1 st in next st; rep from * 3 times—24 sts. Continue in this manner, inc 4 sts every other row, having 1 more st between incs until there are 32 sts. Work even until 4½" from beg. **Last Row:** K 2 tog across. Cut yarn leaving a 10" end; thread through rem 16 sts. Draw up tightly and fasten securely.

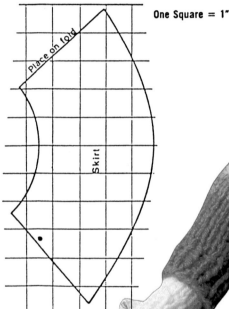

One Square = 1"

Place on fold / Skirt

Finishing
Stuff all pieces as you go. Sew cast-on edge of each foot together, sew back leg seam. Sew body back seam; sew legs in place. Sew arm seam and sew to body. With G hook, join A at body side of hand, ch 3 for thumb, sl st in joining; fasten off. Repeat on other hand. Sew back head and neck seam; sew to body. Embroider Turquoise satin stitch eyes, Red mouth. Cut 14" strands of B for hair. Lay strands across back of head; backstitch along center. Knot 3" strands across front for bangs. Tie a strand of C around each half of hair; tack to side of head. With C, tie bows at wrists for bracelets.

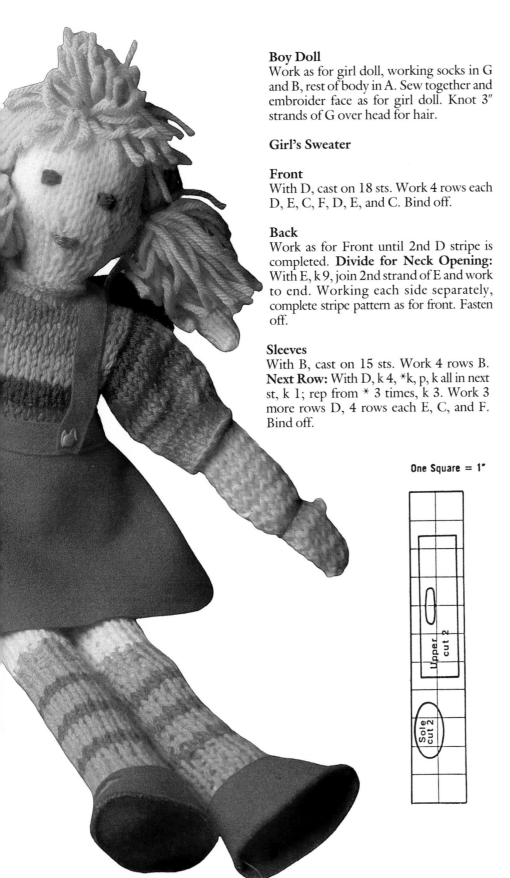

Boy Doll

Work as for girl doll, working socks in G and B, rest of body in A. Sew together and embroider face as for girl doll. Knot 3″ strands of G over head for hair.

Girl's Sweater

Front

With D, cast on 18 sts. Work 4 rows each D, E, C, F, D, E, and C. Bind off.

Back

Work as for Front until 2nd D stripe is completed. **Divide for Neck Opening:** With E, k 9, join 2nd strand of E and work to end. Working each side separately, complete stripe pattern as for front. Fasten off.

Sleeves

With B, cast on 15 sts. Work 4 rows B. **Next Row:** With D, k 4, *k, p, k all in next st, k 1; rep from * 3 times, k 3. Work 3 more rows D, 4 rows each E, C, and F. Bind off.

One Square = 1″

Upper cut 2

Sole cut 2

Finishing

Sew 4 sts together for each shoulder. Centering sleeve cap at shoulder seams, sew in sleeves. **Neck Edging:** From right side, with B, pick up and k 20 sts around neck edge. Work 4 rows; bind off. Sew snap at top of neck opening. Sew button over snap if desired.

Boy's Sweater

Front And Back

Working as for Girl's sweater, work 3″ H, 4 rows each G, B, G, and H. Bind off.

Sleeves

With H, cast on 15 sts. Work in k 1, p 1 ribbing for 6 rows. Continuing in St st, work 10 rows H, 3 rows each G, B, and G. 12 rows H. Bind off. Finish as for Girl's sweater.

Clothing

Girl's Pinafore: Cut skirt and ⅝″ by 9½″ waistband from Magenta felt. Overlap back edges of skirt ¼″; stitch from ● to lower edge. Lap band over skirt; topstitch. Cut one ⅝″ by 3″ and two ½″ by 6″ straps. Lap end of a 6″ strap at right angle over end of other 6″ strap; stitch. Stitch point to end of 3″ strap. Lap other end of short strap under band at back edge; stitch. Cut buttonhole in end of straps and at back of band. Sew on buttons.

Boy's Overalls: Use ⅛″ seams. Cut 2 pant legs from Turquoise felt. Fold each leg in half right sides together; stitch from * to lower edge. Turn right side out. Right sides together, stitch crotch seam, leaving open above ● in back. Turn up ½″ cuff on each leg. Cut ¾″ by 9¼″ waistband. Right sides together, stitch to pants. Cut two ½″ by 8″ straps. Sew one under back band, 1″ from seam. Place pants on doll. Cross straps in back and bring to front. Cut straps even with bottom of waistband. Cut buttonhole in end of each strap and in back waistband. Sew on buttons.

Shoes: Cut felt uppers and soles. Lap back edges of uppers; stitch. Whipstitch sole to upper.

CENTER DIAMOND AMISH QUILT

Approximately 84″ square

Materials

45″-wide cotton or cotton-blend fabrics: 3¾ yds. Turquoise, 2½ yds. Lavender, 1½ yds. Maroon; 5 yds. color desired for Backing; Mountain Mist quilt batting: 90″ by 108″; sewing thread to match fabrics; quilting thread to match fabrics; pencil and paper for patterns; materials for transferring quilting design; quilting frame or hoop.

Marking And Cutting

Press fabric thoroughly. Cut all pieces on lengthwise or crosswise grain of fabric. Draw each quilt piece on the **wrong side** of the fabric with a ruler, a T- or L-square and a sharp pencil. Mark seamlines on pieces—the dimensions given below include ¼″ seam allowance. All marking and cutting must be done accurately if pieces are to fit together properly. From **Lavender,** cut a 31½″ square for **Center,** four 4″ by 48″ strips for **Inner Borders** and 4″-wide strips to piece 340″ long **Binding.** From **Maroon,** cut two 23″ squares; cut in half diagonally to form 4 **Triangles.** From **Turquoise,** cut 2 **Outer Borders** 17″ by 51½″ and 2 **Outer Borders** 17″ by 84½″. Cut **Backing** fabric into two 2½-yd. pieces; stitch together along side edge.

Piecing

Pieces may be sewn together by hand or machine. However, for very complex patterns, hand-sewing usually ensures more accuracy. Sew pieces right sides together, matching seamlines and starting and stopping stitching exactly on seamlines. Press all seams to one side. To set a piece into an angle, clip inside corner to seamline. Sew one side almost to corner; pin second side in place, matching seamlines; turn seam exactly at corner and sew the second side. Stitch **Maroon Triangles** to each side of **Lavender Center.** Matching raw edges at one end, stitch a **Lavender Inner Border** to one edge of center—piece will extend about 3½″ beyond other end. To attach remaining **Inner Borders,** set strips into angle between previous border and center. Stitch shorter **Outer Border** strips to top and bottom of quilt top, longer strips to sides.

Transfer Center Quilting Motif to **Lavender Center.** Using a pencil and ruler, draw quilting lines ¾″ apart on **Maroon Triangles** both parallel and perpendicular to longest edge. Transfer Star Motif to corners of **Inner Border,** and Flower Motifs along sides. Trace Feather and Tulip Motif to **Outer Border** making slight alterations in spacing so that repeat fits between corners.

Assembling Quilt

Lay the **Backing** flat on the floor, wrong-side up; place batting on top of it. Lay quilt top in place, right-side up. Starting at the center of the quilt, baste out to the midpoint of all four edges. Then, starting at the center, baste to the four corners. Trim excess batting; baste around outer edge 1½″ from edge.

Quilting

By Hand

Place quilt in a frame or hoop. Use a short needle and quilting thread. Use a short length of thread and pull knot through to batting. Work small stitches as follows: Place forefinger of left hand over the spot where the needle should come through. With the right hand, push the needle through the quilt, thread through with right hand—left forefinger is now put under the quilt. With right hand, push needle down through quilt to touch forefinger. Pull thread through with right hand. Continue working in this fashion. To fasten end of each thread securely, knot near last stitch and pull through to filling. Bring needle out 1″ away; cut thread close to fabric.

By Machine
Using long stitch (8-10 stitches per inch), stitch along quilting lines.

Finishing
Join **Binding** strips end to end. Right sides together, with ¼″ of **Binding** extending over outer basting line, pin, then stitch along basting line, mitering corners. Fold **Binding** to **Backing** side of quilt. Turn under ¼″ on edge and slip-stitch over seam.

Feather and Tulip Motif   **One square = 1″**

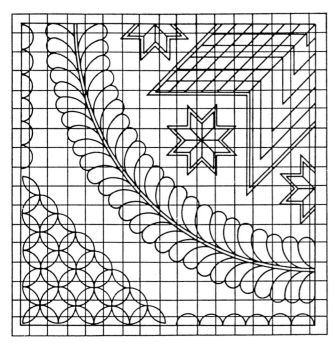

Center Quilting Motif   **One square = 1″**

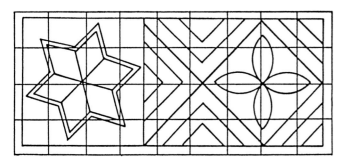

SHAKER MINIATURES

Materials

Wood—fine quality native woods such as pine and maple (Cut them to required thickness or buy miniature lumber. Do not use basswood—it does not have the quality appearance necessary for Shaker furniture.); Toothpicks; White glue; Sandpaper; Brush; Stain; Paint.

Drafting Tools

These items come in handy but are not all necessary. Protractor. T-Square. 30°-60°-90° triangle. Compass. Dividers. Single-edge razor blade. Eraser. Drafting pencil. Oval and circle templates. Graph paper. Flexible rule. Masking tape. Tracing paper. Scotch tape. Scissors. Scale ruler.

Woodworking Tools

(Miniature size tools are available at craft and miniature shops; not all tools are necessary.) Sander. Hand drill and drill set. Coping saw. Spoke Shave. Miter box. Razor saw. X-acto knives. Jeweler's saw. Needle files. Vise. Mini-lamps. Round jeweler's saw. Caliper. Miniature screwdrivers. Miniature turning tools. Small chisel. Hand drill. Keyhole saw. Hand saber saw. Center punch. Moto-Lathe. Moto-Tool and drill press stand. Moto-Saw. Magnifier. Tweezers.

General Directions For Shaker Miniatures

All Shaker Furniture shown here is in the scale of one inch equals one foot. The measurements in the line drawings are all listed in inches. Following measurements on diagrams, make paper patterns for each piece. Cut wood to proper thickness if necessary. Trace each shape to wood and cut along lines using Moto-Saw or small hand saw. Drill any holes indicated on diagrams.

Sanding should be done intermittently through the various stages of furniture construction in order to refine the wood surface. Sand lightly using fine sandpaper or a sander. Always sand flat surfaces with a straight motion following the grain of the wood. Circular motions or sanding against the grain will mar the surface of the wood. Stain the pieces before gluing them together to insure even penetration of stain around the joint area. Where glue seeps

from joint, the wood becomes sealed and stain will not penetrate the wood after that. For painted pieces we recommend a flat paint.

For the bent curves in many pieces, bend the wood by soaking it in warm to hot water for a few hours or overnight if necessary. Be sure the piece of wood is weighted down so it is immersed and will absorb the water. Remove the wood from the water, wrap it around a mold of the particular curve you need and hold it in place with clamps. Allow the wood to dry overnight. When completely dry, sand, stain and assemble the piece.

Scoring means to groove part way into a solid surface. This can be done with a knife or as in the case of the miniature room's floor with a dull pencil to give the effect of planks.

To Weave Chair Seats

Iron-on rug binding closely resembles the "listing" of the Shakers and can be easily woven into a chair seat. If the iron-on variety is not available, use regular rug binding and back it with cloth tape so that it will be stiff and hold its shape. It must then be cut into 1/16-inch-wide pieces. A solid color may be used or two different colors can be alternated to give a more noticeable checkerboard pattern.

The first step in seating the chair is known as *warping*. This simply entails wrapping the binding around the front and back seat rails to provide a warp both on the top and the bottom of the seat. The procedure is as follows: the end (doubled over for strength) of one piece or coil of binding is glued with contact cement to the inner side of the back rail as close as possible to the left back post; this doubled-over end must point toward the top of the chair. The binding is brought over the back rail to the front rail at right angles to both the front and back rails. It is then brought over the front rail and returned to the back rail, which it goes under and over. DO NOT TWIST THE BINDING. Continue until the back right post is reached. Then bring the binding over and under the front rail and back to the back rail and cut off the excess, allowing about 1/4-inch extra length. This end is doubled over and securely tucked in. Do not allow the binding to sag; take out as much of the slack as possible so the seat will be firm.

When the warp is completed, the next step is the actual weaving of the seat. This is begun by securing the end of the piece or coil of binding, which will be the *weft*. The end, doubled over for strength, is glued to the inside of the left side rail as close as possible to the left back post. The free end is then attached to a large needle with thread and

MINISTRY'S SIDE CHAIR

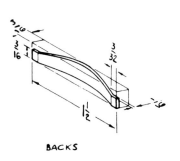

BACKS

ALL MEASUREMENTS ARE IN INCHES

brought over the first warp strip of the top layer, under the next, over one, under one, etc. until the right back post is reached. The full length of the binding is pulled through all the top layers of warp strips. The chair is turned over and the process is repeated on the lower layer of warp strips.

Next, the weft is again woven through the top layer of warp strips, starting under the first strip, over the second, etc. so that the result is the start of a checkerboard pattern. The chair is again turned over and the weft is returned through the lower level of warp strips so as to form, as on the top layer, the beginning of a checkerboard pattern. The process described above is continued until the weft reaches the front posts of the chair. Again, it must be emphasized that the binding must not be twisted. Also, it should be pulled firmly each time it is brought through the warp strips, and the rows should be kept as straight as possible, each touching the last. All ends should be tucked securely into place, and the seat will be finished.

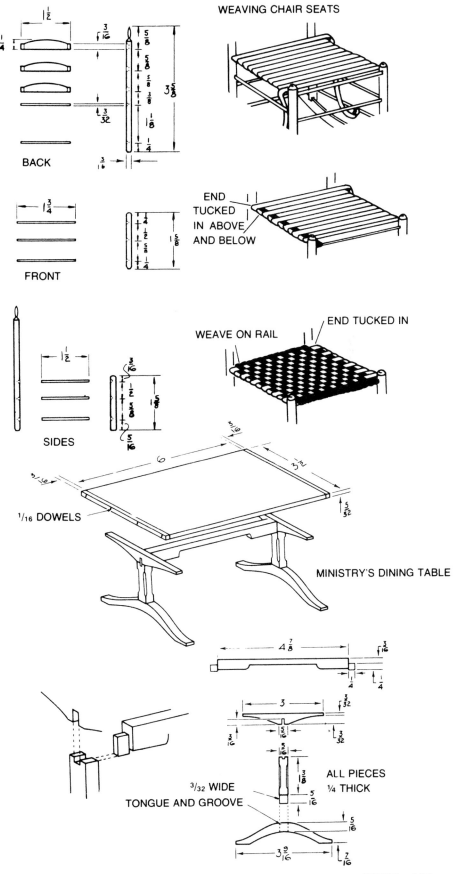

WEAVING CHAIR SEATS

BACK

FRONT

SIDES

END TUCKED IN ABOVE AND BELOW

WEAVE ON RAIL

END TUCKED IN

MINISTRY'S DINING TABLE

1/16 DOWELS

3/32 WIDE
TONGUE AND GROOVE

ALL PIECES 1/4 THICK

THE BIG CHRISTMAS WRAP-UP

The Big Christmas Wrap-Up

1. *Potato-Print Envelope*
2. *"Bakery" Box*
3. *Fancy Fold-Ups*
4. *Origami Basket*
5. *Bandanna Bundle*
6. *Shirt Box*
7. *Tie Box*
8. *Peppermint-Stripe Tubes*
9. *Gardener's Delight*
10. *Quick Kraft-Paper Wraps*
11. *Village-in-the-Round*
12. *Snowflake Box*
13. *"Folk Art" Flowers*
14. *Grocery-Bag Reindeer*
15. *Teddy-Bear Tote*
16. *Dainty Doily Bags*
17. *Patchwork Box*
18. *Baby's Building Block*
19. *Lunch-Bag Specials*
20. *Sweetheart Box*
21. *Gingerbread-Cookie Can*
22. *Pretty Plaid Pouches*
23. *Country Breadbasket*
24. *Stovepipe-Hat Box*
25. *"Wooden" Soldier*
26. *Jumbo-Crayon Tubes*

To Make Boxes

Draw pattern from bottom of box onto **railroad board.** Draw pattern for lid, ⅛" larger all around than bottom; cut out. Check board to see which way it bends without cracking. Cutting circumference in this direction, cut box side desired height by the circumference of the bottom plus 1"; cut lid rim desired height by the circumference of the lid plus 1". Wrap side around bottom until edges match snugly; hold in place with thin strips of **masking tape.** Using a single strand of **heavy-duty polyester thread** and a **quilting needle,** whipstitch edges together ⅛" from edges with stitches ¼" apart. Do not pull thread too tightly or it will rip cardboard. End by weaving end of thread under stitches. Stitch side seam following stitch diagram. For heart-shaped box, begin sewing at point; crease side at indentation and continue sewing other side to point. Trim edges even at point; whipstitch sides together. Sew lid together in same way.

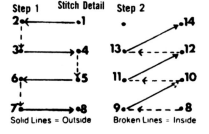

Step 1 Stitch Detail Step 2

Solid Lines = Outside   Broken Lines = Inside

To Cover Round, Oval, Or Heart-Shaped Boxes

Cut top covering ½" larger all around than lid, bottom covering ½" larger all around than bottom. Cut rim and side covering height of lid or box plus ½" by circumference plus 1". Mix ¼ cup **wallpaper paste** with water; stir until smooth and consistency of thick cream. With **paintbrush,** apply paste to bottom of box. Set box in center of covering, turn over and smooth out wrinkles. With **scissors,** slash edge of covering to edge of box every ½" around. Apply paste to lower edge of box side; fold up tabs, pressing smoothly against side. Apply paste to entire box side. Keeping edge of covering even with bottom of box

and lapping on one side, apply covering to side. Slash excess paper at top, paste tabs to inside of box. Cover box lid in same manner. Allow box and lid to dry partially. When outer surface is dry, place box and lid down on a clean surface; place small jars or cans inside to prevent warping. Move weights often to prevent them from marking boxes.

POTATO-PRINT ENVELOPE

1. Cut slice from **raw potato** to make flat surface. Press **heart-shaped cookie cutter** into potato. Cut away potato around heart leaving base as handle; remove cookie cutter. With **stiff brush,** paint surface of heart with **red acrylic paint.** Stamp hearts in even rows on **manila envelope.** Touch up hearts with brush if necessary. Outline flap with **red felt-tip marker.** Make 2 holes in flap, 2 matching holes in envelope beneath flap. Insert **green ribbon** through holes; tie bow.

2. "BAKERY" BOX

Cover top of **4" by 9½" by 12" box** with **white paper.** Enlarge design. Cut roof, doors, and tree trunks from **brown paper;** sign, steps, bow, and doorknob from **shiny red paper;** window frames, wreath, and trees from **shiny green paper;** and windows from **yellow construction paper.** Outline shingles on roof with **brown felt-tip pen. Glue** pieces to box top.

"BAKERY" BOX   One square = 1"

BAKERY

3. FANCY FOLD-UPS

Following diagram, draw pattern for box onto **railroad board.** Dimensions are given for small box; medium and large box are in parentheses. Cut out along solid lines; score and fold along broken lines. Flatten box. Apply **wallpaper paste** to outside of box; place box on wrong side of **cotton print fabric.** Let dry. Trim fabric ⅜″ larger than box; clip to inner corners and along curves. Fold and paste fabric edge to inside of box. Cut handle lining pieces from fabric; paste to inside of handles. Cut fabric from slits. Fold handles to center; close flaps over handles. Tie **ribbon** around box through handles; tie bow.

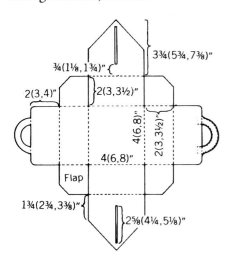

4. ORIGAMI BASKET

Use a **square of paper twice the size of the finished basket desired.** Fold square in half diagonally, then in half again (fig. 1). Bring top right-hand point down to lower point; flatten and crease (fig. 2). Turn over and repeat previous step (figs. 3 and 4). Fold sides to center; crease (fig. 5). Open corners; crease flat (fig. 6). Turn piece over; repeat figs. 5 and 6. Fold left half over right half (fig. 7). Turn piece over and repeat previous step (fig. 8). Fold sides to center (fig. 9). Fold top layer of lower point up; fold lower edge up again (fig. 10). Turn piece over and repeat folds (fig. 11). Fold left half over right. Repeat folds of lower point (fig. 12). Turn piece over;

fold left side over right. Repeat folds (fig. 13). Turn piece upside down (fig. 14). Push sides out; flatten and shape bottom (fig. 15).

ORIGAMI BASKET

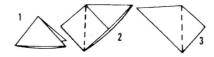

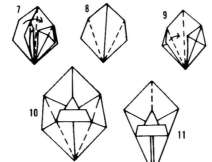

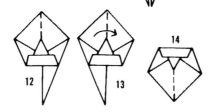

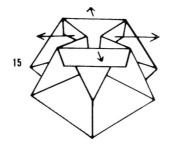

5. BANDANNA BUNDLE

Place gift in center of **red bandanna.** Tie diagonally opposite corners in knot at top; repeat with remaining corners. Insert **thin tree branch** through knot.

6. SHIRT BOX

Cover top of **2″ by 10″ by 15″ shirt box** with **red-and-white-striped fabric, gluing** edges to inside. Enlarge pattern; placing arrows on stripes, cut collar pieces and placket. Using **spray adhesive,** attach collar and placket. Outline pocket and edges of collar and placket with ⅛″-wide **red grosgrain ribbon.** Glue **small shirt buttons** to points of collar, **4 medium shirt buttons** down placket.

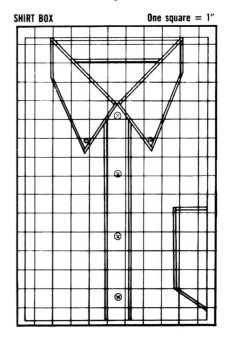

7. TIE BOX

Cover top of **1½″ by 5¼″ by 14¼″ tie box** with **white paper, gluing** edges to inside. Enlarge pattern; lightly trace to top of box. With arrows on grain of fabric, cut tie and knot from **red-, white-, and green-striped fabric.** Attach to box with **spray adhesive.** With **white glue,** glue ⅛″-wide **red grosgrain ribbon** along collar lines; glue on **2 small white shirt buttons.**

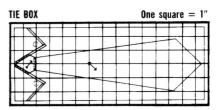

8. PEPPERMINT-STRIPE TUBES

Wrap **candy-striped fabric or paper** diagonally around length of **cardboard tube;** tie a **ribbon bow** at each end.

9. GARDENER'S DELIGHT

Cut **green print cotton 12″ by 14″.** Wrong sides in, seam 12″ edges. With seam at center, stitch across bottom. Turn right-side out. At each side, 3″ below top, stitch 2 perpendicular buttonholes, ¼″ apart. Turn top edge to wrong side below buttonholes; stitch around. Stitch again ½″ above first stitching to form casing. Cut **1 yd. ¼″-wide red grosgrain** in half. Run ribbon through casing into one buttonhole and out the other on same side; repeat from opposite side. Pull up ribbons and tie bows. **Glue 2** bands of ribbon around **clay planter.** Place filled bag in planter.

10. QUICK KRAFT-PAPER WRAPS

Wrap boxes with **brown kraft paper.** Decorate with **ribbon, pinecones, holly berries, dried flowers,** and **Christmas-tree balls.**

11. VILLAGE-IN-THE-ROUND

Cover **large oval hatbox and lid** with **sage green cotton fabric.** Enlarge patterns. From **dark green pin-dot fabric,** cut 32 leaves and ³⁄₁₆″-wide bias strips for stem. Cut **8 red pin-dot fabric** and **8 gold-print fabric** tulips. Cut farm scene, 8 buildings, trees, fence, and building details from **fabric scraps.** With **white glue,** glue details to buildings; with **wallpaper paste,** paste on buildings and rim decoration.

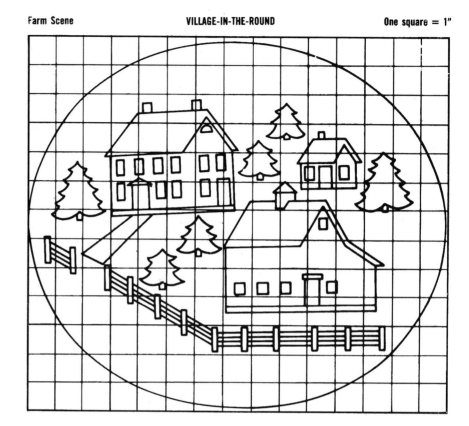

Farm Scene · VILLAGE-IN-THE-ROUND · One square = 1″

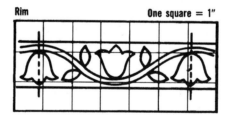

Rim · One square = 1″

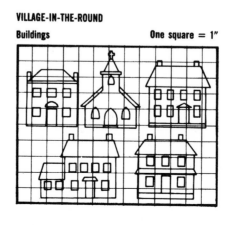

VILLAGE-IN-THE-ROUND
Buildings · One square = 1″

12. SNOWFLAKE BOX

Cover bottom and lid of **5″-high, 10″-diameter round box** with **brown kraft paper.** For each snowflake, fold a **3¾″ square of white bond paper** in half to form a rectangle. With fold at bottom, fold as in fig. 1 to form a triangle. Trace fig. 2 to 6 triangles, fig. 3 to 6 triangles; cut out design. Using **wallpaper paste,** alternating designs, **glue 6** snowflakes evenly spaced around top and 6 around side of box. Cut 12 small hearts from **red construction paper;** glue between snowflakes. Cut four 1″ by 10″ strips of white bond paper; fold each in half 3 times. Trace fig. 4 to one side. Cut out design; slash along lines. Glue strips together matching design. Cut tiny diamond shapes along edges. Weave ³⁄₈″-wide strips of red construction paper through slashes in trim. Glue to rim.

SNOWFLAKE BOX

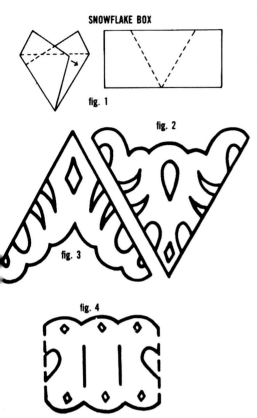

fig. 1

fig. 2

fig. 3

fig. 4

13. "FOLK ART" FLOWERS

Cover top, sides, and bottom of 3½"-high, 9"-diameter round box with white paper. Cover rim with red-and-white dotted paper. Enlarge design for top; cut flowers from dotted paper, leaves and stems from shiny green paper and centers from shiny yellow paper. Cut 5 flowers and 10 leaves for side of box. Glue designs to box.

"FOLK ART" FLOWERS   **¼ of Design**

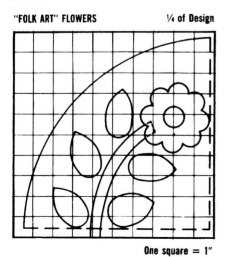

One square = 1"

14. GROCERY-BAG REINDEER

Enlarge patterns. Cut face from paper: red nose and mouth, brown ears and pupils, pink inner ears, white irises, and black eyelids. Draw nostrils with black felt-tip marker. Glue inner ears to outer ears; fold forward on dotted line. Fold 1" at top of brown grocery bag to back; fold again 1½" below first fold. Glue ears inside center side fold of bag, with top of ears at top folded edge of bag; glue face to bag. Cut antlers from lightweight cardboard and light gold velour paper; glue velour paper to cardboard. With masking tape, attach antlers to folded top of bag on back. Insert gift; refold top and tape shut.

GROCERY-BAG REINDEER   **One square = 1'**

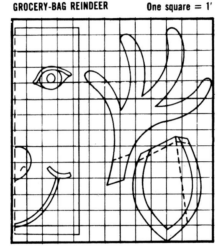

15. TEDDY-BEAR TOTE

From shiny green paper, cut 14 strips ¼"-wide by length of large, heavy-duty brown grocery bag; glue strips down bag about ⅝" apart. Enlarge pattern; cut bear from brown and light gold velour paper, neck bow and package from shiny red paper, package from green paper, and eyes and nose from black paper. Glue to bag. Draw details with black felt-tip pen. Cut two 1½" by 18½" strips of red paper. Starting at center folds of bag, with ½" extending above bag, glue strips to front and back of bag. Fold strip and glue edge to inside. Cut two 2½" by 14½" green paper handles. Fold lengthwise into thirds; glue. Glue ends of handles to inside of bag; glue a 2½" by 8½" piece of brown paper over each handle on inside to reinforce it.

TEDDY-BEAR TOTE   **One square = 1"**

16. DAINTY DOILY BAGS

Wrap paper lace doily place mat around a 2½" by 4½" box, lapping edges; glue overlap. Fold one end as if wrapping box; glue. Remove box. Pleat sides of bag. Decorate with ribbon, pinecones, berries, and ribbon roses.

17. PATCHWORK BOX

Cover sides of 6"-deep, 9¾"-square gift box and top of lid with white paper. Glue 4⅞" square of red-and-white checked paper to center of lid. From red pin-dot paper, cut two 3¾" squares; cut in half diagonally to form 4 triangles. Cut four 2¾" squares. Glue squares at corners and triangles at center of checked square as in photograph—edges extend onto rim. Glue checked paper around rim, folding excess at lower edge to inside of lid. Place lid on box; lightly draw a 4½" by 9" rectangle in center of each side. Divide rectangle into eight 2¼" squares. Remove lid. Outline each rectangle with red felt-tip pen. From pin-dot paper, cut sixteen 2¼" squares; cut diagonally. Glue red triangles into squares as in diagram.

18. BABY'S BUILDING BLOCK

From **2-ply illustration board,** cut 8″-square box top and bottom, 7⅞″ by 8″ box front and back, and two 7¾″ by 7⅞″ box sides. With **white glue,** glue front and back to bottom, holding with **pushpins.** Glue sides to bottom, front, and back. Let glue set. Place top on box. Cut two 3″ by 8″ strips **thin white paper.** Fold 1 in half lengthwise; with fold at edge, glue to top and back of box. Let dry. Trim ⅜″ from remaining strip, glue to inside of top and back. Glue white paper to sides of box. Enlarge patterns. Cut teddy bear from **brown and gold velour paper;** draw details with **black felt-tip pen.** Cut necktie, packages, berries, tree ornaments, and "T" from **shiny red paper;** tree, holly, ribbons, and "B" from **shiny green paper;** star and candle flames from **gold paper;** candles from **white paper.** Glue bear to top, tree to one side. For remaining sides, repeat tree or cut motifs desired. Glue ¾″ by 8″ strips of red paper over edges of box.

Top   One square = 1″

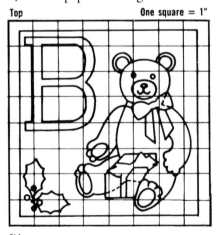

Side

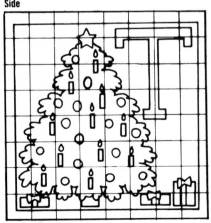

19. LUNCH-BAG SPECIALS

Cut scallops, punch holes, or cut out row of hearts along top of **small brown lunch bags.** Tie on **lace beading, ribbons,** or **Christmas-tree balls.**

20. SWEETHEART BOX

Cover **heart-shaped bandbox and lid** (pattern for top given below) with **red wallpaper striped fabric.** Glue 2 rows of 1¼″-wide white lace edging along center and one row on each side of top of lid. Glue ½″-wide green satin ribbon along center and ¼″-wide green satin ribbon over edge of lace on sides. Glue ⅝″-wide lace edging around rim; glue ¼″-wide ribbon over edge of lace. Sew ⅝″-wide lace edging to each side of a 14″ length of ½″-wide ribbon. Fold into bow; secure center with ribbon. Glue to top of box. Enlarge pattern. Cut 4 holly leaves each from **green calico** and **white holly-print fabric.** Right sides in, stitch leaves together in pairs, leaving opening for turning. Clip curves and corners; turn right-side out. Stuff lightly; slip-stitch opening. Hand quilt along lines. Turn under ¼″ on ends of a **4″ by 20″ strip of red pin-dot fabric.** Right-side out, fold in half lengthwise, inserting a **1¾″ by 19″ strip of quilt batting;** baste along lower edge. Roll strip into rose shape, pleating outer layers for fullness. Stitch bottom together; wrap with thread ¼″ above lower edge. Glue rose and leaves to top of box.

One square = 1″

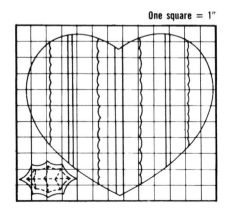

One square = 1″

21. GINGERBREAD-COOKIE CAN

Cover **1 lb. coffee can** with plastic lid with **green-and-white dotted fabric.** Enlarge patterns. From fabric, cut and **glue 3 brown** gingerbread boys, 3 **red-and-white dotted** hearts, 3 **gold print** stars, and 3 **red gingham** candy canes evenly around can. Outline gingerbread boys with **white baby rickrack;** glue on **red fabric** buttons, **white fabric** eyes, **red yarn** mouth. Glue **red baby rickrack** around lower edge of can. Trace gingerbread-boy pattern; add ½″ around. Cut 2 from brown. With **6-strand embroidery floss,** embroider **white** satin-stitch eyes, **red** back-stitch mouth on one. Right sides in, leaving small opening, stitch pieces together in a ¼″ seam. Clip seams; turn right-side out. Fold **8″ pipecleaner** in half; insert 1 end into each leg. **Stuff** figure; slip-stitch opening. Glue on red fabric buttons; slip-stitch white rickrack around edge. Right sides in, matching edges, stitch ⅝″-**wide ruffled eyelet** edging around edge of **4¾″-diameter white eyelet fabric circle;** stitch ends of edging together. Press seam toward center. Baste **4½″ circle of batting** to wrong side of eyelet; sew red rickrack around edge of eyelet. Sewing through plastic, sew circle to lid by hand. Make 1½″ diameter loop of **red-and-white dotted ribbon;** sew flat bow over ends. Tack loop to top. Slip gingerbread boy through loop.

22. PRETTY PLAID POUCHES

Cut **fabric** twice desired width plus seam by height plus seam and deep top hem. Wrong side in, stitch lengthwise seam; press seam. Fold with seam at center; stitch across bottom. Turn right side out; stitch hem. Tie **ribbon** bow.

23. COUNTRY BREADBASKET

Fold **20″ by 30″ dish towel** in half to 15″ by 20″. Stitch about 3″ from fold, to shorten towel to fit around box, checking against the actual box, retaining box pattern; trim seam; press. Back with **thick nonwoven interfacing**. Cut 3″ squares from corners of interfacing. Line with **checked gingham**. Stitch through all layers, 3″ from each edge. On wrong side, raw edges matching, pin 10″ length ¼″-wide **grosgrain ribbon**, 3″ from each corner on all edges. Hem edges. Tie bows at corners.

24. STOVEPIPE-HAT BOX

Enlarge patterns. From **4-ply railroad board**, cut 2 sides, 8″-diameter lower lid, 8¼″-diameter upper lid, 7¾″-diameter base, 11¼″-diameter brim, and a ¾″ by 25½″ rim. Following instructions for making boxes, overlap side pieces and sew together; sew sides to base, rim to lower lid. **Glue** base to center of brim; lower lid to center of upper lid. Cut **black construction paper** coverings—2 upper brims, 2 sides, 9¼″-diameter upper lid, 11″-diameter lower brim, and 1¼″ by 25½″ rim. Slash inner curve of upper brim to line at ½″ intervals; bend up tabs. Paste upper brims to top of brim overlapping edges at seams of sides. Slash paper around outer edge; paste to bottom. Cover remaining surfaces following instructions for covering boxes.

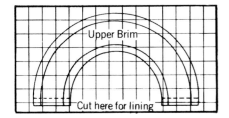

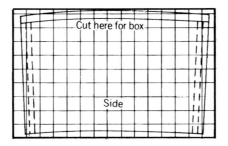

Cut here for box

Side

25. "WOODEN" SOLDIER

Glue 4″-diameter **black construction-paper** circle to top of lid of **3″-diameter, 18″ long cardboard mailing tube**. Slash excess paper to edge of lid; glue to sides. Glue 3¼″ by 9½″ strip of black around sides of lid. Enlarge patterns. Draw features at center of 2½″ by 9½″ **strip of peach construction paper** with **felt-tip pens**. Remove lid, glue face strip around top of lower portion of tube. Cut **yellow construction-paper hair**; glue around tube with ends at edges of face. Cut ¾″ by 1½″ strip of **shiny red paper**; glue on for collar. Cut **blue construction-paper** strap, **gold paper** circles; glue in place. Glue on 7½″ by 9½″ piece of blue paper for trousers. With **blue felt-tip pen**, draw line down center front and back to form legs. Glue ⅜″-wide white construction-paper stripes down sides. Cut 1″-diameter black paper circle in half; glue to lower edge of legs for feet. Glue 5⅞″ by 9½″ strip shiny red paper around middle of tube for jacket. Cut ½″-wide strips of **white construction paper**; glue to front and back to form X. Glue on ½″ by 9½″ white strip for belt. Glue on 5 gold buttons. For arms, cut 3½″ by 6¼″ strips peach paper; roll into ⅞″-diameter, 6¼″ long tubes; glue. Cut two 1¾″-diameter peach circles for each arm; draw a ⅞″-diameter circle in center of each larger circle. Clip to inner circle at ¼″ intervals; fold down tabs. Glue a circle to each end of arm tubes. Glue ¾″ by 3½″ peach strip around one end of each tube, 3½″ by 5⅞″ red paper strip around other end. Cut 1¼″ by 3½″ strip of gold paper for each epaulet; cut ½″-long fringe along one long edge. Fringe down, and ¼″ extending above end of arm, glue gold strip around red end of arm. Clip excess paper to top of tube; glue to end of tube. Glue ⅞″-diameter gold circle over end. Glue on arms.

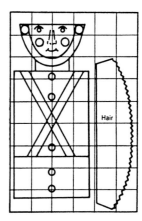

Hair

One square = 1″

26. JUMBO-CRAYON TUBES

Cut 2½″ by 9½″ strip of **shiny red or green paper**. One edge extending ¾″ beyond top, **glue** strip around lid of **3″-diameter, 25″ long mailing tube**. Slash excess paper to edge of tube at ⅜″ intervals, glue tabs to end of tube. Repeat at bottom of tube. Lower edges even, glue 4¾″ by 9½″ strip of **red or green construction paper** around lid. Top edges even, glue 9½″ by 18″ strip around bottom section of tube. Enlarge patterns. Cut 2 of each border from **black construction paper**; glue around tube. From **bristol board**, cut point, a ⅞″- and a 2½″-diameter circle. Lap edges of point and glue; glue circles to ends. Cut 2″ diameter circle of shiny paper, glue to small end of point. Slash excess paper at ¼″ intervals; glue to sides of point. Cut point from shiny paper; upper edges even, glue around bristol-board point. Slash excess paper; glue to bottom. Glue point to top of tube.

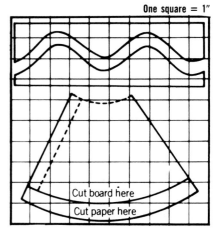

One square = 1″

Cut board here

Cut paper here

V.
BOUNTIFUL BATCHES

*A*t least one month before Christmas, you will want to start creaming butter and sugar and adding the allspice, coconut, molasses, cinnamon and maple that go into the cascades of wreaths, ribbons, crescents, triangles, spirals, ovals and shells that make up our own Christmas Cookie Assortment. Our 'line-up' of seventeen Gingerbread Boys and Girls is just a taste of the fun you can have decorating these creatures. And our finale is, of course, the eighth architectural wonder of the gingerbread world, the Christmas Cottage.

Here's a sampler of the very best holiday cookies, swirled with chocolate, crunchy with nuts and filled with fresh fruit—Coconut Macaroons, Peanut Refrigerator Cookies, Praline Thins, Bonbon Cookies, Fresh Apple Chews, Neapolitan Shell Cookies, Tunnels of Fudge and Ginger Crisps. Recipes on pages 116-117.

GINGER CRISPS

½ cup butter or margarine, softened
¾ cup sugar
3 tablespoons light molasses
1 egg
2½ cups all-purpose flour
1½ teaspoons ground ginger
1½ teaspoons ground cinnamon
1 teaspoon baking soda
½ teaspoon ground allspice

About 4½ hours before serving or up to 1 week ahead:

1. In large bowl with mixer at low speed, beat butter, sugar, molasses, and egg until light and fluffy. Add flour and remaining ingredients. Beat at low speed until well mixed, constantly scraping bowl with rubber spatula. Shape mixture into a ball; wrap with plastic wrap and refrigerate 2 to 3 hours until easy to handle.

2. Preheat oven to 375°F. Lightly grease 2 large cookie sheets. On lightly floured surface with lightly floured rolling pin, roll half of dough ⅛ inch thick, keeping remaining dough refrigerated. Cut dough into as many 3" by 3" squares as possible; cut each square diagonally in half to form two triangles. With dull edge of French knife, lightly make 4 crosswise lines in each triangle (do not cut through dough). Reserve trimmings.

3. With pancake turner, carefully place cookies, ¼ inch apart, on cookie sheets. Bake 8 minutes or until edges of cookies are firm. With pancake turner, remove cookies to wire racks to cool. Repeat with 3 remaining dough and reroll trimmings. Store cookies in tightly covered container. Makes about 5 dozen.

NEAPOLITAN SHELL COOKIES

2 cups all-purpose flour
⅓ cup sugar
½ teaspoon salt
    butter or margarine
⅓ cup cold water
    about ½ cup favorite preserves or jam
1 egg white, beaten

About 3 hours before serving or day ahead:

1. In medium bowl, combine flour, sugar, and salt. With pastry blender or two knives used scissor-fashion, cut in ¼ cup butter or margarine until mixture resembles coarse crumbs. Stir in water until dough holds together, adding 1 more tablespoon water if needed. Shape dough into a ball.

2. In small saucepan over low heat melt 3 tablespoons butter or margarine. Cut dough into 4 equal pieces. On lightly floured surface with floured rolling pin, roll 1 piece into 12" by 12" square; brush with some butter or margarine. Repeat with remaining dough. Arrange squares in one stack. Roll dough, jelly-roll fashion. Cut into twenty-four ½-inch-thick slices.

3. Preheat oven to 375°F. Grease large cookie sheet. Place a slice of dough, cut-side down, on palm of one hand. With thumb of other hand, gently press center through to form a ribbed cone. (Ribs should not separate completely.) Shape cone with fingertips so that it measures about 2 inches at opening and about 2½ inches from opening to tip. Press tip together. Fill each cone with 1 teaspoonful preserves or jam. With hand, gently close opening of cone; place on cookie sheet. Repeat with remaining slices. Brush dough with egg white. Bake 25 minutes or until golden. Remove to wire racks to cool. Store cookies in tightly covered container. Makes 2 dozen.

COCONUT MACAROONS

3 egg whites, at room temperature
½ cup sugar
1 teaspoon vanilla extract
½ teaspoon salt
2 cups flaked coconut
⅓ cup all-purpose flour

About 2 hours before serving or up to 3 days ahead:

1. Preheat oven to 325°F. Lightly grease two cookie sheets.

2. In small bowl with mixer at high speed, beat egg whites until soft peaks form. Beating at high speed, gradually beat in sugar, 2 tablespoons at a time, beating well after each addition until sugar is completely dissolved. Beat in vanilla and salt. (Whites should stand in stiff, glossy peaks.) With rubber spatula, gently fold coconut and flour into egg-white mixture.

3. Drop coconut mixture by heaping teaspoonfuls, about 1 inch apart, onto cookie sheets. Bake 20 minutes or until cookies are lightly browned. With metal spatula, carefully remove cookies to wire racks to cool, about 30 minutes. Store macaroons in tightly covered container. Makes about 2½ dozen.

TUNNELS OF FUDGE

½ 14-ounce can sweetened condensed milk (⅔ cup)
2 squares unsweetened chocolate
½ cup unsalted peanuts, finely chopped
2¼ cups all-purpose flour
1 cup sugar
½ cup shortening
1 teaspoon baking powder
1 teaspoon vanilla extract
½ teaspoon salt
2 eggs

About 5 hours before serving or up to 3 days ahead:

1. In double boiler over boiling water, cook condensed milk and unsweetened chocolate until mixture is smooth and very thick, about 10 minutes, stirring frequently. Remove double-boiler top from heat; stir in peanuts. Refrigerate fudge mixture about 2½ hours or until well chilled and easy to handle.

2. Meanwhile, into large bowl, measure flour and remaining ingredients. With mixer at low speed, beat until well mixed, frequently scraping bowl with rubber spatula. Shape mixture into a ball; wrap with plastic wrap and refrigerate 2 to 3 hours until easy to handle.

3. Preheat oven to 375°F. Lightly grease 2 large cookie sheets. Divide fudge mixture into 4 equal portions; with hands, roll each into a 12-inch-long rope; set aside. On lightly floured surface with floured rolling pin, roll one-fourth of dough into 12" by 5" rectangle. Place a fudge rope on top of dough along one 12-inch side. Roll dough and rope jelly-roll fashion to encase fudge in dough. Place roll, seam-side down, on cookie sheet; repeat with remaining dough and fudge ropes. Bake rolls 15 minutes or until golden. Remove rolls to wooden board; cut each diagonally into ½-inch-thick slices; cool on wire racks. Makes about 8 dozen.

PEANUT REFRIGERATOR COOKIES

1   cup unsalted peanuts
2   cups all-purpose flour
1   cup butter or margarine, softened
¾   cup packed light brown sugar
½   teaspoon vanilla extract
¼   teaspoon salt
¼   teaspoon baking soda
1   egg

About 4 hours before serving or up to 1 week ahead:

1. In blender at medium speed or in food processor with knife blade attached, blend ¾ cup peanuts, a few portions at a time until coarsely ground. Reserve remaining peanuts for garnish later.

2. Into large bowl, measure flour and remaining ingredients. With mixer at low speed, beat ingredients until well blended, occasionally scraping bowl with rubber spatula. With spoon, stir in ground peanuts until well mixed. With hands, on waxed paper, roll dough into three 5-inch-long rolls. Flatten each roll slightly to shape into a rectangle; wrap in waxed paper; refrigerate about 2 hours or up to 1 week.

3. To bake, preheat oven to 350°F. Grease 2 large cookie sheets. Slice rolls crosswise into ¼-inch-thick slices. Place slices, ½ inch apart, on cookie sheets; press a reserved peanut into top of each cookie. Bake 8 to 10 minutes until lightly browned. With pancake turner, remove cookies to wire racks to cool. Repeat with remaining dough and peanuts. Store cookies in tightly covered container. Makes about 5 dozen.

BONBON COOKIES

1¾   cups all-purpose flour
½   cup confectioners' sugar
½   cup butter or margarine
2   tablespoons milk
½   teaspoon almond extract
⅛   teaspoon salt
1   6-ounce package semisweet-chocolate pieces
     Almond Glaze
2   tablespoons light corn syrup

About 3½ hours before serving or up to 3 days ahead:

1. In medium bowl with hand, knead first 6 ingredients until mixed.

2. Preheat oven to 350°F. Reserve 3 tablespoons semisweet-chocolate pieces for garnish later. With hands, shape about 2 rounded teaspoonfuls cookie dough around about 6 semisweet-chocolate pieces; roll into a ball. Place cookie on ungreased cookie sheet, pressing gently to flatten bottom of cookie and shaping dough with fingers into rounded peaks. Repeat with remaining dough and chocolate pieces, placing cookies 1 inch apart on cookie sheet. Bake 15 minutes or until cookies are set, but not brown. (Cookies become firm when cool.) Remove cookies to wire rack to cool, about 1 hour.

3. When cookies are cool, prepare Almond Glaze. Dip cookies into glaze; let dry on wire rack over waxed paper, about 30 minutes.

4. In heavy small saucepan over low heat, heat corn syrup and reserved chocolate pieces until chocolate melts. With spoon, drizzle mixture over glaze on cookies; allow to dry, about 15 minutes. Store cookies in tightly covered container. Makes about 2 dozen.

Almond Glaze

In small bowl with spoon, stir 2¼ cups confectioners' sugar, 3 tablespoons water, 2 tablespoons light corn syrup, 1½ teaspoons salad oil, ¾ teaspoon almond extract and 3 to 4 drops red food color until smooth.

FRESH APPLE CHEWS

2   cups all-purpose flour
¾   cup packed brown sugar
½   cup butter or margarine, softened
3   tablespoons water
1¼   teaspoons ground cinnamon
1   teaspoon baking soda
½   teaspoon salt
1   egg
1   cup California walnuts, chopped
1   cup currants or dark seedless raisins
1   medium apple, peeled, cored, and finely chopped
     about 15 green candied cherries, each cut in half

About 2 hours before serving or up to 1 week ahead:

1. Preheat oven to 375°F. Grease large cookie sheet.

2. Into large bowl, measure first 8 ingredients. With mixer at low speed, beat ingredients until well blended, occasionally scraping bowl with rubber spatula. With spoon, stir in nuts, currants, and apple until well mixed.

3. Drop dough by heaping tablespoonfuls, about 2 inches apart, onto cookie sheet. With back of spoon, spread each cookie into a 3-inch round; place a candied green-cherry half in center of each. Bake 15 to 20 minutes or until lightly browned. Remove cookies to wire racks to cool. Repeat until all dough is used, greasing cookie sheet each time. Store cookies in tightly covered container. Makes about 2½ dozen.

PRALINE THINS

1   6-ounce can or bag pecan halves
4   tablespoons butter or margarine
1¼   cups packed light brown sugar
⅓   cup all-purpose flour
1   teaspoon maple extract
¼   teaspoon salt
1   egg

About 2 hours before serving or up to 3 days ahead:

1. Line large cookie sheet with foil. Reserve 24 pecan halves; chop remaining pecans.

2. Preheat oven to 350°F. In 2-quart saucepan over low heat, melt butter or margarine; remove saucepan from heat; stir in brown sugar and remaining ingredients until well blended; stir in chopped pecans. Drop mixture by tablespoonfuls, 3 inches apart onto cookie sheet; press a reserved pecan half into top of each. Bake 12 minutes. Slide foil with cookies onto wire rack to cool completely.

3. Meanwhile, reline cookie sheet with foil and repeat with remaining mixture and pecan halves. When cookies are cooled, gently peel away foil. Store cookies in tightly covered container. Makes about 2 dozen.

RAINBOW RIBBONS

3½ cups all-purpose flour
1 cup sugar
1 cup butter or margarine, softened
1 teaspoon vanilla extract
½ teaspoon salt
2 eggs
1 teaspoon instant espresso coffee powder
2 teaspoons hot tap water
2 tablespoons cocoa
½ teaspoon anise extract
green food color
red food color

About 4 hours before serving or up to 1 week ahead:

1. Into large bowl, measure first 6 ingredients. With mixer at low speed, beat ingredients until well blended, occasionally scraping bowl with rubber spatula. Divide dough into thirds; place each in a bowl.

2. In cup, stir instant espresso and water until espresso is dissolved. Stir espresso mixture and cocoa into one-third of dough; with hand, knead until well blended. To second third of dough, add anise extract and enough green food color to tint dough a pretty green color; with hand, knead until well blended. To remaining dough, add enough red food color to tint dough a pretty pink color; with hand, knead until well blended. Shape each

dough into a ball; wrap each with plastic wrap and refrigerate 1 hour or until firm enough to handle. (Or, place dough in freezer 30 minutes.)

3. On sheet of waxed paper with floured rolling pin, roll pink dough into 12″ by 7½″ rectangle. On another sheet of waxed paper, roll chocolate dough into 12″ by 7½″ rectangle. On another sheet of waxed paper, roll green dough into 12″ by 7½″ rectangle. Invert chocolate dough onto pink dough; invert green dough onto chocolate dough.

4. Fold dough into thirds: Starting from one 12-inch side, fold one-third of dough over middle one-third; fold opposite one-third over both to make 12″ by 2½″ rectangle. Wrap dough in plastic wrap and refrigerate 1 hour or until firm enough to slice. (Or, place dough in freezer 30 minutes.)

5. Preheat oven to 400°F. Cut dough crosswise into ¼-inch-thick slices. Place slices, cut-side down, on ungreased cookie sheets, about 1 inch apart. Bake cookies 10 minutes or until very lightly browned around edges. With pancake turner, remove cookies to wire racks to cool. Store cookies in tightly covered container to use up within 1 week. Makes about 4 dozen cookies.

BLACK FOREST COOKIES

1 8-ounce package semisweet-chocolate squares
1 16-ounce can pitted dark sweet cherries in light syrup
2¾ cups all-purpose flour
shortening
¾ cup sugar
¾ cup milk
1 tablespoon lemon juice
½ teaspoon baking soda
½ teaspoon salt
½ teaspoon almond extract

About 3 hours before serving or up to 3 days ahead:

1. Grease large cookie sheets. In heavy small saucepan over low heat, heat 2 squares semisweet chocolate until melted and smooth, stirring occasionally. Remove saucepan from heat. With knife, coarsely chop 4 squares of chocolate; set aside.

2. Drain cherries, reserving ¼ cup cherry liquid; coarsely chop cherries. Pat cherries dry with paper towel.

3. Preheat oven to 400°F. Into large bowl, measure melted chocolate, reserved cherry liquid, flour, ½ cup shortening, and remaining ingredients. With mixer at low speed, beat ingredients until blended, occasionally scraping bowl with rubber spatula. Stir in cherries and chopped chocolate.

4. Drop dough by level tablespoonfuls, as many as possible, about 2 inches apart, on cookie sheet. Bake cookies 10 to 12 minutes until lightly browned. With pancake turner, remove cookies to wire racks to cool. Repeat with remaining dough.

5. When cookies are cooled, in small saucepan over low heat, heat 1 teaspoon shortening and remaining 2 squares of chocolate until melted and smooth, stirring occasionally. With spoon, drizzle chocolate mixture over cookies. Let chocolate dry about 30 minutes or until firm. Store cookies in tightly covered container in refrigerator to use up within 3 days. Makes about 5 dozen cookies.

PEANUT-CHOCOLATE CRESCENTS

½   cup salted peanuts, ground
1   cup all-purpose flour
½   cup creamy peanut butter
¼   cup confectioners' sugar
1   teaspoon vanilla extract
*   butter or margarine, softened*
3   squares semisweet chocolate
1   tablespoon milk
1   tablespoon light corn syrup

About 3 hours before serving or up to 1 week ahead:

1. Reserve 3 tablespoons ground peanuts for garnish. In large bowl with hand, mix flour, peanut butter, confectioners' sugar, vanilla, 4 tablespoons butter or margarine and remaining ground peanuts until well blended.

2. Preheat oven to 325°F. With hands, shape 1 teaspoonful cookie dough at a time into a 1½-inch crescent. Place cookies on ungreased cookie sheets, about 1 inch apart. Bake cookies 15 minutes or until golden. Remove cookies to wire racks to cool.

3. When cookies are cool, in 1-quart saucepan over low heat, heat chocolate, milk, corn syrup, and 1 tablespoon butter or margarine until melted and smooth, stirring occasionally; remove saucepan from heat. Dip one end of each cookie into melted chocolate mixture to cover half of cookie. Place cookies on wire rack over sheet of waxed paper; sprinkle chocolate lightly with reserved ground peanuts. Let dry. Store cookies in tightly covered container to use up within 1 week. Makes about 5 dozen cookies.

CANDY TOPS

2¾   cups all-purpose flour
1   cup packed brown sugar
1   cup chunky peanut butter
1   cup butter or margarine, softened
¾   cup sugar
1½   teaspoons baking soda
1   teaspoon salt
1   teaspoon vanilla extract
2   eggs
1   8-ounce package nonmelting chocolate-covered candies

About 2 hours before serving or up to 1 week ahead:

1. Preheat oven to 350°F. Into large bowl, measure all ingredients except candies. With mixer at low speed, beat ingredients until well blended, occasionally scraping bowl with rubber spatula.

2. Shape dough into 1-inch balls. Place balls, about 2 inches apart, on ungreased large cookie sheets. Bake cookies 12 minutes or until lightly browned. Remove cookie sheets from oven; quickly press 3 or 4 candies into top of each cookie. Return to oven and bake 3 minutes longer.

3. With pancake turner, carefully remove cookies to wire racks to cool. Store cookies in tightly covered container to use up within 1 week. Makes about 7 dozen cookies.

MINT TRIANGLES

3   cups all-purpose flour
1½   cups confectioners' sugar
1   cup butter or margarine, softened
1   teaspoon vanilla extract
¼   teaspoon salt
¾   5½-ounce box chocolate-covered mints (48 ¾-inch round mints)

About 2 hours before serving or up to 3 days ahead:

1. Into large bowl, measure all ingredients except mints. With hand, knead ingredients until well blended and mixture holds together.

2. Preheat oven to 350°F. With hands, shape dough into 48 balls. Flatten and pinch each ball to form triangle with all sides measuring 1½ inches. With thumb or tip of spoon, make small indentation in center of each triangle. Place triangles, about 2 inches apart, on ungreased large cookie sheet.

3. Bake cookies 10 minutes or until lightly browned. Remove cookie sheet from oven. Quickly press a chocolate-covered mint into the center of each cookie. Return to oven and bake cookies 2 to 3 minutes longer until mints are slightly melted. With pancake turner, remove cookies to wire racks to cool. Store cookies in tightly covered container to use up within 3 days. Makes 4 dozen cookies.

PIGNOLIA CRESCENTS

1½   cups pine nuts (pignolias), about 9
        ounces
1¾   cups all-purpose flour
¾   cup butter or margarine, softened
½   cup confectioners' sugar
1½   teaspoons vanilla extract
¼   teaspoon salt
1   egg white, beaten

About 1½ hours before serving or up to 1
week ahead:

1. In blender at medium speed or in food
processor with knife blade attached, blend
¾ cup pine nuts until finely ground; place
in large bowl. Reserve remaining pine nuts
for tops of cookies.

2. Into bowl with ground nuts, measure
flour, butter or margarine, sugar, vanilla,
and salt; with hand, knead mixture until
well blended and holds together.

3. Preheat oven to 350°F. With hands,
shape 1 rounded teaspoonful dough at a
time into 2-inch crescent. Place crescents,
about 1 inch apart, onto ungreased cookie
sheets. With pastry brush, lightly brush
crescents with egg white. Gently press remaining pine nuts into crescents. Bake
cookies 15 minutes or until lightly
browned. Remove cookies to wire racks to
cool. Store cookies in tightly covered containers to use up within 1 week. Makes
about 4 dozen cookies.

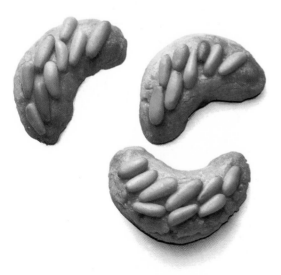

MAPLE WALNUT WREATHS

1   cup sugar
¾   cup butter or margarine, softened
1   tablespoon baking powder
½   teaspoon salt
½   teaspoon maple extract
2   eggs
2½   cups all-purpose flour
½   cup California walnuts, finely
        ground
        green food color
15   red candied cherries

About 3 hours before serving or up to 1
week ahead:

1. Into large bowl, measure sugar, butter
or margarine, baking powder, salt, maple
extract, eggs, and 2 cups flour. With mixer
at low speed, beat ingredients until well
blended, occasionally scraping bowl with
rubber spatula. With wooden spoon, stir
in walnuts and remaining ½ cup flour until
mixture is smooth. Set aside half of dough.
Into dough remaining in bowl, stir a few
drops green food color to tint a pretty
green color. Wrap both doughs with plastic wrap and refrigerate 1 hour or until
doughs are firm enough to handle. (Or,
place dough in freezer 30 minutes.)

2. Preheat oven to 350°F. On lightly
floured surface with hands, roll 2 teaspoonfuls plain dough into 5-inch-long
rope. Repeat, using 2 teaspoonfuls green
dough. Place ropes side by side and gently
twist together. Shape twisted ropes into a
circle, joining ends together to resemble a
wreath. With pancake turner, place cookie
wreath on ungreased large cookie sheets.
Repeat with remaining dough, placing
cookies about 2 inches apart.

3. Cut each candied cherry into 6 slivers.
Arrange 3 slivers on each cookie wreath.
Bake cookies 15 to 18 minutes until lightly
browned. With pancake turner, remove
cookies to wire racks to cool. Store cookies
in tightly covered container to use up
within 1 week. Makes about 2½ dozen
cookies.

TOFFEE BARS

1¾   cups all-purpose flour
1   cup sugar
1   cup butter or margarine, softened
1   teaspoon vanilla extract
1   egg, separated
½   cup California walnuts, finely
        chopped

About 2 hours before serving or up to 1
week ahead:

1. Preheat oven to 275°F. Grease 15½" by
10½" jelly-roll pan. Into large bowl, measure all ingredients except egg white and
walnuts. With mixer at low speed, beat ingredients just until blended, occasionally
scraping bowl with rubber spatula. Increase speed to medium; beat until well
mixed. Pat dough evenly into prepared
pan.

2. In cup with fork, beat egg white slightly;
brush over top of dough and sprinkle with
nuts.

3. Bake 1 hour and 10 minutes or until
golden. Immediately cut lengthwise into 4
strips, then cut each strip crosswise into 12
pieces to make 48 bars in all. Remove bars
from pan to cool on wire racks. Store
cookies in tightly covered container to use
up within 1 week. Makes 4 dozen cookies.

CHRISTMAS TREE COOKIES

2½   cups all-purpose flour
1   cup sugar
1   cup butter or margarine, softened
1½   teaspoons baking powder
½   teaspoon salt
½   teaspoon almond extract
1   egg
       about ¼ cup green sugar crystals
1   1.5-ounce container confetti décors

About 3½ hours before serving or up to 1 week ahead:

1. Into large bowl, measure first 7 ingredients. With mixer at low speed, beat ingredients until blended, occasionally scraping bowl with rubber spatula. (Dough may be crumbly.) With hands, knead dough until mixture holds together. Reserve ⅓ cup dough; wrap in plastic wrap and refrigerate. With hands, roll remaining dough into three 6-inch-long rolls.

2. Place sugar crystals on waxed paper. Roll each roll in sugar crystals to coat well. Form each roll into a triangle-shaped log by gently pressing roll to flatten bottom, then pressing sides of log together into a point. Wrap each log in plastic wrap and refrigerate 2 hours or until dough is firm enough to slice. (Dough can be refrigerated up to 1 week before baking.)

3. To bake, preheat oven to 350°F. Slice one log crosswise into ¼-inch-thick slices. Place slices, about 1 inch apart, on ungreased cookie sheet. For each cookie, shape ¼ teaspoon reserved dough to resemble tree trunk; attach to bottom side of slice. Sprinkle each cookie lightly with some confetti décors. Bake cookies 10 to 12 minutes until lightly browned. With pancake turner, remove cookies to wire racks to cool. Repeat with remaining logs and confetti décors. Makes about 6 dozen cookies.

RICH LITTLE TEA COOKIES

1   cup all-purpose flour
½   cup butter or margarine, softened
¼   cup sugar
¼   teaspoon vanilla extract
⅛   teaspoon salt

About 3 hours before serving or up to 1 week ahead:

1. In large bowl with mixer at low speed, beat flour, butter or margarine, sugar, vanilla, and salt until well blended, occasionally scraping bowl with rubber spatula.

2. Preheat oven to 350°F. On lightly floured surface with floured hands, shape dough into 1½" by ½" pieces, each using about 1 teaspoonful of dough. Place cookies on ungreased large cookie sheets. With side of fork or dull edge of knife, mark each cookie crosswise several times.

3. Bake cookies 10 to 15 minutes until lightly golden. Cool cookies 5 minutes on cookie sheet; then with metal spatula, gently remove cookies to wire racks to cool. Makes about 4 dozen cookies.

COCONUT WREATHS

1¾   cups all-purpose flour
½   cup sugar
½   cup butter or margarine, softened
1   3½-ounce can shredded coconut
1   egg
       red and green candied cherries for
       garnish

About 2 hours before serving or up to 1 week ahead:

1. Into large bowl, measure first 5 ingredients. With mixer at low speed, beat ingredients until well blended, occasionally scraping bowl with rubber spatula. On lightly floured surface with floured rolling pin, roll one-third of dough at a time, ¼ inch thick. With floured 2½-inch doughnut cutter, cut dough into rings. (If necessary, trim excess coconut from edges of rings.)

2. Preheat oven to 375°F. Lightly grease large cookie sheet. Place rings, about 1 inch apart, on cookie sheet. Cut candied cherries into pieces resembling flower petals. Press 3 petals on each cookie wreath to resemble a flower.

3. Bake cookies 10 minutes or until golden. Remove cookies to wire racks to cool. Repeat with remaining dough, trimmings, and cherries. Store cookies in tightly covered container to use up within 1 week. Makes about 2 dozen cookies.

PECAN CRUNCH

2 cups all-purpose flour
1 cup packed light brown sugar
1 cup butter or margarine, softened
1 teaspoon vanilla extract
1 egg
1 6-ounce package semisweet-chocolate pieces
1½ cups pecans, toasted and finely chopped

About 2 hours before serving or up to 1 week ahead:

1. Into large bowl, measure first 5 ingredients. With hand, knead ingredients until blended and mixture holds together.

2. Preheat oven to 350°F. Pat dough evenly into 15½″ by 10½″ jelly-roll pan. Bake 25 minutes or until golden.

3. Meanwhile, in heavy small saucepan over low heat, melt chocolate pieces, stirring frequently. Set aside.

4. Remove jelly-roll pan from oven; pour chocolate over baked layer in pan. With metal spatula, evenly spread chocolate over baked layer; sprinkle with pecans. Cool in pan on wire rack. When cool, cut lengthwise into 6 strips, then cut each strip crosswise into 12 pieces to make 72 bars in all. Store cookies in tightly covered container to use up within 1 week. Makes 6 dozen bars.

SNOW FLOWERS

2½ cups all-purpose flour
1 cup butter or margarine, softened
½ cup sugar
1 teaspoon vanilla extract
3 egg yolks

About 3 hours before serving or up to 1 week ahead:

1. In large bowl with mixer at low speed, beat all ingredients until well mixed, occasionally scraping bowl with rubber spatula. Shape dough into a ball; wrap with plastic wrap and refrigerate 2 hours or until dough is firm enough to handle. (Or, place dough in freezer 40 minutes.)

2. Preheat oven to 375°F. On lightly floured surface with floured rolling pin, roll half of dough ¼ inch thick, keeping remaining dough refrigerated. With floured 1¾-inch flower-shaped cookie cutter, cut dough into as many flowers as possible. Place cookies on ungreased large cookie sheet, about 1 inch apart.

3. Bake cookies 8 to 10 minutes until lightly browned. Remove cookies to wire racks to cool. Repeat with remaining dough and trimmings. Store cookies in tightly covered container to use up within 1 week. Makes about 4 dozen cookies.

SUNBURSTS

¾ cup butter or margarine, softened
½ cup sugar
2 cups all-purpose flour
1 teaspoon vanilla extract
¼ teaspoon salt
2 eggs
about ½ cup apricot preserves

About 1½ hours before serving or up to 1 week ahead:

1. In large bowl with mixer at high speed, beat butter or margarine and sugar until light and fluffy.

2. Reduce speed to low; add flour, vanilla, salt, and eggs. Beat ingredients until well mixed, occasionally scraping bowl with rubber spatula.

3. Preheat oven to 400°F. Spoon half of dough into decorating bag with large rosette tube. Onto ungreased cookie sheet, pipe dough into as many 1½-inch rosettes as possible, about 1 inch apart. Press thumb into center of each rosette to make a ¼-inch-deep indentation. Bake cookies 6 to 8 minutes until golden. With pancake turner, carefully remove cookies to wire racks to cool. Repeat until all dough is used.

4. Store cookies in tightly covered container to use up within 1 week. Just before serving, spoon some apricot preserves into indentation in center of each cookie. Makes about 4½ dozen cookies.

MOLASSES SPIRALS

1⅔ cups all-purpose flour
⅓   cup sugar
⅓   cup shortening
⅓   cup molasses
2   tablespoons cider vinegar
½   teaspoon baking soda
¼   teaspoon ground cinnamon
¼   teaspoon ground ginger
⅛   teaspoon ground allspice
⅛   teaspoon salt
1   egg

About 2 hours before serving or up to 1 week ahead:

1. Into large bowl, measure all ingredients. With mixer at low speed, beat until well blended, occasionally scraping bowl with rubber spatula.

2. Preheat oven to 350°F. Grease large cookie sheets. Spoon dough into decorating bag with ¼-inch writing tube. For each cookie, pipe some dough in a continuous spiral beginning with a 2-inch circle and narrowing the spiral to a point in the center. Pipe cookies, about 2 inches apart, onto cookie sheet.

3. Bake cookies 8 to 10 minutes until golden brown. With pancake turner, remove cookies to wire racks to cool. Store cookies in tightly covered container to use up within 1 week. Makes about 3 dozen cookies.

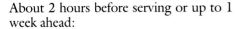

ALMOND LACE ROLLS

⅔   cup blanched slivered or whole
    almonds, finely ground
½   cup sugar
½   cup butter
1   tablespoon all-purpose flour
2   tablespoons milk

About 1½ hours before serving or up to 3 days ahead:

1. Preheat oven to 350°F. Grease and flour large cookie sheet. Into 10-inch skillet, measure all ingredients (do not use margarine because it separates from sugar during cooking). Cook over low heat, stirring, until butter is melted and mixture is blended. Keep mixture warm over very low heat.

2. Drop 1 heaping teaspoonful mixture onto cookie sheet. Repeat to make 3 more cookies, about 2 inches apart. (Do not place more than 4 on cookie sheet because, after baking, cookies must be shaped quickly before hardening.) Bake 5 minutes or until golden.

3. Remove cookie sheet from oven; let cool about 1 minute to let cookies set slightly. Then, with pancake turner, quickly loosen and turn cookies over, one by one, and roll around handle of wooden spoon. (If cookies get too hard to roll, reheat in oven a minute to soften.) Cool cookies on wire racks. Repeat until all batter is used, greasing and flouring cookie sheet each time. Store cookies in tightly covered container to use up within 3 days. Makes about 2½ dozen cookies.

ROCKY ROAD

1¼ cups all-purpose flour
½   cup butter or margarine, softened
¼   cup packed light brown sugar
1   teaspoon vanilla extract
½   teaspoon baking soda
¼   teaspoon salt
1   egg
½   cup California walnuts, chopped
½   cup dark seedless raisins
½   cup butterscotch-flavor pieces
½   cup milk-chocolate pieces
    about ½ cup miniature marshmallows

About 2½ hours before serving or up to 1 week ahead:

1. Into large bowl, measure first 7 ingredients. With mixer at low speed, beat ingredients until well blended, occasionally scraping bowl with rubber spatula. Stir in walnuts, raisins, butterscotch-flavor pieces, and milk-chocolate pieces.

2. Preheat oven to 375°F. Grease large cookie sheets. Drop mixture by heaping tablespoonfuls, about 2 inches apart, onto cookie sheets. Bake cookies 10 minutes.

3. Remove cookie sheet from oven; lightly press two or three marshmallows into center of each cookie.

4. Bake cookies 2 minutes longer or until cookies are golden and marshmallows are very slightly melted and stick to cookies. Remove cookies to wire racks to cool. Store cookies in tightly covered container to use up within 1 week. Makes about 2 dozen cookies.

ANISE OVALS

2 cups all-purpose flour
⅔ cup sugar
⅔ cup shortening
2 teaspoons anise seeds, crushed
2 teaspoons baking powder
2 eggs

About 2 hours before serving or up to 1 week ahead:

1. Into large bowl, measure all ingredients. With mixer at low speed, beat ingredients until well blended, occasionally scraping bowl with rubber spatula.

2. Preheat oven to 350°F. Shape 2 teaspoonfuls dough at a time into 2-inch-long ovals. Place cookies, about 1 inch apart, on ungreased cookie sheets. Bake cookies 15 minutes or until very lightly browned. Remove cookies to wire racks to cool. Store cookies in tightly covered container to use up within 1 week. Makes about 4 dozen cookies.

PRETZEL COOKIES

3 cups all-purpose flour
1 cup butter or margarine, softened
½ cup confectioners' sugar
1 tablespoon baking powder
1 teaspoon vanilla extract
¼ teaspoon salt
2 eggs
1 1.75-ounce container chocolate décors

About 1½ hours before serving or up to 1 week ahead:

1. Into large bowl, measure first 6 ingredients, 1 egg, and 1 egg yolk (reserve remaining egg white for brushing on cookies later). With mixer at low speed, beat ingredients until well blended, occasionally scraping bowl with rubber spatula. Stir in chocolate décors.

2. Preheat oven to 400°F. With hands, roll 2 level tablespoonfuls mixture into a 12-inch-long rope. Shape rope into loop-shaped pretzel. Repeat with remaining dough. Place pretzels, about 1 inch apart, on ungreased large cookie sheets. Brush pretzels with reserved egg white.

3. Bake pretzel cookies 10 to 12 minutes until golden. With pancake turner, carefully remove pretzel cookies to wire racks to cool. Store cookies in tightly covered container to use up within 1 week. Makes about 1½ dozen cookies.

DATE-NUT CHRISTMAS ROCK COOKIES

2 cups all-purpose flour
½ cup sugar
½ cup butter or margarine, softened
1 teaspoon ground cinnamon
1 teaspoon baking soda
¼ teaspoon ground cloves
3 eggs
1½ cups California walnuts, chopped
1 10-ounce container pitted dates, chopped
   about 15 green candied cherries, each cut in half
   about 15 red candied cherries, each cut in half

About 1½ hours before serving or up to 1 week ahead:

1. Preheat oven to 375°F. Into large bowl, measure first 7 ingredients. With mixer at low speed, beat ingredients until well blended, occasionally scraping bowl with rubber spatula. With spoon, stir in walnuts and dates.

2. Drop dough by tablespoonfuls, about 1½ inches apart, onto ungreased cookie sheets. Place a green and red cherry half on top of each cookie, pressing gently into center of cookie. Bake cookies 10 minutes or until golden. With metal spatula, remove cookies to wire racks to cool. Store cookies in tightly covered container to use up within 1 week. Makes about 2½ dozen cookies.

MAPLE WALNUT CUPS

1   cup all-purpose flour
    butter or margarine, softened
    sugar
¼   cup dark corn syrup
¼   teaspoon maple extract
1   egg
½   cup California walnuts, finely
    chopped

About 1½ hours before serving or up to 3 days ahead:

1. Preheat oven to 350°F. In medium bowl with hand, knead flour, 6 tablespoons butter or margarine and ¼ cup sugar until well blended. Divide dough into 16 pieces. Press dough pieces into bottoms and up sides of sixteen 1¾-inch muffin-pan cups.

2. In 1-quart saucepan over low heat, melt 1 tablespoon butter. Remove from heat; stir in corn syrup, maple extract, egg, and 1 tablespoon sugar.

3. Sprinkle chopped walnuts evenly into each pastry cup; spoon syrup mixture on top. Bake 20 to 25 minutes until crust is lightly browned and toothpick inserted in center comes out clean.

4. Cool cookie cups in pans on wire racks about 5 minutes or until firm. With tip of knife or small metal spatula, loosen cookie cups from muffin-pan cups and place on wire racks to cool completely. Store in refrigerator to use up within 3 days. Makes 16 cookie cups.

SPRITZ

This famous cookie is so named because the buttery dough is "spritzed" through a cookie press into a long narrow strip, cut into cookies after baking.

3   cups all-purpose flour
1½   cups butter or margarine, softened
¾   cup sugar
¼   cup orange juice
1   egg

About 2 hours before serving or up to 1 week ahead:

1. Into large bowl, measure all ingredients. With mixer at low speed, beat ingredients until well mixed, occasionally scraping bowl with rubber spatula.

2. Preheat oven to 375°F. Using part of dough at a time and bar-plate tip, press in long strips, about 1 inch apart, down length of ungreased cookie sheet.

3. Bake cookies 8 minutes or until light golden, being careful not to overbake. Immediately cut each strip crosswise into 2½-inch cookies. With pancake turner, immediately remove cookies to wire racks to cool. Repeat with remaining dough. Store cookies in tightly covered container to use up within 1 week. Makes about 9 dozen cookies.

MACADAMIA MELTAWAYS

2   7½-ounce jars macadamia nuts
2   cups all-purpose flour
1   cup butter or margarine, softened
¼   cup confectioners' sugar
1   teaspoon almond extract

About 2 hours before serving or up to 1 week ahead:

1. In blender at medium speed or in food processor with knife blade attached, blend 1 cup macadamia nuts until finely ground; place in large bowl. Reserve remaining nuts for tops of cookies.

2. Into bowl with ground nuts, measure flour, butter or margarine, confectioners' sugar, and almond extract; with hand, knead until mixture is well blended and holds together.

3. Preheat oven to 350°F. With hands, shape scant tablespoonfuls dough into balls. Place balls about 1 inch apart on ungreased cookie sheets. Press a reserved macadamia nut into top of each ball. Bake cookies 12 to 15 minutes until lightly browned. Remove cookies to wire racks to cool. Store cookies in tightly covered container to use up within 1 week. Makes about 5 dozen cookies.

CHRISTMAS COTTAGE

2   batches gingerbread
3   batches Ornamental Icing
    red food color
    cocoa
    decorations:
4   peppermint sticks
4   or 5 small candy canes
2   packages assorted-flavor Life Savers
1   package peppermint-stick Life Savers
2   16-ounce packages round peppermint
      candies
    silver dragées
    cinnamon red-hot candies
    heavy cardboard, 15" by 15" for base

1. **Enlarge diagrams and cut patterns** from lightweight cardboard. In addition to pieces given in diagrams you will need: top of step, 4½" by 1½"; side of step, 1⅜" by ½" (cut 2); front of step, 4½" by ½"; porch floor, 7½" by 3"; porch front, 7½" by 1"; porch side, 2⅞" by 1" (cut 2); back of house, 12" by 6"; roof of shed, 2½" by 2¾"; front of shed, 2" by 3½"; side of chimney, two pieces 8½" by ¾", two pieces 1½" by ¾", and two pieces 5" by ¾"; 12" by 13" for floor of balcony.

2. **Make two batches gingerbread.**

3. Line four 17" by 14" cookie sheets and four 15½" by 12" cookie sheets with foil, moistening surface under foil to prevent sliding. Place 3 cups dough on each larger sheet. With damp cloth under sheet, to prevent sliding, roll out dough on each sheet to 16" by 14". Roll out 2⅓ cups dough to 14" by 11" on each of the smaller sheets.

4. Refrigerate 30 minutes. (If you don't have the 8 cookie sheets needed, roll out dough to size on foil and slide foil onto tray or large piece of cardboard to refrigerate, then slide foil onto cookie sheet for baking. Cookie sheets of rolled dough can be

Christmas Cottage, irresistible gingerbread house, straight out of a fairy tale, with second-story porch, child's-dream peppermint roof. On one side, a "stone" chimney pokes up; on the other a lean-to holds logs for the Christmas hearth.

stacked in the refrigerator.)

5. Dust all patterns **except doors and windows,** with flour. Remove dough from refrigerator and arrange patterns, leaving ½" between each. With sharp, pointed paring knife, carefully cut out each piece. Carefully remove patterns and all excess dough (reserve for use later). Bake in 350°F. oven 12 to 15 minutes or until cookies are set and lightly browned. Cool completely before removing from foil.

6. **To make stained-glass doors, windows:** Put three to four Life Savers of one color in small plastic bag and crush with rolling pin; repeat with two other colors. Bake gingerbread doors and windows on foil-lined cookie sheet for five minutes, or until set. Then sprinkle cut-out areas with crushed candies, two or three colors in each cut-out. Brush off excess. Bake 3 minutes or until candy melts. Let cool before removing from foil.

7. **To assemble house:** Following Construction Tips, attach front, side, and back pieces of house on heavy 15" by 15" cardboard. Rest 12" by 13" balcony floor across front and back so 12-inch-wide front extends about 2½" beyond front wall to create floor for balcony (see photo).

Attach porch pieces and step pieces; frost in place. Frost shed pieces together and frost in place. Frost chimney pieces together and frost in place.

Attach front and back roofs with frosting, propping them up under sides of eaves to keep them from slipping as they dry. Then attach balcony sides, back walls of balcony, and balcony doors (opened out slightly). Let dry.

8. **To decorate with icing:** With light pink icing, using medium writing tube and following photo, pipe on horizontal lines to simulate logs. Pipe on chimney "stones."

Attach front door and window with icing.

Cover roof and shed roof with white icing and, before it dries, press on peppermint candies. Using medium rosette tube, pipe on rosette of white icing between each candy. Make small rosette on each candy; place silver dragée on center.

Pipe on rosettes along ridge of roof and line with cinnamon red-hot candies.

With brown icing (made with cocoa and white icing), pipe medium rosettes along edges of house, chimney, shed, and balcony, smaller rosettes along steps.

Attach candy-cane porch posts; decorate with white frosting at base of each. Cut small candy canes to make balcony railing, with 2 peppermint Life Savers as base of each post; decorate with icing, silver dragées. Cover base with white-icing "snow."

GINGERBREAD

9   cups all-purpose flour
1   tablespoon grated lemon peel
2   teaspoons ground ginger
½   teaspoon salt
2   cups light corn syrup
1½ cups packed light brown sugar
1¼ cups butter or margarine

1. In large bowl, combine flour, lemon peel, ginger, and salt. In 3-quart saucepan, stir together corn syrup, brown sugar, and butter or margarine. Stirring constantly, cook over medium heat until butter or margarine is melted. Stir into flour mixture until well blended.

ORNAMENTAL ICING

1   16-ounce package confectioners' sugar
½   teaspoon cream of tartar
3   egg whites at room temperature
½   teaspoon vanilla extract

Combine all ingredients in medium-size bowl. With mixer, blend until smooth, then beat at high speed until very stiff and knife drawn through mixture leaves a clean-cut path. Makes 2 cups. **Note:** Because the icing dries very quickly, make each batch just before you are ready to use it. If you must store for a few hours or overnight, cover tightly with plastic wrap. When using, keep container covered with damp cloth or paper towel. Mix in food colors as needed. If icing is too thick when using fine tubes, add a few drops of water. For thicker icing, beat in some extra confectioners' sugar.

Diagrams and **Constructions Tips** on page 130.

GINGERBREAD
BOYS & GIRLS

1	cup butter or margarine, softened
2/3	cup packed brown sugar
1/2	cup light molasses
1	egg
3½	cups all-purpose flour
1	teaspoon salt
1	teaspoon baking powder
1	teaspoon ground ginger
1	teaspoon ground allspice
1	teaspoon ground cinnamon
1	teaspoon ground cloves
	Frosting "Paint"

Up to 1 week ahead:

1. In large bowl with mixer at low speed, beat butter or margarine, brown sugar, and molasses until light and fluffy. Add egg and remaining ingredients except Frosting "Paint"; beat at low speed until well mixed, constantly scraping bowl with rubber spatula. Shape dough into a ball; wrap dough with plastic wrap or waxed paper and refrigerate 3 to 4 hours until firm.

2. Preheat oven to 350°F. Lightly grease 2 large cookie sheets. Cut dough in half. On lightly floured surface with lightly floured rolling pin, roll one half of dough ¼ inch thick (keep remaining dough refrigerated). With 8-inch-long gingerbread-boy cookie cutter, cut as many cookies as possible; reserve trimmings.

3. With pancake turner, carefully place cookies on cookie sheets. Bake 12 minutes or until edges of cookies are lightly browned. Remove cookies to wire racks to cool. Repeat with remaining dough and reroll trimmings.

4. Prepare Frosting "Paint."

5. Decorate gingerbread people: Place cookies on waxed-paper-lined cookie sheets. With small and medium artist's brushes and decorating bag with decorating tubes, decorate gingerbread people as desired. Set aside to allow frosting to dry completely, about 2 hours. Makes 12.

Frosting "Paint"

In large bowl with mixer at low speed, beat *5 cups confectioners' sugar, ½ teaspoon cream of tartar,* and *4 egg whites* until just mixed. Increase speed to high and beat until mixture is stiff and knife drawn through mixture leaves a clean-cut path. Divide frosting into small bowls. Tint each bowl of frosting with *food color* as desired, and if necessary, add a little *water* so icing will spread easily. Keep all bowls covered with plastic wrap to prevent frosting from drying out.

CHRISTMAS COTTAGE

CONSTRUCTION TIPS

When assembling pieces of gingerbread, work with icing in decorating bag with medium tip. Pipe a line along edge of one piece; press it against adjoining piece and hold in place for several minutes until icing has set. (It may be necessary to shave edges with a sharp knife to assure proper fit.) Before adding pieces that put weight on other pieces (as when adding a roof to house walls), be sure walls are iced together solidly before proceeding.

Smooth seams with damp cloth; fill in any space with more icing. For extra stability, pipe icing along inside seams of house.

If you're not planning to eat the house, you can use toothpick "nails" for even sturdier construction. Cut toothpicks diagonally into ½" lengths. With real nail or skewer, pierce edge of two pieces to be joined. Insert toothpick "nail" into one hole. After applying icing on edge of one piece, put two pieces together with "nails" in place.

If you have leftover dough, make cookies. Roll ⅛" thick; cut out; arrange on cookie sheet ¼" apart and bake 15 to 20 minutes. Decorate with any remaining frosting.

Five o'clock Christmas afternoon. Candy no longer appeals to the Children.

Maud Tousey

VI. SWEET TOUCHES, NIBBLES, BREADS AND PASTRIES

*O*ur 'catch-all' chapter includes Holiday recipes that are synonymous with Christmas. Here are cakes and pies and breads that will fill each household with the perfumes and spices of December baking: toasted almonds, baked caraway, gingered muffins, and sherry- and brandy-laced fruitcakes. Unable to pick a favorite fruitcake, we are offering five delightfully different variations on the classic Christmas cake, including one with chocolate. And if mincemeat is your weakness, here are more than 15 suggestions for including it in every meal you eat on Christmas Day!

Walnut Ice-Cream Roll, vanilla ice cream and fudge-truffle center wrapped in chocolate cake, garnished with toasted walnuts.
Recipe on page 144.

HOT & SPICY WALNUTS

    4   cups water
    1   8-ounce can California walnuts
    1   tablespoon salad oil
    1   tablespoon sugar
 1½   teaspoons Worcestershire
  ½   teaspoon ground red pepper
  ¼   teaspoon salt

About 1½ hours before serving or up to 2 weeks ahead:

1. In 3-quart saucepan over high heat, heat water to boiling; add walnuts and heat to boiling; cook 1 minute. Rinse walnuts under running hot water; drain; pat dry with paper towels. Wash saucepan and dry.

2. In same saucepan over medium heat, in hot salad oil, cook walnuts and remaining ingredients about 5 to 7 minutes until browned, stirring constantly.

3. With slotted spoon, remove walnuts to paper towels to drain and cool completely. Store walnuts in tightly covered container to use up within 2 weeks. Makes 2 cups.

MIXED SUGARED NUTS

  ½   6-ounce can frozen orange-juice
        concentrate, thawed
    2   egg whites
 1¾   cups sugar
    5   teaspoons ground cinnamon
 2¼   teaspoons ground allspice
  ¾   teaspoon salt
    2   12-ounce cans salted cashews
    1   6-ounce can pecan halves
    1   4½-ounce can whole blanched
        almonds

About 2½ hours before serving or up to 2 weeks ahead:

1. In large bowl with fork, beat undiluted orange-juice concentrate and egg whites until blended. In pie plate, mix well sugar, cinnamon, allspice, and salt.

2. Preheat oven to 300°F. Stir nuts in orange-juice mixture in bowl. With slotted spoon, remove nuts, about ½ cup at a time, to pie plate with sugar mixture; toss to coat well. Spread sugar-coated nuts on two 15½" by 10½" jelly-roll pans; bake 30 to 35 minutes until nuts are golden, stirring occasionally.

3. Cool nuts in jelly-roll pans 5 minutes; then with pancake turner, transfer to waxed paper to cool completely. Store sugared nuts in tightly covered container to use up within 2 weeks. Makes about 10 cups.

CHRISTMAS WALNUT BRITTLE

    1   cup sugar
  ½   cup light corn syrup
  ¼   cup water
  ¼   teaspoon salt
    1   cup California walnuts, coarsely
        chopped
    1   tablespoon butter or margarine,
        softened
    1   teaspoon baking soda
  ⅓   cup diced mixed candied fruit

About 1 hour before serving or up to 1 week ahead:

1. Grease large cookie sheet. In heavy 2-quart saucepan over medium heat, heat sugar, corn syrup, water, and salt to boiling, stirring frequently until sugar is completely dissolved. Stir in chopped walnuts. Carefully set candy thermometer in place and continue cooking, stirring frequently, until temperature on candy thermometer reaches 300°F. or hard-crack stage (when a small amount of mixture dropped into a bowl of very cold water separates into hard and brittle threads), about 20 minutes.

2. Remove saucepan from heat; immediately stir in butter or margarine and baking soda; pour mixture at once onto cookie sheet. With two forks, lift and pull walnut mixture into a rectangle about 14" by 12". Sprinkle candied fruit over mixture. Place cookie sheet on wire rack; cool walnut brittle completely.

3. With hands, gently snap candy into small serving-size pieces. Store candy in tightly covered container to use within 1 week. Makes about 1 pound.

A baker's bounty of everyone's favorites—Braided Marble Bread, Little Honey Loaves, Gingerbread Muffins, Pumpkin-Raisin Nut Bread, Onion-Cheese Bread and Holiday Cranberry Quick Bread. Recipes on pages 138-139.

ONION-CHEESE BREAD

2   tablespoons sugar
1   teaspoon salt
1   package active dry yeast
    about 2¾ cups all-purpose flour
¼   cup water
4   tablespoons butter or margarine
1   8-ounce container creamed cottage
    cheese
1   egg
2   teaspoons dill seeds
2   teaspoons grated onion

About 4 hours before serving or up to 2 days ahead:

1. In large bowl, combine sugar, salt, yeast, and ½ cup flour. In 1-quart saucepan over low heat, heat water and butter until very warm (120° to 130° F.). (Butter does not need to melt completely.)

2. With mixer at low speed, gradually beat liquid into dry ingredients just until blended. Increase speed to medium; beat 2 minutes, occasionally scraping bowl with rubber spatula. Beat in cottage cheese, egg, and ½ cup flour to make a thick batter; beat 2 minutes, scraping bowl often. With spoon, stir in 1 cup flour to make a soft dough. Stir in dill seeds and onion.

3. Turn dough onto well-floured surface and knead until smooth and elastic, about 10 minutes, adding more flour while kneading (about ½ to ¾ cup). Shape dough into ball and place in greased large bowl, turning dough over to grease top. Cover and let rise in warm place (80° to 85°F.), away from draft, until doubled, about 1 hour. (Dough is doubled when two fingers pressed into dough leave a dent.)

4. Grease 1½-quart soufflé dish or round casserole. Punch down dough. Shape dough into a ball; place in soufflé dish. In center of ball, cut a 4-inch cross about ¼ inch deep. Cover; let rise in warm place until doubled, about 45 minutes. (Dough is doubled when one finger very lightly pressed against dough leaves a dent.)

5. Preheat oven to 350°F. Bake 35 minutes or until loaf sounds hollow when lightly tapped. Remove loaf from dish; cool on rack. Makes one 1½-pound loaf.

LITTLE HONEY LOAVES

2¼ cups all-purpose flour
¾   cup packed dark brown sugar
1¼ teaspoons salt
1   teaspoon baking powder
¾   teaspoon baking soda
⅓   cup shortening
2   eggs
½   cup milk
⅓   cup honey
2   teaspoons grated lemon peel

About 2½ hours before serving or up to 3 days ahead:

1. Preheat oven to 350°F. Grease and flour three 5¾" by 3¼" loaf pans or one 9" by 5" loaf pan. In bowl, mix first 5 ingredients. With 2 knives used scissor-fashion, cut in shortening to resemble coarse crumbs.

2. In small bowl with fork or wire whisk, beat eggs, milk, honey, and lemon peel until well mixed. Stir honey mixture into flour mixture just until flour is moistened. Spoon batter evenly into loaf pans.

3. Bake small loaves 40 minutes, large loaf 1 hour or until toothpick inserted in center comes out clean. Cool bread in pans on wire rack 10 minutes; remove from pans. Cool bread completely on rack. Makes three ½-pound loaves or one 1½-pound loaf.

GINGERBREAD MUFFINS

2½ cups all-purpose flour
1   cup light molasses
1   cup buttermilk
1   cup pecan halves, chopped
½   cup sugar
½   cup shortening
1½ teaspoons baking soda
1   teaspoon ground cinnamon
1   teaspoon ground ginger
½   teaspoon salt
¼   teaspoon ground nutmeg
1   egg

About 45 minutes before serving or early in day:

1. Grease and flour twenty-four 2½-inch muffin-pan cups; set aside.

2. Preheat oven to 375°F. Into large, bowl measure all ingredients. With mixer at low speed, beat ingredients just until blended, constantly scraping bowl with rubber spatula. Increase speed to medium; beat 2 minutes, occasionally scraping bowl.

3. Spoon batter into muffin pans to come about halfway up each cup. Bake 20 to 25 minutes until toothpick inserted in center of muffin comes out clean. Cool muffins in pans on wire rack 10 minutes; remove from pans. Serve muffins warm or cool muffins on wire rack to serve later. Makes 24 muffins.

PUMPKIN-RAISIN NUT BREAD

6   cups all-purpose flour
1   tablespoon salt
4   teaspoons baking powder
2   teaspoons baking soda
2   teaspoons ground cinnamon
½   teaspoon ground cloves
4   eggs
1   29-ounce can pumpkin
1   16-ounce package brown sugar
½   cup apple cider
½   cup salad oil
1   cup dark seedless raisins
½   cup California walnuts, chopped

About 2½ hours before serving or up to 3 days ahead:

1. Preheat oven to 350°F. Grease two 9" by 5" loaf pans. In large bowl with fork, mix first 6 ingredients. In another large bowl with fork, beat eggs with pumpkin, brown sugar, cider, and oil until well blended. Stir pumpkin mixture into flour mixture just until flour is moistened. Gently stir raisins and walnuts into batter; spoon evenly into loaf pans.

2. Bake 1 hour and 10 minutes or until toothpick inserted in center comes out clean. Cool in pans on wire rack 10 minutes; remove from pans; cool completely on rack. Makes two 2½-pound loaves.

BRAIDED MARBLE BREAD

Dark Dough

2¼   cups whole-wheat flour
2¼   cups rye flour
       about 2¾ cups all-purpose flour
1   tablespoon sugar
1   tablespoon salt
2   packages active dry yeast
2¼   cups water
⅓   cup dark molasses
3   tablespoons butter or margarine
1   tablespoon caraway seeds (optional)

Light Dough

3   tablespoons sugar
2   teaspoons salt
1   package active dry yeast
       about 5¾ cups all-purpose flour
2   cups water
3   tablespoons butter or margarine
1   egg white, beaten

About 5 hours before serving or up to 2 days ahead:

1. Prepare dark dough: In medium bowl, combine whole-wheat flour, rye flour, and 2½ cups all-purpose flour; set aside. In large bowl, combine sugar, salt, yeast, and 1½ cups flour mixture. In 2-quart saucepan with spoon, mix water and molasses; add butter or margarine and caraway seeds; over low heat, heat mixture until very warm (120° to 130°F.). (Butter or margarine does not need to melt completely.)

2. With mixer at low speed, gradually beat liquid into yeast mixture just until blended. Increase speed to medium; beat 2 minutes, occasionally scraping bowl with rubber spatula. Gradually beat in 1 cup flour mixture to make a thick batter; continue beating 2 minutes, scraping bowl often. With wooden spoon, stir in 3 cups flour mixture to make a soft dough.

3. Lightly sprinkle work surface with all-purpose flour; turn dough onto surface. With floured hands, knead dough about 10 minutes, until smooth and elastic, working in remaining flour mixture while kneading. Shape dough into a ball and place in greased large bowl, turning dough over so that top is greased. Cover and let

rise in warm place (80° to 85°F.) away from draft, until doubled, about 1½ hours. (Dough is doubled when two fingers pressed lightly into dough leave a dent.)

4. Meanwhile, prepare light dough: In another large bowl, combine sugar, salt, yeast, and 2 cups all-purpose flour. In 1-quart saucepan over low heat, heat water and butter or margarine until very warm (120° to 130°F.). (Butter or margarine does not need to melt completely.)

5. With mixer at low speed, gradually beat liquid into dry ingredients just until blended. Increase speed to medium; beat 2 minutes, occasionally scraping bowl with rubber spatula. Gradually beat in ¾ cup flour to make a thick batter; continue beating 2 minutes, scraping bowl often. With wooden spoon, stir in 2½ cups flour to make a soft dough.

6. Turn dough onto well-floured surface and knead until smooth and elastic, about 10 minutes, adding more flour while kneading (about ¼ to ½ cup). Shape dough into a ball and place in greased large bowl, turning dough over so that top is greased. Cover and let rise in warm place (80° to 85°F.), away from draft, until doubled, about 1 hour. (Dough is doubled when two fingers pressed lightly into dough leave a dent.)

7. Punch down dark dough and turn onto lightly floured surface; cut into four equal pieces; cover with towel and let dough rest 15 minutes for easier shaping. Repeat with light dough.

8. Grease two large cookie sheets. On floured surface, with hands, roll each dough piece into a 15-inch-long rope. Place four dough ropes, two dark and two light, side by side, alternating colors. Pinch ropes together at one end to seal. Braid ropes by weaving far right rope over, under, then over ropes to left. Repeat weaving, always starting with far right rope, until end; pinch end of ropes together to seal. Place braid diagonally across cookie sheet; tuck ends under. Repeat with remaining dough, placing it on second cookie sheet. Cover each braid with a towel; let rise in warm place until doubled when one finger very lightly pressed against dough leaves a dent.)

9. Preheat oven to 350°F. With pastry brush, brush loaves with some egg white.

Place loaves on cookie sheets on two oven racks; bake 20 minutes; switch cookie sheets between upper and lower oven racks so both loaves brown evenly; bake about 20 minutes longer, or until loaves sound hollow when lightly tapped with fingers. Remove loaves from cookie sheets and cool on wire racks. Makes two 2½-pound loaves.

HOLIDAY CRANBERRY QUICK BREAD

4   cups all-purpose flour
2   cup sugar
1   tablespoon baking powder
2   teaspoons salt
1   teaspoons salt
1   teaspoon baking soda
½   cup shortening
2   eggs
1¾   cups orange juice
2   tablespoons grated orange peel
2   cups fresh or frozen cranberries, coarsely chopped
1   cup California walnuts, chopped

About 2½ hours before serving or up to 3 days ahead:

1. Preheat oven to 350°F. Grease and flour two 9" by 5" loaf pans. In large bowl, mix first 5 ingredients. With pastry blender or 2 knives used scissor-fashion, cut in shortening until mixture resembles coarse crumbs.

2. In medium bowl with fork, beat eggs, orange juice, and grated orange peel until blended; stir into flour mixture just until flour is moistened. Gently stir cranberries and walnuts into batter. Spoon batter evenly into loaf pans.

3. Bake 55 minutes or until toothpick inserted in center comes out clean. Cool bread in pans on wire rack 10 minutes; remove from pans. Cool bread completely on rack. Makes two 1½-pound loaves.

To Freeze And Serve Up To 1 Month Later

Wrap each loaf tightly with foil or freezer-wrap; seal; label; and freeze. To thaw, remove wrap; let bread stand at room temperature about 2 hours.

Four of our five fruitcakes on pages 142-143 are shown here: Chocolate, Fresh Cranberry, Miniature and English.

CHOCOLATE FRUITCAKE

3   6-ounce cans pecan halves
1   7.5- to 8-ounce container red candied
    cherries
1   cup golden raisins
1   cup dark seedless raisins
¼   cup dry sherry
1   3.5- to 4-ounce container diced
    candied citron
    all-purpose flour
1¼ cups sugar
1   cup water
¾   cup butter or margarine, softened
1½ teaspoons baking soda
1   teaspoon vanilla extract
½   teaspoon baking powder
½   teaspoon salt
4   squares unsweetened chocolate,
    melted
3   eggs
¼   cup light corn syrup

Day ahead or up to 1 month ahead:

1. Line 10-inch tube pan with foil; press out wrinkles as much as possible so cake surface will come out smooth.

2. Coarsely chop 4 cups pecan halves; reserve remaining pecans for garnish. Cut each red candied cherry in half.

3. In large bowl, combine chopped pecans, red-cherry halves, raisins, sherry, and candied citron; let stand 30 minutes until sherry is absorbed, stirring occasionally. Stir in ¼ cup flour until fruit and nuts are evenly coated.

4. In another large bowl with mixer at low speed, beat sugar, next 8 ingredients, and 2 cups flour until blended, occasionally scraping bowl with rubber spatula. Increase speed to high; beat 3 minutes, occasionally scraping bowl. Stir fruit mixture into batter until mixed.

5. Preheat oven to 300°F. Spoon batter into prepared pan, packing down batter evenly to eliminate air pockets. Bake 1¾ to 2 hours or until toothpick inserted in center of cake comes out clean. Remove cake from oven but do not turn oven off. Cool cake in pan on wire rack; remove cake from pan and carefully peel off foil.

6. Meanwhile, place remaining pecan halves in 9″ by 9″ baking pan. In oven, toast pecans until lightly browned, stirring nuts occasionally. Cool.

7. In small saucepan over medium heat, heat corn syrup to boiling: boil 1 minute. With pastry brush, brush top of fruitcake with syrup. Arrange toasted pecan halves on top of cake until top is completely covered. Wrap cake tightly with foil or plastic wrap. Refrigerate to use up within 1 month. Makes one 4½-pound fruitcake. 32 servings.

FRESH CRANBERRY FRUITCAKE

6   large oranges
4   cups all-purpose flour
1½ cups sugar
1   tablespoon baking powder
1   teaspoon baking soda
1   teaspoon salt
½   cup shortening
2   eggs
½   cup cream sherry
2   cups cranberries, coarsely chopped
1½ cups dark seedless raisins
1½ cups California walnuts, coarsely
    chopped
    Frosted Cranberries for garnish
¼   cup light corn syrup for garnish
    small nontoxic leaves for garnish

Early in day or up to 1 week ahead:

1. From oranges, grate 2 tablespoons peel, squeeze ½ cup juice, and chop orange pulp to make 2 cups.

2. Grease well and flour 12-cup oven-safe ring mold. In large bowl, mix flour and next 4 ingredients. With pastry blender or two knives used scissor-fashion, cut in shortening until mixture resembles coarse crumbs.

3. Preheat oven to 325°F. In medium bowl with fork, beat eggs, cream sherry, and orange juice until well blended; stir egg mixture, orange peel, orange pulp, chopped cranberries, raisins, and walnuts into flour mixture just until flour is moistened. Spoon batter evenly into prepared ring mold. Bake 1½ hours or until toothpick inserted in center comes out clean. Cool

cake in pan on wire rack 10 minutes; remove from pan; cool cake completely on wire rack.

4. If you like, when cake is cool, prepare Frosted Cranberries for garnish; set aside. In small saucepan over medium heat, heat corn syrup to boiling; boil 1 minute. Use corn syrup to attach Frosted Cranberries and leaves in a wreath on top of cake. Makes 32 servings.

Frosted Cranberries

In pie plate with fork, beat *1 egg white* slightly. Onto waxed paper, measure *¼ cup sugar*. Coat *1 cup cranberries* with egg white; then coat cranberries completely with sugar. Place frosted cranberries on wire rack over waxed paper to dry, about 1 hour.

ENGLISH FRUITCAKE

2   16-ounce containers mixed candied
    fruit (about 4 cups)
    all-purpose flour
¾   cup butter or margarine, softened
1   cup sugar
2   tablespoons brandy or orange juice
2½ teaspoons baking powder
1   teaspoon salt
6   eggs
1   cup pecans, chopped
1   cup California walnuts, chopped
1   cup semisweet-chocolate mini pieces
1   cup dark seedless raisins
⅓   cup apple jelly
½   teaspoon almond extract
2   7-ounce packages marzipan
    confectioners' sugar
    red and green candied cherries for
    garnish

Day ahead or up to 1 month ahead:

1. Preheat oven to 300°F. Lightly grease 10″ by 3″ springform pan.

2. In large bowl, toss mixed candied fruit with 1 cup flour; set aside.

3. In another large bowl with mixer at high speed, beat butter or margarine and sugar until light and fluffy. Add brandy, baking powder, salt, eggs, and 1 cup flour; at low

speed, beat until well mixed, constantly scraping bowl with rubber spatula. Increase speed to medium; beat 2 minutes, occasionally scraping bowl.

4. With rubber spatula, fold fruit mixture, pecans, walnuts, chocolate mini pieces, and raisins into batter. Spoon batter into prepared pan, packing down batter to eliminate air pockets. Bake 1¾ hours or until toothpick inserted in center of cake comes out clean. Cool cake in pan on wire rack 10 minutes; remove side from pan and cool cake completely on wire rack.

5. When cake is cool, with metal spatula, loosen cake from pan bottom; remove pan bottom. Place cake on cake plate. In small saucepan over low heat, melt apple jelly; stir in almond extract. Brush mixture over top and side of cake.

6. Knead marzipan into a ball. Lightly sprinkle work surface with confectioners' sugar. With rolling pin, roll marzipan into a 14-inch round; carefully place over cake; gently press onto top and side of cake, smoothing out pleats with fingers moistened with some water. Trim edge of marzipan even with bottom of cake. Wrap cake with foil or plastic wrap. Refrigerate to use up within 1 month.

7. To serve, if desired, decorate cake with candied cherries. Makes one 6-pound fruitcake, 48 servings.

CHRISTMAS CAKE

1	large orange
1	3.5- to 4-ounce container diced candied citron
1	3.5- to 4-ounce container red candied cherries, chopped
½	cup golden raisins
½	cup pitted prunes, chopped
½	cup pecans, chopped all-purpose flour
1	cup butter or margarine, softened
1	cup sugar
1	teaspoon baking powder
¼	teaspoon salt
3	eggs dry sherry
1	cup confectioners' sugar
4	teaspoons milk
¼	teaspoon almond extract

Early in day or up to 1 week ahead:

1. From orange, grate 3 tablespoons peel and squeeze ¼ cup juice. Cover orange juice and refrigerate. In small bowl, mix 1 tablespoon each of candied citron, cherries, and orange peel; cover and refrigerate for garnish.

2. Preheat oven to 300°F. Grease and flour six 1-cup Bundtlette cake pans. In medium bowl, toss raisins, prunes, pecans, remaining citron, candied cherries, and orange peel with ⅓ cup flour.

3. In large bowl with mixer at high speed, beat butter or margarine and sugar until light and fluffy. Add baking powder, salt, eggs, 1¼ cups flour, and ½ cup sherry; at low speed, beat until well mixed, constantly scraping bowl with rubber spatula. Increase speed to medium; beat 2 minutes, occasionally scraping bowl. With rubber spatula, fold fruit mixture into batter. Spoon batter into prepared pans, packing down batter to eliminate air pockets. Bake 45 minutes or until toothpick inserted in center of a cake comes out clean. Cool cakes in pans on wire racks 30 minutes. Remove from pans. Cool completely on wire racks.

4. When cakes are cool, return cakes to pans. In cup, mix reserved orange juice and 2 tablespoons sherry; sprinkle 1 tablespoon orange-juice mixture over each cake in pans.

5. In small bowl, mix confectioners' sugar, milk, and almond extract until easy spreading consistency. Place sheet of waxed paper under wire racks. Remove cakes from pans. Spoon icing over cakes on racks. Garnish tops of cakes with reserved fruit mixture. Store fruitcakes in tightly covered container to use up within 1 week. Makes 6 cakes. 12 servings.

Turn **leftover fruitcake** into an elegant dessert—here's how: Slice the cake to fit into wine goblets or small custard cups; moisten lightly with fruit juice or sherry; top with whipped cream. Delicious!

BANANA FRUITCAKE

3	3½- to 4-ounce containers candied red cherries (about 1½ cups)
1	8-ounce package dried figs, chopped (1 cup)
1	3.5-ounce container diced candied citron (about ½ cup)
1	4-ounce container diced candied orange peel (½ cup)
1	4-ounce container diced candied lemon peel (½ cup)
2	cups golden raisins
1½	cups pecans, chopped
½	cup dark seedless raisins
3¾	cups all-purpose flour
1½	cups sugar
1	cup butter or margarine, softened
¾	cup orange juice
¾	cup mashed bananas (about 2 ripe medium bananas)
2	teaspoons baking powder
1	teaspoon orange extract
½	teaspoon salt
6	eggs

Early in day or up to 1 month ahead:

1. Line 10-inch tube pan with foil; press out wrinkles as much as possible so cake surface will come out smooth. Cut each red cherry in half; reserve about 18 cherry halves for garnish. In large bowl, combine remaining cherry halves, figs, next 6 ingredients, and ¾ cup flour until fruits and nuts are evenly coated with flour.

2. In another large bowl with mixer at low speed, beat remaining 3 cups flour with remaining ingredients just until blended, constantly scraping bowl with rubber spatula. Increase speed to medium; beat 4 minutes longer, occasionally scraping bowl. Stir batter into fruit mixture until well mixed.

3. Preheat oven to 300°F. Pour batter into prepared pan, packing down batter evenly to eliminate air pockets. Bake 2½ hours or until toothpick inserted in center of cake comes out clean. Cool cake in pan on wire rack 30 minutes; remove from pan and carefully peel off foil. Cool cake completely on rack. Arrange reserved cherry halves on top of cake in clusters. Wrap fruitcake tightly with foil or plastic wrap. Refrigerate. Makes one 5½-pound fruitcake. 40 servings.

6. When pudding is done, cool in bowl on wire rack 5 minutes. With metal spatula, loosen pudding and invert onto platter; garnish with strawberries. Serve pudding warm with warm Brandied Chocolate Sauce. Makes 12 servings.

Brandied Chocolate Sauce

In 1-quart saucepan over low heat, heat *3 squares semisweet chocolate, ½ cup heavy or whipping cream, ¼ cup sugar, 4 tablespoons butter or* margarine *and ¼ teaspoon salt* until melted and smooth, stirring occasionally. Remove saucepan from heat; stir in *1 tablespoon brandy.*

To Do Ahead

Up to 2 days ahead, prepare steamed pudding and chocolate sauce as above. Refrigerate sauce in covered small bowl. When pudding is done, remove from bowl and refrigerate until cool. Wrap pudding with plastic wrap or foil; return to refrigerator. To serve, resteam pudding in lightly greased bowl, covered, as directed above, for 1½ hours. Reheat sauce in heavy 1-quart saucepan over low heat, stirring constantly, until heated through. Serve as above.

STEAMED CHESTNUT PUDDING

1	*pound chestnuts*
	water
½	*cup butter or margarine, softened*
½	*cup packed brown sugar*
¼	*cup sugar*
4	*eggs*
2	*cups all-purpose flour*
⅔	*cup milk*
3	*tablespoons brandy*
2	*teaspoons baking powder*
1	*teaspoon vanilla extract*
½	*teaspoon salt*
	Brandied Chocolate Sauce
	strawberries for garnish

About 3 hours before serving:

1. In 4-quart saucepan over high heat, heat chestnuts and enough water to cover to boiling. Reduce heat to medium; cover saucepan and cook 10 minutes. Remove saucepan from heat. With slotted spoon, remove chestnuts, 3 or 4 at a time, from water to cutting board. Cut each chestnut in half. With tip of small knife, scrape out chestnut meat from its shell. (Skin will stay in shell.) In blender at medium speed or in food processor with knife blade attached, blend chestnuts in batches until finely ground; set aside.

2. Heavily grease deep 2½-quart heat-safe bowl. Cut foil 1 inch larger than top of bowl to use as cover; grease one side of foil very well; set aside.

3. In large bowl with mixer at medium speed, beat butter or margarine, brown sugar, and sugar until light and fluffy, occasionally scraping bowl with rubber spatula. Add eggs, flour, milk, brandy, baking powder, vanilla extract and salt; beat at low speed just until blended. Increase speed to medium; beat 1 minute, occasionally scraping bowl with rubber spatula. Stir in ground chestnuts. Spoon pudding mixture into prepared bowl. Cover bowl with foil, greased-side down, tying tightly with string.

4. Set bowl on trivet in saucepot (8 to 12 quart). Pour in enough water to come halfway up side of bowl; over high heat, heat to boiling. Reduce heat to low; cover and simmer 2 to 2½ hours until toothpick inserted through foil into center of pudding comes out clean.

5. About 15 minutes before pudding is done, prepare Brandied Chocolate Sauce; keep warm.

WALNUT ICE-CREAM ROLL

Picture on page 133

4	*eggs*
	sugar
½	*cup cake flour*
1	*teaspoon baking powder*
	cocoa
	salt
2	*pints vanilla ice cream*
½	*6-ounce package semisweet-chocolate pieces (½ cup)*
¼	*cup sweetened condensed milk*
2	*tablespoons orange-flavor liqueur*
½	*12- to 12.5-ounce jar butterscotch-flavor topping (½ cup)*
2½	*cups California walnuts, toasted and coarsely chopped*
	small holly leaves or other nontoxic leaves for garnish

Early in day or up to 2 weeks ahead:

1. Preheat oven to 375°F. Grease 15½″ by 10½″ jelly-roll pan; line pan with waxed paper.

2. Separate eggs, placing egg whites in small mixing bowl and yolks in large mixing bowl. With mixer at high speed, beat egg whites until soft peaks form. Beating at high speed, gradually sprinkle in ¼ cup sugar, beating until sugar is completely dissolved and whites stand in stiff peaks.

3. To bowl with egg yolks, add ½ cup sugar; with mixer at high speed, beat until mixture is very thick and lemon colored. Add flour, baking powder, ⅓ cup cocoa, and ¼ teaspoon salt; with mixer at medium speed, beat until blended. With wire whisk or rubber spatula, gently fold beaten egg whites into yolk mixture. Spread batter evenly in prepared pan. Bake 12 to 15 minutes until cake springs back when lightly touched with finger.

4. Sprinkle clean cloth towel with some cocoa. Immediately invert cake onto towel. Carefully peel waxed paper from cake. Starting at a narrow end, roll cake with towel, jelly-roll fashion. Place cake roll, seam-side down, on wire rack; cool completely, about 30 minutes.

5. Place vanilla ice cream in refrigerator to soften slightly, about 30 minutes. Meanwhile, in 1-quart saucepan over low heat, heat semisweet-chocolate pieces until melted and smooth, stirring occasionally; remove from heat. Stir in sweetened condensed milk, orange-flavor liqueur, and dash of salt until blended. Refrigerate chocolate mixture until slightly cooled, about 15 minutes.

6. Unroll cooled cake; spread top evenly with softened ice cream. Spoon chocolate mixture in crosswise strip along narrow edge, leaving 2-inch border. Starting at same narrow end, roll cake without towel. Cover and freeze ice-cream roll until firm enough to handle, about 2 hours.

7. Spread butterscotch-flavor topping over ice-cream roll. Pat walnuts into topping; cover; freeze until firm, at least 4 hours.

8. To serve, place ice-cream roll on chilled platter. Let stand 10 minutes for easier slicing. Garnish platter with holly leaves. Makes 16 servings.

(Bûche de Noël)

> 5   eggs, separated
> 1   cup confectioners' sugar
>   cocoa
>   Mocha Filling
>   Chocolate Butter Cream

Early in day or day ahead:

1. Grease 15½″ by 10½″ jelly-roll pan; line bottom of pan with waxed paper; grease and flour paper.

2. Preheat oven to 400°F. In large bowl with mixer at high speed, beat egg whites until soft peaks form. Gradually sprinkle in ½ cup confectioners' sugar; beat until stiff peaks form.

3. In small bowl with mixer at high speed, beat egg yolks until thick. At low speed, beat in ½ cup confectioners' sugar and 3 tablespoons cocoa, occasionally scraping bowl. Fold yolk mixture into whites. Spread batter in pan; bake 15 minutes or until top springs back when touched.

4. Sprinkle towel with some cocoa. Invert cake onto towel; peel off paper. Starting at narrow end, roll cake with towel, jelly-roll fashion; place, seam-side down, on rack to cool.

5. Meanwhile, prepare Mocha Filling and Chocolate Butter Cream.

6. Unroll cake; spread top with filling. Starting at same narrow end, roll cake without towel. Place cake seam-side down on platter. Spoon butter cream into decorating bag with large star tip; use to pipe lengthwise lines on roll. Refrigerate. Makes 14 servings.

Mocha Filling

In small bowl with mixer at medium speed, beat *1 cup heavy or whipping cream, ¼ cup confectioners' sugar, ¼ cup cocoa, and 1 tablespoon instant coffee granules* until stiff peaks form.

Chocolate Butter Cream

In bowl, beat *2 cups confectioners' sugar, 4 tablespoons butter,* softened, *2 tablespoons milk, 1 teaspoon vanilla extract, 1 egg yolk,* and *1 square unsweetened chocolate,* melted, until good spreading consistency.

MINCEMEAT SUNDAES

1   pint vanilla ice cream
8   ladyfingers
2   small bananas
½   28-ounce jar ready-to-use mincemeat

1. Remove ice cream from freezer; let stand at room temperature to soften slightly, about 10 minutes.

2. Meanwhile, split each ladyfinger horizontally in half; then cut each crosswise in half. Slice bananas into ¼-inch-thick slices. Arrange ladyfingers around side of each of 4 dessert dishes, allowing rounded end to extend just to rim of dish. Arrange banana slices inside of ladyfingers.

3. Scoop a ball of ice cream into each dessert dish; top with mincemeat. Serve immediately. Makes 4 servings.

It's the traditional time to enjoy **mincemeat**—that thick, richly delicious mixture of raisins, apples, and spice. Buy it in jars, ready to use, or in condensed form in packages, to be reconstituted with water before using. Serve it as the season's special pie, topped with hard sauce, ice cream, or Cheddar cheese. And try the suggestions below for perking up favorite foods with holiday goodness. In each, add ready-to-use or reconstituted condensed mincemeat to individual taste.

Main-Course Treats
Stir **mincemeat** into baked beans or pork and beans; heat.

Add **mincemeat** to bread or corn-bread stuffing for poultry, pork.

Serve as one of condiments with curried chicken or seafood.

Stir into mashed sweet potatoes or butternut squash.

Stir into hot buttered rice or rice pilaf as meat accompaniment.

Stir into cottage cheese; serve as part of salad plate with tuna, chicken, or shrimp salad.

Sauces
Stir into honey or maple syrup; serve on pancakes or waffles.

Heat and use in place of raisin sauce for ham.

Stir into gravy for roast turkey, duckling, chicken, goose, pork, lamb, or braised pork chops.

Stir into dressing for fruit salads.

Serve warm over ice cream, vanilla or butterscotch pudding, bread or rice pudding.

Desserts
Stir into softened frozen vanilla yogurt; freeze until firm.

Use as topping for cheesecake.

Use instead of apples in Brown Betty recipe.

Use as crêpe filling; serve crêpes topped with whipped cream.

Use as filling for meringue shells; top with vanilla ice cream.

Cook's Guide To Nuts

The favorite kinds

These are the different varieties generally available and most popular for snacks and recipes:

Almonds are California's major tree crop, producing more than half the world's supply. They come whole in the shell, or shelled with brown skin left on (natural) or with skin removed (blanched); also sliced, slivered, and chopped. Some almonds have soft shells that can be cracked with finger pressure; harder shells must be cracked with a nutcracker or hammer.
One pound in the shell yields about 1½ cups nut meats.

Black walnuts, because of their extremely hard shells, are sold shelled; in-shell nuts, available where black-walnut trees grow, must be cracked with a hammer and the meats picked out with a nut pick.
One 2-ounce bag shelled black walnuts measures about ½ cup coarsely broken nut meats.

Brazil nuts are large, rich, and oily white kernels covered by a thin brown skin, inside a three-cornered, dark brown, rough shell. Buy them whole, in shell or shelled, unblanched or blanched.
One pound in-shell nuts yields about 1½ cups nutmeats.

To shell Brazil nuts, cover with cold water in saucepan and heat to boiling; boil 3 minutes. Drain, cool in cold water 1 minute, then crack shells. Or, freeze nuts a few hours, then crack.

To slice shelled Brazil nuts, cover with cold water and heat to boiling; boil 5 minutes. Drain; cut lengthwise into thin slices. If a vegetable parer is used, slices will curl attractively.

Cashews are kidney-shaped nuts imported from tropical countries. The nut hangs from the bottom of an applelike fruit as it grows and has an inedible skin that is removed before nuts are processed. Cashews are sold roasted and salted, or unroasted and unsalted, whole, in halves, or in pieces.
One pound cashews measures 3 to 3⅓ cups.

Chestnuts, once grown in this country, are imported today, mainly from Italy. They are best cooked before eating. Unlike most other nuts, they are seasonal, available fresh from mid-September to March. They are sold in the shell, and also canned: whole or pureed, and whole, preserved in syrup (called *marrons glacés*).
One pound in-shell chestnuts yields about 2½ cups nutmeats.

To shell and blanch chestnuts at the same time, cover nuts with cold water in a saucepan and heat to boiling; cover pan and cook chestnuts 15 minutes. Remove saucepan from heat. For whole chestnuts, remove 3 or 4 nuts at a time from hot water and, with kitchen shears, carefully cut each chestnut on flat side through shell; with fingers, peel off shell and skin, keeping nuts whole (leave rest of nuts in hot water until ready to peel, or inner skin won't come off). For chopped chestnuts, boil chestnuts in the same way; remove 3 or 4 at a time to cutting board; cut each in half. With tip of small knife, scrape out meat from shell; inner skin will stay in shell.

Coconuts are fruits of a tropical palm tree, available all year with peak supplies from October to December. Canned coconut—shredded, flaked, or toasted—is also available.
One medium coconut yields about 3½ cups grated meat plus about ⅓ cup coconut milk.

The easiest way to shell coconuts: Pierce eyes (three rings at one end) with a skewer and hammer, and drain liquid into cup. Then, bake coconut in a 350°F. oven 30 minutes; it will break open easily when tapped with a hammer. Remove white meat; peel off dark skin with vegetable parer; slice meat thin or dice and grate in blender or shred in food processor.

Filberts are cultivated varieties of the wild hazelnut shrub or tree. Buy by the pound, unshelled.
One pound nuts in shell yields about 1½ cups nutmeats.

Macadamia nuts are named for Dr. John Macadam, who first discovered they were edible. Slightly sweet and very crisp, they are sold shelled and lightly roasted, in jars, cans, and packages.
One seven-ounce jar nuts measures about 1½ cups.

Peanuts are really legumes not nuts—they belong to the bean and pea family. They are a rich source of vegetable protein. Buy them unshelled or shelled; raw; roasted, salted or unsalted; with skins left on or removed.
One pound peanuts in shell yields about 2⅓ cups shelled nuts.

Pecans, native to this country, are available all year with best supplies from September to November. They come in shell, or shelled in halves or pieces, or as meal.
One pound in-shell nuts yields about 2¼ cups nutmeats.

Pine nuts are also known as pignolias, piñons, and Indian nuts. They are seeds of varieties of pine growing in Southwestern United States, Mexico, and southern Europe. Buy them in shell or, more readily, shelled.
One-fourth pound pine nuts, shelled, measures about ¾ cup.

Pistachios are seeds of a small evergreen tree. The shell is naturally sand-colored; some shells are dyed to achieve a red color. Buy them in shell or shelled, roasted and salted or unsalted.
One pound in-shell nuts yields about 2¼ cups nutmeats.

Walnuts are America's most popular nut for cooking. Over 95 percent of this country's supply is grown in Calfiornia. Walnuts come in shell or shelled and in pieces.
One pound in-shell nuts yields about 2 cups nut meats.

To shell walnuts so halves are perfect, stand nut on flat end, hold by its seam, and carefully strike pointed end sharply with hammer so halves will be exposed.

Roasting and toasting
Almonds, Brazil nuts, filberts, pecans, pine nuts, and **walnuts** can be roasted in the oven or in a skillet.

Oven method: Preheat oven to 350°F. In jelly-roll pan, spread whole, sliced, slivered, or chopped nuts in a single layer; bake 5 to 20 minutes (depending on size of pieces), stirring occasionally, until just lightly browned (nuts will brown a little more after being removed from oven). Cool in pan on wire rack.

Skillet method: In small skillet over low heat, brown nuts in a little butter, margarine, or salad oil, stirring constantly. Drain on paper towels.

Chestnuts: Cut an X in flat side of each nut and place, cut-side up, on cookie sheet in one layer. Bake in oven preheated to 400°F. about 20 minutes or until tender when fork is inserted through cut in shell.

Peanuts in shell: Roast in oven as for almonds (above) 15 to 20 minutes.

VII. TREES, TREATS AND TRIMMINGS

While the Christmas spices and perfumes are filling the house, it is time to deck the halls as well as the table top, the walls, the tree and even the front door. Creating a holiday atmosphere is as traditional as cooking the Christmas turkey. Our suggestions include decorative items to keep, to give and to pass along through the family year after year. Some are simple; others are more elaborate; but all are designed to bring Christmas into your heart.

In the study, originally the farmhouse kitchen, a sleigh of pretty packages stands before the fireplace. On the mantel: a rope of greens arranged with little bake tins, wrapped around a big plumpudding pan at the center; below, set of silvery rings—they're really the sides of springform pans—each one holding a little lighted candle.

PAPER PLACE MATS

Materials (for 4)
Four 18″ by 24″ sheets of medium-weight white drawing paper; stencil or X-acto knife with sharp new blade, or small, sharp scissors (do not use curved or cuticle scissors); French curve (optional), dressmakers' carbon; several large sheets of tracing paper.

To Make
For each place mat, enlarge and trace design sections onto sheet of tracing paper, joining them along broken lines A and B to form half of design. A French curve will make it easier to trace the curved lines. Tape a sheet of white paper to a hard, flat surface and position the half-design on the left half of the paper, leaving enough room for the other half of the design to be traced later. Slip carbon paper between design and white paper; tape design in place and transfer it lightly to paper using sharp pencil. To complete design, turn and position the half-design pattern on the right half of the paper—do not turn it over—aligning it with the part that has been traced (the narrow ends of the two half-designs should meet). Refer to diagram to be sure curved lines go in the right direction. Transfer design as before. Repeat for four place mats. Cut out design beginning with small areas around flowers. Cut out scalloped edge of place mat after other areas have been completed. If you're using a knife, tape paper to hard, flat surface and use a French curve for cutting curved lines.

Pretty dessert-party table is dressed for the occasion with sweets. "Peppermint candies" trim the tree, which is circled with hand-painted jelly jars you fill with your own homemade goodies, topped off with tiny paper doilies. Lacy paper place mats, set off against a green cloth, are cut out in flower design to match the delicate china pattern. Project instructions on page 152.

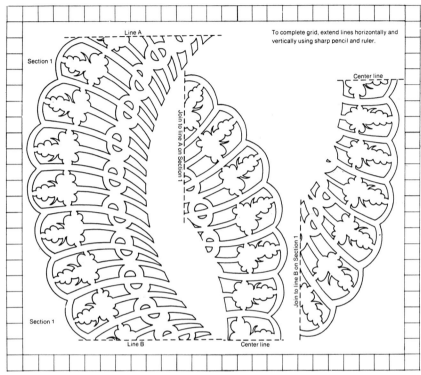

1 square = ½″

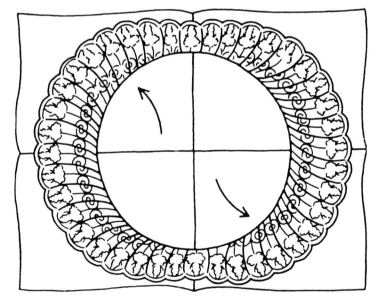

PLACEMENT OF DESIGN

HAND-PAINTED JELLY JARS

Materials
Glass jelly jars; china decorating paints, fine sable brush, brush cleaner, slower; jar of glaze (optional), tiny paper doilies; ribbon; white cotton gloves.

To Make
Use designs below or create your own. The paints are easy to use, but be careful to follow these general directions. For the paint to adhere properly, it is extremely important that the jars are clean, dry, free of fingerprints—wear cotton gloves when handling them. When painting one color over another, be sure the first dries thoroughly. Clean the brush with brush cleaner before using different color. Because the paints dry quickly, you may want to add "slower" to slow down drying time. To do this, put a few drops of paint on a piece of waxed paper, mix in a drop of slower. To "erase" what you have painted, quickly wipe paint away with cotton swab. After the jars have air-dried, put them in the oven, then turn it on to 150°F. and "bake" for one hour. Let them cool in oven. If desired, for more sheen, brush on glaze, let dry, then bake in oven for an hour and cool, as before. After filling jars, cover with doilies held on with ribbon. To use designs shown:

A. Pattern is repeated on each panel of jar. Paint broken line at bottom in red, dotted border in white. Add flowers, red scalloped edge. Paint green dot at center of each white dot at rim.

B. On each panel, paint red stripes first, then white dots, rim.

C. Draw outline of bow, freehand, with white paint. Add red stripes.

JELLY-JAR DESIGNS

HOLIDAY TABLE SETTING

For each place setting: Small and large springform-pan bottoms are stacked with tin mold (or cookie cutter) in between, topped with carved-wood napkin holder, pretty napkin.

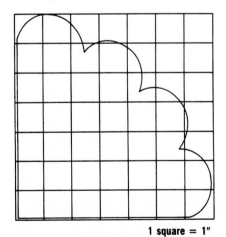

1 square = 1"

To make scalloped place mats, 13" in diameter, cut from red felt, using pattern above.

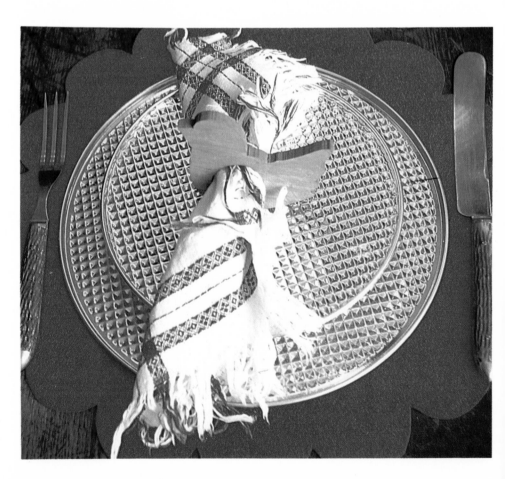

Maid's Apron

From piqué, cut 6″-square skirt and 3½″-square bib. Turn ¼″ to wrong side at bottom of skirt and sides of bib. Stitch fold over eyelet edging. Turn ¼″ to wrong side at sides of skirt and top of bib. Gather top of skirt to 5″ width. Cut two 5½″-strips of bias tape. Raw edges matching, and leaving ¼″ of bias extending at each end, sandwich gathered edge of skirt between bias strips. Stitch across. Cut two 8″ lengths of wider White ribbon. Matching raw edges, sandwich ribbon between ends of strips of bias tape for ties; stitch. Turn to right side. Fold a ¼″ pleat at each side of lower edge of bib. Right sides together, matching raw edges, center and pin lower edge of bib to upper strip of bias tape; stitch. Slip-stitch edges of other strip over seam. Cut a 6″ length of ribbon; sew ends to inside at top of bib. Sew on holly sprig.

CHRISTMAS "CRACKERS"

Cut **cardboard tubes** (from paper towels, gift wrap, etc.) to 4″ lengths and fill with **tiny tissue-wrapped gifts.** Then cut piece of **foil gift wrap** 7″ by 21″. With shiny sides in, fold back both short ends four inches (see sketch) and cut each end, as pictured, into ⅜″ wide fringe, 3½″ deep, to within ½″ from ends. Turn fringed ends foil-side out and **tape** in place as shown, then roll foil around cardboard tube and tie with **yarn** at each end.

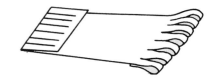

AT-YOUR-SERVICE BOTTLE BIBS

Materials (For both)
¼ yd. each White waffle piqué and lightweight cotton.

For Butler
½ yd. ⅛″-wide White satin ribbon; ½ yd. ¼″-wide Black velvet ribbon; 3 tiny Black ball buttons.

For Maid
¾ yd. ½″-wide White satin ribbon; ¾ yd. ½″-wide White eyelet edging; ½ yd. ½″-wide Single Fold White Bias Tape; tiny sprig fake holly with berries.

To Make
Enlarge and trace pattern.

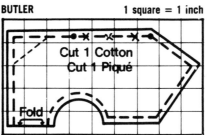

BUTLER　　　　　　　　1 square = 1 inch

Cut 1 Cotton
Cut 1 Piqué

Fold

Butler's Apron
Cut fabrics as indicated; transfer all marks. Right sides in, pin cotton pieces to piqué along all edges. Leaving open on right front edge, stitch ¼″ from edge all around. Clip and notch seam as required; turn right-side out through front opening. Press edge flat. Lap left front over right; topstitch from ● to ●. Cut White ribbon in half and sew a tie to each side at "waist". Sew on buttons. Make velvet bow and sew on 1½″ from top. Press lapels to right side.

PINE-TREE PATCHWORK CLOTH

63″ in Diameter

Materials

45″-wide cotton fabrics—2 yds. each Dark Green with White pin dots and Red-and-Light-Green tiny print on Off-White background, 1 yd. each solid Red and Off-White, ⅛ yd. Brown with White pin dots; cotton fabric for backing—4 yds. 36″-wide or 3 yds. 45″-wide; 66″ square Morning Glory quilt batting; sewing thread; Red, Off-White, and Dark Green quilting thread; quilting hoop; lightweight cardboard for templates.

Tree Block   **One square = 1″**

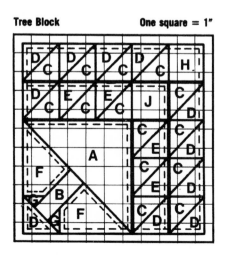

To Make

Enlarge and trace patterns. Stitch pieces right sides together using ¼″ seams. Press seams before joining to other pieces. Match seams when joining pieces. To make templates, trace large (A), medium (C, D, E), and small (G) triangles; square (H, J), trunk and side shapes (F); trace patterns onto cardboard; add ¼″ seam allowance to all edges; cut templates. From Dark Green fabric, cut 5 lower border pieces, 4 upper border pieces, 10 large triangles (A), and 140 medium triangles (C). From Off-White, cut 20 trunk side shapes (F), 110 medium triangles (D), and 10 squares (H). From Red, cut 40 medium triangles (E) and 10 squares (J). From Brown, cut 10 trunks (B) and 20 small triangles (G). From print, cut a 29″ circle, 10 inner points, and 10 outer points. **BLOCKS:** Start and end stitching where seam allowances meet. Stitch 100 Green medium triangles to Off-White medium triangles along longest edge to form a square. Stitch remaining Green medium triangles to Red medium triangles in same manner. Following bold lines on block pattern, join triangles and squares to form strips. Stitch strips to large triangles starting with shortest inner strip, then longer one. Join outer strips in same manner. Stitch small Brown triangles to Off-White side shapes, making 5 each for left and right sides of trunks. Join Brown and Off-White pieces to sides of trunks. Stitch Off-White me-dium triangles to bottom end of trunks to form triangles. Stitch upper and lower sections of blocks together. For top of cloth, stitch upper border strips together to form a circle. Stitch inner edge of border around printed fabric center circle; press seam toward border. For sides of cloth, stitch upper edges of tree blocks to straight edges of print fabric inner point pieces. Join ends to form circle. Pin and stitch top edge of sides to outer edge of upper Dark Green border, adjusting so side lies flat. Pin and stitch straight edges of outer print fabric point pieces to lower edges of tree blocks adjusting seams so cloth lies flat. Stitch outer Dark Green border strips to-gether. Pin and stitch to edge of cloth adjusting so border lies flat. Using a ruler and pencil, lightly trace quilting lines to inner and outer points. Piece backing fabric to make a 65″ square. Right sides out, place quilt batting between tablecloth and back. Pin all layers together. Baste from center to outer edge horizontally and vertically. Baste around inner and outer borders, along outer edge, and from top to bottom of each tree block. With matching thread, quilt parallel lines across center circle, 4½″ apart; repeat in opposite direction to form squares. Quilt along inner and outer edges of upper border, edges and lines of print side pieces, and inner edge of outer border. With Red thread, quilt around outer edge of quilt blocks. Quilt remaining lines with matching thread. For binding, from Red fabric, cut and join 1½″ bias strips to make binding 202″ long. Raw edges matching, stitch around ¼″ from edge. Turn bias strip to back; turn in ¼″ on raw edge; slip-stitch to first stitching.

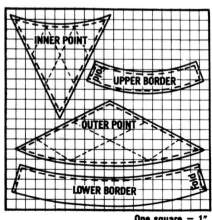

One square = 1″

PINECONE BASKET

Materials

10″ wire pine cone basket frame or a footed garden basket available at florist or garden supply shops. Wire coat hanger. About 235 assorted pine cones. Silicone glue. Clear acrylic spray. 1 yd. ⅞″-wide plaid taffeta ribbon.

To Make

Use a pinecone basket or make a handle from coat hanger and attach to garden basket. Starting at bottom, insert flat bottom cones such as Ponderosa, Scotch red or pitch pine, by sharply turning clockwise, forcing cones between wires. Trim cone edges and fill in spaces with small balsam fir, Douglas fir, hemlock or larch cones. Glue to secure all cones. Coat with acrylic spray.

Preparation

For lasting arrangements, pinecones should be baked to remove moisture, insects and to dry out seeds. Bake for 20 minutes in a 200 degree oven in a **disposable** aluminum pan or foil-lined pan. Newly harvested cones containing a lot of pitch, such as white pine or Norwegian spruce, can be soaked in luke-warm water then baked at high temperatures to form interesting partially opened shapes and more glossy natural glazes. To increase variety, pinecones can be cut into rosettes by either cutting off the bottom or top with sharp garden or lopping shears.

PINECONE HOLIDAY HEART

Materials

About 100 pinecones, 1″-2″ long; silicone glue **OR** hot glue gun; clear acrylic spray; 16″ by 18″ heavy cardboard **OR** light wood (if heart is to be hung outdoors); wire for hanging; long cinnamon sticks; Pink/Red check linen dish towel; matching thread; nylon fishing line and needle.

Preparation

For lasting wreaths, pinecones should be baked to remove moisture, insects and to dry out seeds. Bake for 20 minutes in a 200°F. oven in a disposable aluminum pan or foil-lined pan.

To Make

Enlarge diagram. Cut heart base from cardboard or wood. Make 2 small holes at X's; pull wire through from back to front; secure ends in front. Glue larger pinecones around edge of heart base; fill in center.

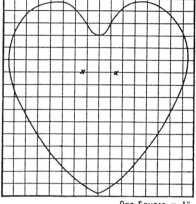

One Square = 1″

Glue smaller cones to fill in spaces between cones. Let dry; coat with acrylic spray. Cut 6½″-wide strip from length of towel. Right sides in, using ¼″ seam, stitch long edges together. Turn right side out with seam at center back. Turn raw ends under ¼″; slip-stitch. Tie strip into a bow inserting cinnamon sticks through knot. Thread needle with fishing line; attach bow to cones by winding line around cones and stitching through bow.

ROSE OF SHARON WALL HANGING

Materials

Cotton or cotton-blend fabrics—1 yd. Off-White, ½ yd. Dark Green, ⅜ yd. Red, ½ yd. Red-and-White print for binding; 1 yd. muslin for backing; 31″ square firm non-woven interfacing; matching sewing thread.

To Make

Enlarge and trace patterns. Add ¼″ seam allowance to all edges of appliqué pieces. Cut Off-White fabric and muslin 31″ square. From Green, cut 4 large leaves, 48 small leaves, 8 curved stems, and 4 straight stems cut on bias. From Red, cut 1 small, 4 medium, and 1 large flower, and 4 medium-flower center circles. From Off-White, cut 4 medium flowers, 1 large flower, and center circle for large flower. From print, cut and piece 1¼″-wide bias strips to make piece 126″ long. Clipping curves and corners and trimming seam allowance as required for smooth turning, turn under ¼″ seam allowance on all edges of appliqué pieces; press. Following diagram, appliqué stems and leaves to Off-White square. Starting with centers, appliqué flower layers together, then appliqué flowers in place. Wrong-side in, pin appliquéd piece to interfacing and backing. Press under ¼″ on one long edge of binding. Right sides together and edges even, sew raw edge of binding to appliquéd piece. Cut off excess; turn under and lap ends. Fold binding to back, matching pressed edge to stitching line; slip-stitch in place.

One square = 1″

VINE AND BERRY WREATH

18″ in Diameter

Materials

45″-wide cotton fabrics—2 yds. Off-White, ½ yd. Red, ¼ yd. Red with White dots, ¼ yd. Dark Green with White dots, ⅛ yd. or scraps each Dark Red and Medium Green-and-White print; two 30″ squares quilt batting; thread to match fabrics; 1 skein each Dark Green and Medium Green 6-strand embroidery floss for stems; Off-White quilting thread; fusible bonding web; polyester stuffing; 2 yds. cotton cord for cording.

To Make

Enlarge pattern. Cut two 30″ squares Off-White fabric. Trace wreath and appliqué design onto one 30″ square. Make pattern for leaf. From Green with White dots, cut and join ⅞″-wide bias strips to make strip 40″ long. From same fabric, cut 8 leaves. From Green print, cut 16 leaves. Cut and join 1½″-wide Red bias strips to make a 66″ length. Cut 24 Red and 24 Dark Red ½″-diameter berries. Cut fusible web for all leaves and berries. Turn in and press ¼″ to wrong side on both long edges of Green bias strip. Pin and baste strip along center line of appliqué design; slip-stitch edges of bias strip neatly and invisibly by hand. Fuse pairs of Green print leaves and single Dark green leaves in place on fabric. Fuse berries in place. With matching thread zig-zag stitch in place. With backstitch and 3 strands of floss, embroider stems of berries using Green for Red berries and Dark Green for Dark Red berries. Place appliquéd piece, right-side up, on top of quilt batting and second 30″ square of fabric under batting. Baste through all layers along seamlines and vertically and horizontally across wreath. Place piece in quilting hoop. By hand, quilt along both edges of bias stem, around leaves and berries. Quilt ¼″ from inner and outer seamlines of wreath. Cut out wreath. Open ends will be seamed at bottom later. For back, from remaining Off-White fabric, cut two wreaths, piecing as required. Cut wreath from quilt batting. Place fabric wreaths right-side out with batting between; baste along edges. Stitch Red bias strips together to make one long piece. To make piping, fold in half lengthwise inserting cotton cord inside fold. With zipper foot, stitch along edge of cord. Raw edges matching, stitch piping along inner and outer seams. Right sides together, stitch front to back. Clip and trim seams; turn right-side out through opening at end. Turn in seam allowance at one end and lap over other end. Slip-stitch seam on front of wreath leaving open on back. Stuff wreath firmly; complete slip-stitching of seam. For bow, right-side in, fold Red and White dotted fabric in half lengthwise; trim ends diagonally. Stitch with ¼″ seam, leaving opening for turning at center. Turn right-side out; slip-stitch opening. Tie a bow; sew to lower front of wreath over seam.

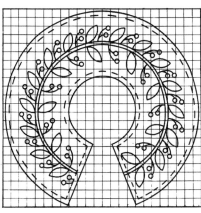

One square = 1″

TINY SALT-DOUGH WREATH

Materials

Salt dough made with 2 cups all-purpose flour, 1 cup salt, about one cup water (recipe below); aluminum foil; varnish; small amounts of acrylic paints—green, red, yellow, purple; picture hanger.

To Make

For salt dough, add about ¾ cup of water to flour and salt. Mix and knead five to seven minutes, until dough is smooth, adding water as necessary. Roll out. Form a 6″ wreath of crumbled aluminum foil; place on cookie sheet. To make dough leaves: pull off small balls of dough in teardrop shapes, in sizes from ½″ to 1″. Flatten into leaf shapes; create veining with table knife. Lay leaves around outer and inner edges of wreath, moistening lightly where one leaf joins another. Form fruits and berries from balls of dough. Place on wreath, moistening with water to bond. Texture may be added by pricking dough shapes with toothpick. Fill in open areas with smaller leaf shapes. Cover loosely with foil; bake in oven preheated to 325°F. for 1½ hours, until rock-hard. Cool. Apply varnish, using serveral coats on all sides to seal out humidity. Paint with acrylics. Glue picture hanger on back.

PINECONE CANDY-CANE WREATH

Materials

22″ natural evergreen wreath; 4 yards velvet ribbon; beading wire; for each candy cane: miniature fruit cluster, 24 miniature pinecones, 8″ length of red velvet tubing, short lengths of thread, thin wire, white glue.

To Make

Enlarge diagram of candy cane. Trace onto cardboard and cut out 7. Liberally apply glue to one side of canes; attach pinecones to cover surface; let dry thoroughly. Dip end of fruit cluster into glue and attach. Make bow out of tubing, secure at middle with thread, glue to candy cane. Attach candy canes to wreath with short lengths of thin wire. Make four-loop bow with velvet ribbon and attach with wire.

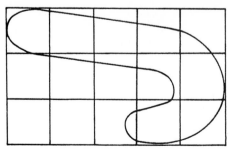

1 square = 1″

GUMDROP-RIBBON WREATHS

Materials (for each)

10″ Styrofoam wreath; 9 yds. of 1¼″-wide green satin ribbon, 18″ of 1½″-wide red satin ribbon, 24″ of 1″-wide plaid ribbon; two 1-lb. bags of large gumdrops; one ½-lb. bag of small spice drops; long straight pins.

To Make

Cut 5-yd. length of green satin ribbon and wrap tightly around wreath. Secure ends on back with pins. Insert pins through large gumdrops and attach to front of wreath leaving 3″ space at top of wreath. Insert pins through spice drops and attach to front of wreath on top of gumdrops. Cut 18″ length of green satin ribbon and make bow without streamers; do same with red satin ribbon. Make bow with streamers from plaid ribbon. Loop remaining length of green ribbon around top of wreath. Attach all three bows and hang.

With natural greens, attach materials by wrapping them with a length of wire about 12″ long, which can then be wrapped around the branches of the wreath.
With Styrofoam wreaths, push stiff-stemmed materials into surface of the form; wire other materials onto florist picks first. (Homemade wired picks can be made with thin wire and heavy wooden toothpicks.)

Make your kitchen a feast for the eyes with our gumdrop-and-ribbon wreaths and ready-for-giving old-fashioned print tins, boxes, and "antique" canning jars, to fill with the luscious sweets and savories of the season.

To Assemble Basic Lined Stocking

Enlarge Stocking Pattern. Adding ½" seam allowance around, cut front and back, being sure to reverse pattern for stocking back. Cut lining. Cut heel, toe and cuff or mark for placement of trim as indicated in individual instructions. Decorate stocking front. For hanging loop, cut a 1½" by 5" or 6" strip of fabric. Turn in ¼" on each long edge. Wrong side in, fold in half lengthwise; stitch close to edge. Fold strip to form a loop. Right sides in, stitch stocking front to back, leaving open at top. Trim seam. Turn right side out. Turn in seam allowance around top edge. Right sides in, stitch front and back lining together; turn seam allowance around top edge to wrong side. Wrong sides together, slip lining into stocking. Inserting loop at back edge, slip-stitch top edges together.

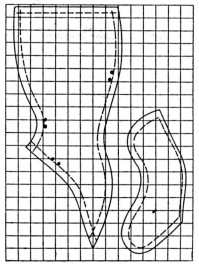

one square = 1"

CALICO STOCKING WITH ANTIQUE DOILY

Materials

¾ yd. each red calico lining, fabric and batting; 3½" by 8½" strip white cotton; one 3" by 8" and one 4" by 8" band crocheted lace; 1½ yds. ¾"-wide white beading with red ribbon; two 5" lace doilies; 2 yds. 1"-wide face edging.

To Make

Fold calico and batting in half. Using Pattern , cut two calico and two batting stocking shapes. Baste a layer of batting to wrong side of each calico piece. Stitch white strip along top edge of wrong side of one calico piece, using ½" seam. Turn to right side of calico; hem to calico to form cuff. One inch down from top, pin 3" band of lace across. One inch below this band, pin 4" band of lace. Stitch strip of beading over top of each band of lace. Pin doilies over heel and toe so that center of doilies will show on stocking. Stitch in place. Slightly gather lace edging. Baste gathered edge on seamline of stocking with free edge of lace toward heel. Assemble stocking. Make bow of beading and sew to center top of decorated side of stocking.

one square = 1"

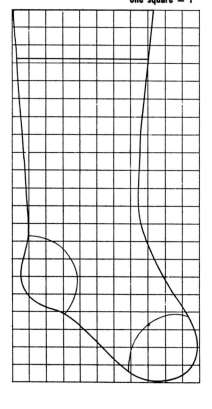

BALLERINA'S TOE SHOE

Materials

45"-wide cotton or cotton blend fabrics—½ yd. dark green stripe, ¼ yd. solid red; ½ yd. ½"-wide ruffled white lace; 5" of ¼"-wide white ribbon; ½ yd. unbleached muslin; 3 yds. ½"-wide red ribbon.

To Make

Enlarge pattern; cut 2 slippers from red and 2 from muslin; cut 2 legs from green and 2 from muslin. Baste muslin to wrong side of each piece. Press under ¼" on top edge of slipper. Cut two 22" lengths of red ribbon. Pin slipper to leg, inserting ribbon between marks; machine-zigzag over edge of slipper. Repeat for back. With right sides in, stitch front to back, leaving open at top. Trim curves; turn; press. Turning under edge of lace, pin lace to upper edge of stocking; stitch. Fold white ribbon in half and sew to side seam at top. Criss-cross red ribbon around leg as in photograph. Tack in place. Tie bow. Make separate bow; attach at toe.

TINIEST CHRISTMAS TREE

Materials

12″ high Styrofoam cone with 5″ diameter base; Styrofoam cylinder 1½″ high by 2½″ diameter for trunk; small pieces of Styrofoam for boxes from about ¼″ by ½″ by 1″ to 2½″ by 2½″ by 1″ (can be cut from a block of Styrofoam using a serrated knife or hacksaw); 2½ yds. ⅜″-wide Red satin ribbon; 1 yd. ¼-wide Gold braid; small pieces of assorted Christmas gift wrapping paper (preferably with small prints); scraps of Gold wrapping paper; small pictures cut from magazines or greeting cards (food, toys, gift ideas, Christmas motifs, etc.); white glue; straight pins and toothpicks; scrap of lightweight cardboard.

To Make

Using glue, cover cone and trunk with scraps of wrapping paper arranged in patchwork fashion. Glue trunk to center bottom of cone; allow to dry. Wrap Styrofoam boxes as if they were small packages; secure with glue, holding paper in place with straight pins until dry. Glue a picture on top of each box. Alternating shapes and sizes, arrange boxes on cone, with larger boxes toward bottom; attach by inserting end of toothpick into glue, then into box; insert other end into cone. Tie tiny bows from 9″ lengths of ribbon. Make knots from small lengths of Gold braid; trim braid about ½″ from knot. Stick straight pin through knot; tuck ends under. Then stick pin through center of bow. Attach to tree at random. Glue Gold paper to each side of cardboard; cut out star. Glue to top of tree.

RUDOLPH THE RED-NOSED REINDEER

Materials

Three flat-sided wooden clothespins; brown wood stain; ¼" paint brush; spare shoe box; 5" length of red rattail for hanging loop; glue; ball of absorbent cotton for tail; scrap of green felt for ears; two small gold sequins; one small red sequin for nose; pair of movable eyes; tweezers.

To Make

Paint clothespins with wood stain. Straddle over side of shoe box to dry. Fold rattail in half to form loop and glue ends together. For body glue two clothespins together, rattail hanging loop between at top. Glue on third clothespin in opposite direction for face and antlers, with bottom of chin ½" above crotch of clothespin at a very slight angle so head is slightly cocked. Using pattern, below, cut green-felt ears. Glue in place; glue on gold sequins on front. Glue on eyes and red-sequin nose. Shape a 1" ball of absorbent cotton and glue to back for tail.

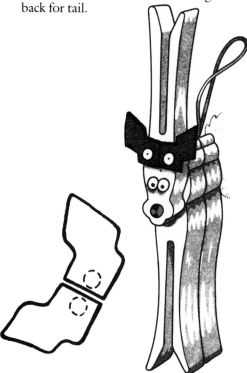

LITTLE RED SLED

Materials

8 Popsicle sticks; X-acto knife; white glue; red acrylic paint; small paintbrush; green and white felt-tip markers; 6" gold cord; awl or nail; waxed paper.

To Make

Cut ½" from end of two sticks. Cut ¾" from end of two other sticks, then cut at slant. For steering bar, cut ½" from both ends of one stick; cut slant on both ends. With awl or nail, punch hole ¾" from each end. Cut 1½" from another Popsicle stick and split this piece in two. With slanted ends on outside, lay the four sticks with cut ends together on waxed paper. 1½" from each end, glue a 1½" strip of Popsicle stick across the four sticks to hold them together. Position steering bar at front of sled. Glue scrap of Popsicle stick over joining of steering bar and sled. ¾" apart, glue runners to crosspieces, extending runners ¾" beyond front of sled. Paint sled red. Let dry thoroughly. "Paint" decorations with green and white felt markers. Run cord through holes; knot ends underneath.

WOODEN TOY SOLDIERS

Materials

Round-head clothespins with large heads; ⅝"-diameter wooden dowel; one Popsicle stick for each soldier; wood saw; pencil; white, blue, red, gold, and pink model paints; ¼" paint brush; fine-point paint brush; one spare shoe box; waxed paper; glue; 3 inches ⅛" plain gold braid for hanging loops; brass thumbtacks.

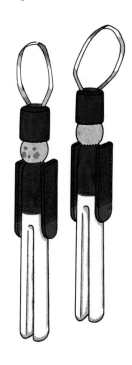

To Make

Saw curved ends off base of clothespins to make flat bottom. Saw dowel into ¾″ lengths. Saw Popsicle sticks in half. Draw a line around clothespin ⅛″ above crotch. Draw a second line around clothespin ⅛″ above first line. Draw a line ½″ from curved end of each piece of Popsicle stitck. Draw a second line ⅛″ above first line.

Note: Complete all painting with one color before proceeding to next color. Let each color dry thoroughly before going to next color or paint will bleed. With ¼″ brush, paint all trousers white as far up as lower pencil line. Place, straddling sides of shoe box to dry. When dry, paint coats above upper line. Paint half of coats and half of dowel pieces (hats) red, other half blue. Paint Popsicle sticks above upper pencil line. Place on waxed paper to dry. Paint hats placing on waxed paper with flat end down. With fine point brush, paint red-dot mouths, blue-dot eyes, pink -dot cheeks. With gold, paint ⅛″ wide cuffs, waistband, buttons, crossed straps on back, plumes on hats. Glue on arms. Glue blue hats on soldiers with red coats, red hats on soldiers with blue coats. When thoroughly dry, place 3″ gold-braid loop on top of hat with thumbtack.

HEAVENLY ANGEL, CHOIRBOY, PRETTY LADY, RACE CAR, "WOODEN" SOLDIER, SPIFFY SANTA

To Make

All the ornaments are based on two shapes; cylinders (cut-down cardboard tubes from paper toweling, covered with colored construction paper), and doilies or paper shaped into cones. Follow the photograph on page, and use materials listed below plus any trims you may have on hand to make the ornaments. Use pieces of thin wire for hangers.

Heavenly Angel and Choirboy

Make cone-shaped bodies from half-circles of construction paper and doilies. Make arms from paper doilies cut into quarter-circles. Simply twist into cone shapes, overlapping as much as necessary. Secure with white glue. Attach arms to body.

Heads are Styrofoam balls. Choirboy's eyes are straight pins with colored tips; angel wings are doilies backed with colored paper, halo is wire hanger.

Pretty Lady

You can use lacy bits of gold-paper doily for jewelry, scraps of colored paper for bow, eyes, mouth.

Race Car

Enlarge pattern for fender to fit length of tube; cut out two from colored paper. Cut wheels from colored paper; glue onto fender and attach to tube. Cut out windshield, circle for driver's "seat"; attach with glue.

"Wooden" Soldier

Use scraps of colored paper for uniform, gold self-sticking decals for buttons. Let construction paper covering tube extend slightly at top for hat; trim so it curves upward in front.

Spiffy Santa

Enlarge pattern for Santa's cap to fit circumference of tube, then cut out on colored paper. Place around top of tube, attach ends, top of hat, with white glue as shown in photograph. Glue on white-paper pompon. Use colored paper for features, beard, and mustache; a small Christmas ball for nose.

To attach wire hangers to Pretty Lady and *"Wooden" Soldier:* Cut circles of cardboard to fit end of tube, cover with colored construction paper, and insert wire loop at center. Tape ends of wire to back of paper insert. With white glue, attach circle to inside of tube end. Hanger on *Spiffy Santa* is attached to hat; hanger on *Race Car* is attached to "seat." *To attach wire hangers to Heavenly Angel and Choirboy:* Twist a few inches of wire to form loop; insert ends through foam head and tape to inside of paper-cone body.

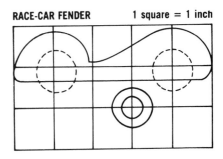

RACE-CAR FENDER   1 square = 1 inch

1 square = 1 inch

GOLDEN LEAF WREATH

½ 12-ounce package peanut-butter chips
    (1 cup)
½ cup butter or margarine
½ cup sugar
1 cup all-purpose flour
1 cup whole-wheat flour
1 teaspoon baking powder
½ teaspoon salt
½ teaspoon baking soda
½ teaspoon ground nutmeg
½ teaspoon ground ginger
1 egg
⅓ cup milk
1 teaspoon vanilla extract
    14" by 1" heavy cardboard ring
    assortment of 1" to 2½" silk or plastic
        leaves
    ribbon

About 2 hours before serving or up to 2
weeks ahead:

1. In heavy 1-quart saucepan or in double
boiler over hot, **not boiling,** water, melt
peanut-butter chips and butter or margarine. Remove saucepan from heat; stir in
sugar. Cool mixture until lukewarm.

2. Meanwhile, enlarge holly leaf pattern
and trace outline on waxed paper. Place a
piece of cardboard under waxed paper; cut
waxed paper and cardboard along traced
outline.

3. In large bowl with spoon, mix all-purpose flour, whole-wheat flour, baking
powder, salt, baking soda, nutmeg, and
ginger. Stir egg, milk, vanilla, and peanut-
butter-chip mixture into flour mixture until smooth.

4. Preheat oven to 350°F. Grease large
cookie sheet. On lightly floured surface
with floured rolling pin, roll half of dough
¼ inch thick. Using cardboard pattern and
knife, cut as many leaves as possible; cut
lines into leaves to resemble veins.

5. Place cookies on cookie sheet. Bake 8 to
10 minutes until lightly browned. With
pancake turner, remove cookies to wire
racks to cool. Repeat with remaining
dough and reroll trimmings. If not using
right away, store cookies in tightly covered
container to use up within 2 weeks. Makes
about 4 dozen.

Holly
Mix **red food coloring** into **1 tablespoon
almond paste** to tint a pretty red color.
Roll into balls, using ¼ teaspoonful al-
mond-paste mixture for each ball. Set
aside.

Decorative Icing
In small bowl with mixture at low speed,
beat **1 cup confectioners' sugar** and **1 egg
white** just until mixed. Increase speed to
high and beat mixture until very stiff and
knife drawn through mixture leaves a
clean-cut path. Keep bowl covered with
plastic wrap to prevent frosting from
drying out.

To Assemble Wreath
Spread a little of the Decorative Icing on
the bottom of each cookie and arrange 14
to 16 cookies around the cardboard ring,
as pictured. Arrange marzipan holly berries
and leaves using additional icing. Fasten
bow. Allow to dry 24 to 48 hours. **Do not
hang until completely dry.**

MARZIPAN ROSE WREATH

2   7-ounce packages almond paste
5½ cups confectioners' sugar
2   egg whites
    red food color
    14" by 1" heavy-duty-cardboard ring
    silk or plastic leaves
    ribbon

2 days ahead or up to 1 month ahead:
Prepare marzipan dough: In large bowl,
knead almond paste, confectioners' sugar,

and egg whites to make a stiff dough. (Or
use food processor with knife blade attached.) Keep dough covered with plastic
wrap until ready to use to avoid drying out.
To make holly berries: In small bowl,
combine ¼ cup marzipan dough with
enough red food color to tint a pretty red
color. Divide mixture into eight pieces; roll
each into a ball. Place in jelly-roll pan to
dry.
To make roses: Roll some of remaining
dough, 2 teaspoonfuls at a time, into thirty
1-inch balls. Lightly dust the counter or
cutting board with confectioners' sugar.
Using a rolling pin, roll each dough ball
into a 3" strip. Remove carefully with a
metal spatula. **To make 30 rosebuds:** Roll
each strip jelly-roll fashion. **To make full
roses:** Roll remaining dough, a teaspoonful at a time, into a ½" to 1" ball and press
into the palm of your hand with your
thumb to make individual petals. Press
petals around rosebuds to make roses as
pictured. Leaving 6 to 8 plain rosebuds,
make 24 roses. Place roses and rosebuds in
same jelly-roll pan with berries to dry
overnight. Wrap remaining marzipan with
plastic wrap to avoid drying out.

Second Day:
Press remaining marzipan evenly around
cardboard ring to create base for the roses,
holly, and leaves. Arrange on base, and
press firmly into base. Fasten bow. Allow
to dry 24 to 28 hours. **Do not hang until
completely dry.**

dip the knife in very hot water first and cut around leaf pattern carefully. With a metal spatula, remove each leaf onto waxed paper to dry. **Note:** Do not peel foil from back of leaves until ready to assemble wreath. It will act as backing to help leaves keep their shape. Keep leaves refrigerated until ready to assemble wreath; they will soften at room temperature.

Chocolate Leaves

1	*12-ounce package chocolate chips*
¼	*cup butter or margarine*
¼	*cup mixed chopped nuts*
¼	*cup flaked coconut*

Follow directions given for Peanut Leaves.

Candy Mint Leaves

2	*cups confectioners' sugar*
2	*teaspoons light corn syrup*
½	*teaspoon mint extract*
1	*egg white*
½	*teaspoon green food coloring*

Into medium bowl, measure 1 cup confectioners' sugar and remaining ingredients. With mixer at low speed, beat ingredients until just mixed; increase speed to high and beat until soft peaks form, occasionally scraping bowl with rubber spatula. With spoon, stir in 1 cup confectioners' sugar to make a stiff mixture.

Between two 12-inch sheets of waxed paper, with rolling pin, roll piece of dough ¼ inch thick. Lift top sheet of waxed paper from rolled dough. Using sharp knife and small leaf pattern (above), make 14 mint leaves. With small spatula, lift out leaves; set aside. (Leaves will store well in tightly covered container up to 1 week.)

To Assemble Wreath

Dab a teaspoon or two of Decorative Icing on the back of each leaf, coating the entire back, and arrange on the cardboard ring as pictured. Fasten ribbon, cherries, and remaining ornaments with additional icing. Allow to dry 24 to 48 hours. **Do not hang before completely dry.**

Note: If you wish to use wreath as a centerpiece, keep refrigerated until ready to serve meal. If you wish to use as door ornament, be sure to keep it out of direct sunlight.

CHOCOLATE FANTASY WREATH

14	*Peanut Leaves*
16	*Chocolate Leaves*
	Decorative Icing (see recipe for Golden Leaf Wreath)
	14" by 1" heavy cardboard ring
	ribbon
	decoration:
	7 kumquats, fresh or jarred
	7 maraschino cherries
	14 almonds
	7 cinnamon sticks (broken in half)
	12 to 14 candy mint leaves (see below)

Peanut Leaves

1	*teaspoon ground ginger*
1	*teaspoon ground cinnamon*
⅓	*cup sesame seeds*
¼	*cup butter or margarine (shortening)*
⅓	*cup grated apple*
1	*12-ounce package peanut-butter chips*

In top of double boiler, combine all ingredients. Over hot, **not boiling,** water, melt mixture. Stir until smooth. Spoon mixture into foil-lined 15″ by 12″ cookie sheet; spread evenly with spatula. Place in refrigerator 1 hour or until solid. Place cookie sheet on a hot towel briefly to loosen bottom of the peanut mixture. Enlarge and cut out leaf pattern and place over hardened peanut mixture. Using sharp paring knife,

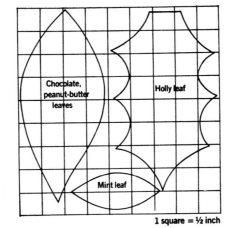

1 square = ½ inch

The Kiddyland Movie Cut-outs
By Thomas B. Lamb

Paste the theater on heavy cardboard or bristol board before cutting the slits. Then paste the strips of film together as indicated or else cut off the "Paste here" sections and mount on adhesive tape as suggested on the Discoveries page in the August issue

Good Housekeeping   December 1922

INDEX

Page numbers in *italics* refer to illustrations.

almond(s)
  bonbons, frozen, 36–37, *37*
  cranberry muffins, *28*, 30
  cream pie, 34, *34*
  crunch, 82, *82*
  curried, 84, *84*
  eggnog, 58
  lace rolls, 123, *123*
  See also marzipan
angel, heavenly, 163, *163*
anise ovals, 124, *124*
appetizers
  buffet, 42–46, *45*
  dinner, 12–15
  microwave, 75–76
apple(s)
  chews, fresh, *115*, 117
  cranberry relish cups, *49*, 50
  date steamed pudding, 77
  poached, 66, *67*
  rings, gingery, 26
artichoke(s)
  and mushroom salad, 27
  shrimp and scallops with, 76
aspic, pâté in, 12–13, *12*
avocado(s)
  filling, peppery, 42
  and orange salad, 27, 73
  seasoned, *41*, 47
  and shrimp in butter sauce, 13, *13*

baby's building block, *107*, 112
baked goods, 29–30
"bakery" box, *106*, 108
ballerina's toe shoe, 160, *161*
banana
  fruitcake, 143
  orange nog, *53*, 55
bandanna bundle, *106*, 109
beef
  bourguignon with chestnuts, 21, *22*
  celebration filet mignon, *64*, 65
  country pot roast with winter vegetables, 24
  and oyster pie, 21
  roast, carving, 23
  tenderloin en croute with caper sauce, 23
  tenderloin with flavored butters, 65, *65*
beets, orange-glazed, 76
biscuits, rich, 19
Black Forest cookies, 118, *118*
bonbon cookies, *115*, 117
boots, crocheted, 99, *99*
bottle bibs, at-your-service, 153, *153*

bread(s)
  braided marble, *136–37*, 139
  colonial oatmeal, *28*, 29
  flowers, crusty, 14, *14*
  Greek Christmas, *28*, 29
  holiday cranberry quick, *136–37*, 139
  little braided herb, 88, *86–87*
  little honey loaves, *136–37*, 138
  onion-cheese, *136–37*, 138
  pumpkin-raisin nut, *136–37*, 138
  ring, pumpkin, 78
  rye, stuffing, *16*, 17
  steamed fig, *49*, 51
  sweet Christmas wreath, *87*, 89
  zucchini-carrot loaves, 91
breadbasket, country, *107*, 113
broccoli puffs, 26, 72
buffets, 40–59
butters, flavored, 65

cabbage
  red, sautéed, 25
  and sour cream pie, 14, *14*
cake(s)
  carrot, *49*, 51
  cranberry-orange coffee, 77
  microwave, 78
  raspberry-strawberry cream, 33, *33*
  spicy crumb, 35, *35*
canapés, quick, 75
candy-cane pinecone wreath, 158, *158*
candy-making, 79
candy tops, 119, *119*
cappuccino, mint, *53*, 54
caramels, 82
caviar and cheese fingers, 43, *45*
celery
  braised hearts of, 70
  stalks, pickled, *87*, 89
champagne punch, holiday, 58
cheese
  blue, pinwheels, 44, *45*
  caramelized Brie, 14
  caraway, crisps, 43, *45*
  and caviar fingers, 43, *45*
  Cheddar straws, *87*, 88
  cream-, scrambled eggs, *41*, 47
  filled crepes with chocolate sauce, 35
  onion bread, *136–37*, 138
  party Brie, 46, *46*
  Roquefort butter, 65

cheese (*Cont.*):
  soup, Cheddar, 48, *49*
  triangles, creamy, 36
  and wine tastings, 56, *56–57*
cheesecake
  chocolate swirl, 77
  Christmas wreath, 31, *31*
chestnut(s)
  beef bourguignon with, 21
  pudding, steamed, 144, *144*
chicken legs, with rice-sausage stuffing, 17
chocolate
  butter cream, 145
  creamy, *53*, 55
  dipped oranges, 91
  fantasy wreath, 165, *165*
  fruitcake, *140–41*, 142
  glaze, 82
  leaves, 31, *31*, 165, *165*
  peanut brittle, double, 79
  peanut crescents, 119, *119*
  sauces, 35, 144, *144*
  swirl cheesecake, 77
choirboy, 163, *163*
Christmas Day sit-down menus, 8–39, *9*, *10–11*
chutney, cranberry, 70
cider, mulled, *53*, 54
clarion angel rug, 97–98, *98*
cocoa nuts, 84–85, *85*
coconut wreaths, 121, *121*
coffee punch, spirited, 58
cookie can, *107*, 112
cookies, 86, 89, 91, 114–25. *See also* gingerbread
corn bread, cranberry, 68
crab
  strudel, 12, *12*
  stuffed mushrooms, festive, 75
"crackers," Christmas, 153, *153*
cranberry(ies)
  almond muffins, *28*, 30
  chutney, 70
  corn bread, 68
  frosted, *140–41*, 142
  fruitcake, fresh, *140–41*, 142
  ginger relish, 70
  orange coffee cake, 77
  and peach relish, spiced, 70
  quick bread, holiday, *136–37*, 139
  relish apple cups, *49*, 50
  sauce, 76
  tea punch, 52, *53*
crayon tubes, jumbo, *107*, 113
crepes, cheese-filled, with chocolate sauce, 35

currant punch, *53*, 54
custard
  filling, raspberry, 33, *33*
  sauce, 77

date
  apple steamed pudding, 77
  nut Christmas rock cookies, 124, *124*
desserts
  dinner, 31–39
  microwave, 77–79
  variety, 132–47
doily
  antique, calico stocking with, 160, *160*
  dainty bags, *107*, 111
dolls
  dainty, *81*, 92
  darling duo knitted, 100–1, *100–1*
  pig pals, 99, *99*
duckling, breast of, with green peppercorns, 23
dump truck, 94, *94*

eggnog
  banana-orange, *53*, 55
  coconut, *53*, 53
  espresso, 39, *39*
  tips, 58
  toasted almond, 58
eggs, scrambled, cream-cheese, *41*, 47
endive, savory, 42, *42*, 45
entrees, 16–24
envelope, potato-print, *106*, 108

fig bread, steamed, *49*, 51
flowers, "folk art," *106*, 111
fold-ups, fancy, *106*, 109
fruit
  and champagne, 33
  fresh, in orange cups, *41*, 47
  glazed ham, 76
  spiced, 91
  See also specific fruits
fruitcakes, *32*, 33, *140–41*, 142–43
fudge
  coffee-walnut, 79
  tunnels of, *115*, 116

gardener's delight, *106*, 110
garlands, 164–65
gift boxes, 106–13, *106–7*

gifts
food as, 82–91
handicrafts as, 92–105
mailing home-baked, 89
wrapping, 106–13
gingerbread, 126–31
boys & girls, 128–29, 129–30
Christmas cottage, 126, 127, 130
cookie can, 107, 112
muffins, 136–37, 138
ginger crisps, 115, 116
goose with glazed oranges, Christmas, 16, 17
grapefruit peels, candied, 83, 83
Greek Christmas bread, 28, 29
grocery-bag reindeer, 106–7, 111
gumdrop-ribbon wreaths, 158, 159

ham, fruit-glazed, 76
hat box, stovepipe, 107, 113
herb-and-spice mix, no salt, 74
honey loaves, little, 136–37, 138

ice cream
frozen almond bonbons, 36–37, 37
roll, walnut, 133, 144–45

jelly jars, hand-painted, 150, 152

kabobs, scallop, 43
kitchen decorations, 149, 159

lady, pretty, 163, 163
lamb, Sunday leg of, 66, 67
lamb, woolly little, 95, 95
liqueurs, 59
liverwurst filling, creamy, 42
low calorie dishes, 72–74, 91
lunch-bag specials, 106–7, 112

macadamia meltaways, 125, 125
macaroons, coconut, 115, 116
maple
meltaways, 88, 86
walnut cups, 125, 125
walnut wreaths, 120, 120
marzipan
apples, 36, 37
rose wreath, 164, 164
mayonnaise
caper, 15, 15
green, 67
menus, sit-down Christmas Day, 8–39, 9, 10–11
microwave dishes, 75–79, 85, 85
mincemeat
pie, 74
uses of, 146, 146
mint leaves, candy, 165, 165
mint triangles, 119, 119
moccasins, crocheted, 98–99, 99
mocha
filling, 145
frosty, 53, 55
truffles, meltaway, 85, 85
molasses spirals, 123, 123
mousse
espresso nut, 36, 36, 73
salmon-sole, 15, 15
muffins
cranberry-almond, 28, 30
gingerbread, 136–37, 138
raisin-bran, 75
mushroom(s)
and artichoke salad, 27
chilled lemony, 13, 13
festive crab-stuffed, 75
sauce, 16, 17
sautéed, 41, 47
mustard
caraway horseradish, 90
gingered orange, 90
no-salt, 74, 74

Neapolitan shell cookies, 115, 116
nuts
guide to, 147
mixed sugared, 134
See also specific nuts

oatmeal
bran cookies, 91
bread, colonial, 28, 29
onion(s)
cheese bread, 136–37, 138
creamed, 49, 50–51
twists, crunchy, 28, 30, 73
orange(s)
and avocado salad, 27, 73
banana nog, 53, 55
chocolate-dipped, 91
cranberry coffee cake, 77
cream punch, 39, 39, 73
cups, fresh fruit in, 41, 47, 47
glazed, Christmas goose with, 16, 17
glazed beets, 76
peels, candied, 83
origami basket, 106, 109
ornaments, 161–63
oyster and beef pie, 21

paper wraps, 106, 110
pastry(ies), 140–47
Russian, 42, 45
shells, 78
patchwork box, 107, 111
patchwork cloth, pine-tree, 154, 154
pâté
in aspic, 12–13, 12
country, 46, 46
peach(es)
and cranberry relish, spiced, 70
fizz, 59
gingered, 19, 72
pear pie, holiday, 34, 34
sauce, 76
peanut
brittle, double-chocolate, 79
chocolate crescents, 119, 119
leaves, 165, 165
refrigerator cookies, 115, 117
pecan crunch, 122, 122. See also praline(s)
pickles, zucchini, 90, 90
pies, dessert
almond cream, 34
coconutty cream, 79
holiday pear-peach, 34, 34
mincemeat, 74
pies, dinner
beef and oyster, 21
sour cream and cabbage, 14, 14
sweet potato, 78
pie shells, 78
pignolia crescents, 120, 120
pig pals, 99, 99
pinafore, little girl's, 81, 92
pinecone
basket, 155, 155
candy-cane wreath, 158, 158
holiday heart, 155, 155
pine-tree patchwork cloth, 154, 154
pizza snacks, 75
place mats, paper, 150, 151
popcorn and nuts, 84, 84
pork
loin, stuffed, prune-pear, 68
loin chops with prune stuffing, 24
roast, with parsley crumb crust, 20, 20
shoulder rolls, glazed, with cranberry corn bread, 68
potato
casserole, party, 25, 25
fans, roasted, 26
frills, crispy, 66, 67
skin hors d'oeuvres, 42
potato-print envelope, 106, 108
pouches, pretty plaid, 107, 113
praline(s)
sweet, 83, 83
thins, 115, 117
pretzel cookies, 124, 124
prune stuffing
pear, pork loin with, 68
pork loin chops with, 24
pudding
apple-date steamed, 77
colonial, 48, 49
steamed chestnut, 144, 144

pumpkin
bisque, velvety, 15, 15, 72
bread ring, 78
butter, 49, 51
raisin nut bread, 136–37, 138
punches
buffet, 52–59
dinner, 39

quiches, bite-sized bacon, 44, 45
quilt, center diamond Amish, 102–3, 102

race car, 163, 163
raisin sauce, 76
raspberry
custard filling, 33, 33
strawberry cream cake, 33, 33
reindeer, grocery-bag, 106–7, 111
relish
cranberry, apple cups with, 50
cranberry-ginger, 70
spiced peach and cranberry, 70
sweet-and-sour, 90, 90
remoulade, julienne of vegetables, 27
Reubens, miniature, 44, 45
rice
festive white and wild, 70
jasmine, 26
saffron, 69, 69
sausage stuffing, 17
Rock Cornish hens, holiday, 19, 72
rocky road cookies, 123, 123
rolls, old-fashioned dinner, 28, 30
Rose of Sharon wall hanging, 156, 157
Rudolph the Red-Nosed Reindeer, 162, 162
rug, clarion angel, 97–98, 98

salad dressing
calorie-wise herb, 74
zucchini, 27
salads, 27
salmon
buffet, 67
filling, lemony, 42
sole mousse, 15, 15
salt-dough
for Santa family portraits, 96, 97
wreath, tiny, 158, 158
salt-free herb-and-spice mix, 74
salt-free mustard, 74, 74
sangria, mock, 53, 54
Santa, spiffy, 163, 163
Santa family portraits, 96, 97
sauce(s)
brandied chocolate, 144
butter, 13
caper, 23
chocolate, 35
confetti, 67
custard, 77
for fish, 67
for ham, 76
mincemeat, 146
mushroom, 17
mustard, 67
sausage
rice stuffing, 17
stuffed veal with saffron rice, 69, 69
stuffing, 49, 50
triangles, 44, 45
scallop(s)
kabobs, 43, 45
and shrimp with artichokes, 76
seafood Newburg, 18, 19
Shaker miniatures, 104–5, 104
shirt box, 106, 109
shrimp
and avocado in butter sauce, 13, 13
and scallops with artichokes, 76
side dishes, 25–26
sled, little red, 162, 162
snowflake box, 106, 110–11
snow flowers, 122, 122
soldier(s)
"wooden" (gift wrapping), 107, 113
"wooden" (paper ornament), 163, 163

soldier(s) (Cont.):
wooden toy (ornament), 162–63, 162
sole-salmon mousse, 15, 15
soup
Cheddar cheese, 48, 49
serving piping-hot, 15
velvety pumpkin bisque, 15, 15
sour cream and cabbage pie, 14, 14
spice-and-herb mix, no salt, 74
spritz, 125, 125
stocking, calico, with antique doily, 160, 160
strawberry-raspberry cream cake, 33, 33
stuffing
prune, 24, 68
rice-sausage, 17
rye-bread, 16, 17
sausage, 49, 50, 69, 69
savory vegetable, 61, 62
sunbursts, 122, 122
sundaes, mincemeat, 146, 146
sweetheart box, 107, 112
sweet potato
bake, 49, 51
pie, 78

table trimmings, 150–54
tea cookies, 121, 121
teddy-bear tote, 107, 111
tie box, 106, 109
toffee bars, 120, 120
tomato
boats, 14, 14
sip, 53, 54
traditional favorites, 60–79
low calorie, 72–74
microwave, 75–79
tree, Christmas
cookies, 121, 121
tiniest, 161, 161
trimmings, 161–63
trimmings, 150–63
table, 150–54
tree, 161–63
wall, 155–60
truffles, meltaway mocha, 85
tubes, gift, 106–7, 110, 113
turkey
garnishes for, 63
roast, with savory vegetable stuffing, 61, 62
with sausage stuffing, 49, 50

veal, sausage-stuffed, with saffron rice, 69, 69
vegetables
remoulade, julienne of, 27
salad, cold, with zucchini dressing, 27
stuffing, savory, roast turkey with, 61, 62
winter, country pot roast with, 24
See also specific vegetables
village-in-the-round, 106, 110

wall trimmings, 155–60
walnut(s)
brittle, Christmas, 134, 134–35
coffee fudge, 79
crisp Chinese fried, 82, 82
hot & spicy, 134
ice-cream roll, 133, 144–45
maple cups, 125, 125
maple wreaths, 120, 120
wassail bowl, 59
wine(s)
butter, 65
and cheese tastings, 56, 56–57
dessert, 57
wreaths, 156–59, 164–65

yule log, 145, 145

zucchini
carrot loaves, 91
dressing, 27
pickles, 90, 90
rounds, zesty, 43, 45